Play and Curriculum

Play and Curriculum

Play & Culture Studies

Volume 15

Edited by
Myae Han and James E. Johnson

HAMILTON BOOKS
Lanham • Boulder • New York • London

Published by Hamilton Books
An imprint of The Rowman & Littlefield Publishing Group, Inc.
4501 Forbes Boulevard, Suite 200, Lanham, Maryland 20706
www.rowman.com

6 Tinworth Street, London SE11 5AL, United Kingdom

British Library Cataloguing in Publication Information Available

Library of Congress Cataloging-in-Publication Data Available

Library of Congress Control Number: 2019952351

ISBN 978-0-7618-7176-7 (pbk. : alk. paper)
ISBN 978-0-7618-7177-4 (electronic)

∞™ The paper used in this publication meets the minimum requirements of American National Standard for Information Sciences—Permanence of Paper for Printed Library Materials, ANSI/NISO Z39.48-1992.

Dedicated to
Jim Christie, my forever mentor
Kern and Minjie, loving family and gifts from God
From Myae Han

Jim Christie, my forever friend
Karen McChesney Johnson, loving wife
From Jim Johnson

Contents

List of Tables and Figure

TABLES

List of Tables and Figure

FIGURE

Preface

As series editor of *Play & Culture Studies* I am delighted to introduce you to volume 15 *Play and Curriculum*, co-edited by Myae Han and myself. We have worked over the year reviewing many brief abstract submissions that came our way in a call for papers on this general and important topic, selecting a subset to invite chapter submissions to more carefully consider for publication. The initial show of interest in this topic was so great that we have decided on a sequel to this volume that will be devoted to play and literacy, viewed as a critically important separate branch of the topic of this volume.

Both volumes 15 and 16 are dedicated to the memory of James F. Christie Past President of The Association for the Study of Play, cherished friend and mentor, who pioneered research and was a leading scholar in both areas, and a wonderful colleague championing causes in early education to improve the lives of young children and their parents and teachers, and leaving a lasting legacy and imprint on our continuing work on the study and uses of play.

Brian Sutton-Smith decades ago keyed in on the peculiarities of mixing play and schooling and considered this strand of our grand narrative under the play-as-progress rhetoric, grappling with theoretical questions about the validity of transfer effects from playing to real world performances (e.g., does playing teacher as a child contribute to your later becoming a good teacher as a grown-up?). He also raised philosophical objections to what could easily become an exercise in the sanitizing of play, the domestication of its spirit and energy, harnessing it for ulterior motives. Nevertheless, he welcomed clashes between those who were sometimes called the play prudes and the play purists, and the largest group falling somewhere in between.

The majority of play scholars whose work is represented in this book most likely are best described as falling in between, shying away from the purists who eschew spoiling play with curriculum, and the prudes or puritans who do not want to spoil the curriculum with play. They would tend not to follow in the footsteps of Pinocchio heading off to Playland instead of school and the ruination and a longer and longer nose. Nor would play scholars likely be led astray by the temptation to smell the roses only within the narrowest of confines of what constitutes the proper learning environment.

The work represented in this volume is very current and important and can be aptly termed a third alternative to reductionistic and expansive approaches to the topics at hand. In the composite they represent the best of the tradition of *Play & Culture Studies* and *The Association for the Study of Play* in that they chapters reflect breadth and depth of scholarship across nations using multiple models and methods and addressing intergenerational needs, challenges and aspirations in the world of play and curriculum. Please play and learn from the pages that follow as we have been able to do working and playing with many others in making this volume happen; and now it's available to you, the reader. Enjoy, tell others what you read, but don't let your nose grow too long!

James Johnson

Acknowledgments

We would like to thank the following people, who reviewed chapters for this edited collection. They have shared their expertise with us and provided valuable comments for the chapters. This volume couldn't be completed without their support.

Dr. David Kushner, University of Cincinnati
Dr. Thomas Hendricks, Elon University
Dr. Nesrin Isikoglu Erdogan, Pamukkale University, Turkey
Dr. Karen M. Johnson, Penn State University, University Park
Dr. Lynn Hartle, Penn State University, Brandywine
Dr. Jennifer Vu, Early Childhood Consultant
Dr. Jason Hustedt, University of Delaware
Dr. Dorit Randal-Griffin, University of Delaware
Dr. Rick Worch, Bowling Green State University

Introduction

James Johnson and Myae Han

The connection between play and the educative-social environment is of obvious interest. It entails many important questions having to do with pedagogical-psychological models, the adult's role in supporting play, materials, and the design of situations and activities for teaching, playing, and learning. This connection becomes intriguing and even perplexing when thinking deeply about the tensions that arise. There is an obvious one between 'fabula,' or the soul of play, the free spirit, on the one hand, and the sturdiness of focus and the seriousness of intent typical in planning and implementing the curriculum. Almost like an irresistible force meeting an immovable object.

A question then becomes, can we balance levity with gravity? Can there be a happy tension between serious-playful, grave-merry? There is a Germanic expression for this. It is *Spoudogeloios*. *Spoudos* translates "serious." And *gelein* translates 'to laugh." Perhaps this unusual expression captures something about this book. How many of us have an urge to reach this ideal, such an evenness of spirit, a *Spoudogeiloios* in the practice of the art of connecting play and curriculum? Perhaps oil and water do mix.

The study of play has been fruitful. So too the study of the uses of play. Educators have long been pursuing and applying ways that play can be a context and even a medium for teaching and learning. Play and curriculum accordingly has received a great deal of attention by researchers and theorists. To be sure, the lion's share of the play world does not intersect with curriculum, or intentional teaching. Playing and learning is happening *without* curriculum. This book, however, is concerned with play and learning *with* curriculum. The present volume draws attention to when curriculum is in play, when flexible, creative teachers, and teachers of teachers, are deliberately setting up curriculum and instruction for play to happen, for certain kinds of quality play to happen, because such play, it is believed, can be a positive influencer on the well-being of the players, their intentions and actions, their learning and development.

The topic under the spotlight in this volume is complex and with many dimensions, and rests upon a voluminous literature. Given the response of our initial call for papers and the winnowing process that we employed, the final set of chapters of the volume were found to be suitably organizable into three sections: I Play, Curriculum and Culture; II Play and Curriculum in STEM; and III Play, Teachers and Higher Education.

PLAY, CURRICULUM AND CULTURE

It seems appropriate for *Play & Culture Studies* to begin with three chapters having to do with culture and contextual factors relating to play and curriculum. More importantly, this topic is currently attracting a great deal of attention because of what is called the global learning crisis and attempts to alleviate it using play as learning strategies. For example, *Sesame Street* is the longest street in the world with scores of nations adapting its television program because of its educational and entertainment value that relies for its effectiveness in part on blending the shows' content and delivery forms in ways that are consistent with child development science and play studies. *Lego Foundation* sponsors annual conferences and supports play-based curriculum development in developing countries, motivated by the fact that curriculum for early learning must foster a breadth of skills and be personally meaningful, and that this is the play curriculum, the one needed to address the global learning crisis.

Pathways and networks must be forged to succeed in making play-based learning work, helping parents and other adults in unique situations understand the universal applicability and local adaptability of play-based learning. External factors of various kinds can facilitate or impede going for the play way to do curriculum and instruction, as the three chapters in this section exemplify. Also, we see the significance of the teacher in relation to other adults, be they parents, administrators, other teachers, in communicating and coming to a shared understanding about the importance of play. Play pedagogy and relationship pedagogy both are needed; they go together in work having to do with professional differences and cultural and generational variability.

In the first chapter, "Incorporating play into the preschool curriculum in a Kogi community in the Sierra Nevada de Santa Marta," S. Lynneth Solis proclaim *saber propio y saber universal,* "own knowledge and universal knowledge" as a saying to reflect a driving force to generate and employ play curriculum that includes indigenous knowledge as well as non-indigenous knowledge. Parental and local community buy-in is revealed in this ethnography to be key to achieving this, and the key to this is the relationship between the teachers and the parents. Many rich details are provided, such as young children's collecting natural specimens for use as manipulatives in learning and illustrating relevant concepts, integrating subjects such as math and social studies. The chapter includes discussion of many important concepts and topics and brings home the point about the criticality of the ethno-education for establishing and developing play pedagogy in developing cultural contexts in our rapidly changing world.

The next chapter, "A case study of a New York City elementary school's adoption of the Playworld activity" by Beth Ferholt, relates a multilayered account of the first adoption not just implementation of the comprehensive and ambitious playworlds in a U.S. school, hinting that perhaps the time is right to begin to do something about the lack playworlds in American Early Childhood Education. The reader sees the classroom of 25 preschool and kindergarten age children with their teachers becoming a magical place where imaginations are ignited and fanned for learning and creativity through the dramatic 'The Trolls' playworld. The case conveys the feel of how interconnected and dynamic are the various dimensions internal to playworld's workings (e.g., careful listening to children, documentation, children's voices in inter-session dialogues and planning, etc.), as well as setting factors and the flow of time. Clues are offered to help the reader to better understand this major world -famous approach and what it might take to see it spread across the educational landscape in the U.S.

In chapter 3, "Home-based child care providers' perspectives about play, curriculum, and quality improvement initiatives," Alison Hooper, Juana Gaviria-Loaiza, and Cailin Kerch set the reader's focus on the often neglected culture of home-based child care, and its distinctive advantages for play and the curriculum such as small group sizes and multi-age enrollment. External systemic pressures can also work against play-based pedagogy and child care. As a subset of a larger study the chapter reports the results informing the reader about how 29 providers described their curriculum and play practices, a very valuable contribution since this research is new and original in its focus, and how they perceived external quality improvement initiatives (In U.S. Quality Rating and Improvement Systems or QRIS) in relation to their views on integrating play and curriculum. Together the two main research questions and the findings and how they are discussed indicate how important external factors are for rendering the curriculum a positive context for play.

PLAY AND CURRICULUM IN STEM

The twenty-first century brings with it a new urgency for educators to prepare students for an uncertain future. Social cognitive skills, creativity, confidence, persistence among others are needed. Problem solving and thinking like a scientist or mathematician are often foregrounded as especially critical. Balancing play with technology, and play with nature, and integrating technology and nature play, have been noted among the primary goals of this century's education with the use of play. Science, technology, engineering, and mathematics (STEM) in play pedagogy are commonly linked to other areas of the curriculum like art (STEAM). Play and STEM are a great combination for such linkages or curricular networking.

This section's three chapters recognizing this new urgency are about STEM curricular issues and play. They are also about the different kinds of play that occur in educational settings that put special emphasis on math, science and nature. A common pattern is for exploratory play, inquiry play, and constructive and construction play to unfold, often sequentially and cyclically as students examine, re-examine, and transform or construct with materials. Dramatic and art/sensory play and game play including ones involving physical activity are also common.

Across the many different play forms, teachers are important in the play. They have various roles such as observing, assessing and documenting the play, or negotiating play decisions with the children, or even co-playing with them. Teachers are responsible for the curriculum and the situational arrangements for STEM-related play, whether the aim is free play, also called spontaneous play or student-initiated play, or teacher-guided play or teacher directed play. The chapters in this section describe this in the research reported concerning play and children and learning math, science and nature.

In the first chapter in this section, "Facilitating mathematical thinking in preschool play: Findings of The CECE Math-Play studies" (chapter 4), Sudha Swaminathan and Jeffrey Trawick-Smith summarize the results of a series of six related studies valuable because they examined math learning and play in naturalistic free play classroom settings and not artificial laboratory settings. Naturalistic video-recorded observations of children and preschool teachers were carefully coded, and when appropriate variables were studied in relation to children's math learning tapped by Tools for Early Assessment in Mathematics (TEAM) employing hierarchical multivariate regression. This chapter's wealth of information about play and teaching and curriculum is based on the systematic research findings leading to sometimes surprising and definitely nuanced answers to six research questions: (1) Which aspects of block play lead to math learning? (2) How do teachers engage children in mathematical thinking in play? (3) Which types of teacher-child interaction influence math learning? (4) Do increases in teacher math talk during play predict greater math learning? (5) Which math topics (e.g., number, geometry, measurement, patterning) do teachers talk about, how and why? (6) Which domains, structures, and purposes of math talk influence math learning?

In chapter 5, "Exploring the role of free play in elementary science," Brian Stone, Lora Lorentsen, and Meghan Schmidt examine empirically in a descriptive field study how free play during third and fourth grade science lessons on static electricity affects learning and student behaviors. Following a comprehensive review of the literature, the methods and procedures of the research are described with results and discussion following. The researchers were focused on the value of child-initiated spontaneous play with select materials, not teacher guided or directed play, and they reported evidence for the benefits of free play in science. Noting how play is undervalued typically in elementary science, they recommend the free play approach be added because of its value for children's creativity, problem-solving, and concept learning.

In chapter 6, "Thinking outside the woods: Teacher's story of urban nature and inviting the wild into the city classroom," Heather Pinedo-Burns discusses the importance of nature play (natural materials lead to explorations and inquiry into the sciences, states of matter, gravity, etc.) , and how to achieve nature play in urban early childhood settings. She describes in rich detail using narrative inquiry her memories and records of how nature and children's and teacher's play and activities with nature unfolded over the years, how she worked with parents her "loved ones," and other stakeholders advocating for a nature mindset. Eschewing fixed romantic conceptions of nature play, she pragmatically embraces the future and the challenges of working to help all children benefit from the nature play and experiences, something of unsurpassed importance in today's world.

PLAY, TEACHERS AND HIGHER EDUCATION

Although the play studies literature includes seminal books that include adult play, such as Henricks (2015) *Play and the human condition,* Sutton-Smith (1997) *Ambiguity of Play* , Kerr and Apter (1991) *Adult play: Reversal theory-telic and paratelic states*), and Huizinga (1950) *Homo Ludens: Play element in culture,* little is known about adult and youth and late adolescence periods and play in educational settings. Playful classrooms for these older students would appear welcomed for the safety and flexibility and freedom they would offer during the learning experience. Mental health issues such as suicides and suicide attempts among young people during their tertiary educations reflect the intense and increasing stress levels felt by members of the forgotten generation. Play based pedagogy could serve well as an antidote to this. In addition to serving emotional and intrapersonal needs, play in the college curriculum could benefit students interpersonally, not to mention their continuing brain development of the executive function (see chapter 9).

In addition, there is growing interest in the effects of having play curriculum experiences at the college level on the beliefs and ideas about play, depth of understanding of play pedagogy, of future teachers, especially those who will be working with young children. Recent work has examined what is known about preparing teachers to enact play pedagogy (Ryan & Northey-Berg,2014), in terms of candidate teachers' views of play, and in terms of what courses and professional development opportunities exist. The value of play in higher education is not just for the teachers and students, but the future students of the new teachers. But are playful methods actually used that are play for play's sake, and not for some ulterior instrumental reason? Chapter 7 examines this using Wood's (2014) play pedagogy distinction between play *in* education (instrumentalism) and play *as* education (play for play's sake).

The first chapter in this section (chapter 7), "Play in higher education: Emergent understandings of play pedagogy for adult learners in early childhood teacher education programs," Marleah Blom and Miranda D'Amico first note that human beings do not stop playing nor lose the capacity to play when they become young adults in the college classroom. Play pedagogy has a place in higher education, especially in training teachers of young children who will employ play with their students. The chapter shares methodological details and findings of a carefully done study in Canada in which early childhood teacher educators from 13 institutes of higher education provided survey and interview data of their beliefs about play and learning related to teaching, and of perceived institutional affordances and barriers to the use of play in higher education teaching and learning. The study's discussion of findings is usefully framed using Wood's (2014) notions of play *as* education versus play *in* education within her play-pedagogy interface.

In chapter 8 "Learning, NOT playing: Mixed method analysis of early childhood preservice teachers' perceptions on children's play," Ilfa Zhulamanova investigated empirically university students' beliefs about play and child development and early education. These students were early childhood teacher candidates and at different semesters in their preparatory program, and they(N = 241) completed on-line surveys using Future Professional's Survey(FPS) developed by Jung and Jin (2014); using mixed methods, interviews were completed on two students who were earlier on in the program

(Cohort 3) and two further along (Cohort 5). Results and interpretation from the qualitative data yielded valuable information relating students' beliefs about play and curriculum to personal childhood play experiences, as well as helping explain quantitative results showing statistically significant cohort differences in beliefs about the role of play in the curriculum.

Finally, chapter 9, "Games at college: Furthering pedagogical and co-curricular goals through play," Abby Loebenberg, Robert Mack, and Laurel Bongiorno report on the case study each co-author performed using games (not to be confused with gamification) with college students. As a group they agree that executive function (EF) is critical in cognition and academic success, and that play supports the developing brains of college age students (EF development continues until age 25 years according to the latest brain science research). The first case study (Loebenberg) involved Role-Playing Games to help each student generate and process and study game playing data over the semester. Research methods in anthropology were learned as the students engaged in this experiment, earning college credits in research methods with this clever use of game play, which students found very attractive making the course in demand on campus. Case 2 (Mack) explored how the principles of modern Eurogame design (German-style board games that appeal to players of board games post childhood) can be usefully adapted making discussion groups run more smoothly and be more enjoyable, for instance, for first year college students thereby enhancing their learning experiences. Case 3 (Bongiorno) reports rich descriptions and illuminating discussions on the use of a modified *Game of Life* as a co-curricular (not a course but put on as a program since 2012 by the career center at the college) play pedagogy for first year students. The three cases demonstrate how games scaffold important learning and support executive function.

Play and curriculum viewed within ever-changing philosophies of education brings a new ingredient to the mix connected to an idealistic dualism commented upon by none other than the American sage Benjamin Franklin who shared this wisdom concerning what should be directed the student's way: "It would be well if they could be taught everything that is useful and everything that is ornamental: but art is long and their time is short. It is therefore proposed that they learn those things that are likely to be most useful and most ornamental" (cited in Bruner,1960, p.4). As Bruner (1960) observed, Franklin considered specific skills to be useful, general understanding as ornamental. This paradox plays itself out in the classroom and other educational settings over and over again, not just with respect to content but also methods. Playful teaching and learning, new emerging play pedagogies, are not just the spices of classroom life (like a spoonful of sugar helping the medicine go down); but they are also needed substances, its ingredients fitting many recipes that can enrich the educational experiences of learners in many situations and across different cultural contexts.

SPECIAL ACKNOWLEDGMENT

This volume would not have been possible without the help of many people, both those of whose names appear in the book and others not mentioned. Among all these people, Jim Christie is front and center. Both co-editors had very special and long-lasting relationships with Jim and learned so much from him and cherish the relationship and the many memories. As we conversed and worked together on this project, we could not help but think of Jim as our strong supporter and teacher. Many feel the same way for sure. We dedicate our work on this volume and the next to him.

REFERENCES

Bruner, J. (1960), *The process of education.* Cambridge, MA: Harvard University Press.

Henricks, T. (2015) *Play and the human condition.* Chicago: University of Illinois Press.

Huizinga, J. (1950). *Homo Ludens*. Boston: Beacon Press.

Jung, E. & Jin, B. (2014). Future professionals' perceptions of play in early childhood classrooms. *Journal of Research in Childhood Education, 28*, pp. 358–376.

Kerr, J.H. & Apter, M.J. eds. (1991). *Adult play*. Amsterdam: Swets & Zeitlinger.

Ryan, S. & Northey-Berg, K. (2014). Professional preparation for a pedagogy of play. In L. Brooker, M. Blaise, & S. Edwards (Eds.) *The Sage handbook of play and learning in early childhood.* (pp.204–215). Los Angeles, CA: Sage.

Sutton-Smith, B. (1997). *The ambiguity of play.* Cambridge, MA: Harvard University Press.

Wood, E. (2014). The play-pedagogy interface in contemporary debates. In L. Brooker, M. Blaise, & S. Edwards (Eds.) *The Sage handbook of play and learning in early childhood.* (pp.145–156). Los Angeles, CA: Sage.

Section I

PLAY, CURRICULUM AND CULTURE

Chapter One

Incorporating Play into the Preschool Curriculum in a Kogi Community of the Sierra Nevada de Santa Marta

S. Lynneth Solis

Studies conducted in small-scale societies provide accounts of indigenous children's play activities and the cultural and social factors that influence them (e.g., Boyette, 2016; Gaskins, 1999; Nyota & Mapara, 2008). Even so, research on indigenous children's play is limited and can simplify or miss the complex ways in which indigenous children engage in play differently than what is typically documented in the literature (Dender & Stagnitti, 2011). More recently, as indigenous children across the world enter formal schooling, questions arise about how to incorporate play into the curriculum in ways that honor local knowledge and tradition (Ames, 2012; Eisazadeh, Rajendram, Portier, & Peterson, 2017; Peterson, Madsen, San Miguel, & Jang, 2016; Taheri & Chahian, 2015). If implemented without regard for the local context, playful learning approaches can become part of a toolbox of educational practices that have historically operated explicitly and implicitly to reject indigenous ways of knowing (May & Aikman, 2003; Romero-Little, 2010). Studying how play is incorporated into the curriculum in small-scale communities can shed light on how local experiences, language, and pedagogical practice can be leveraged to equip children to face contemporary challenges (Moland, 2017; Roopnarine, Patte, Johnson & Kushner, 2015).

This chapter reports on the playful learning experiences of young children of the Sierra Nevada de Santa Marta (SNSM), Colombia. While largely preserving their way of life, the Kogi of the Sierra Nevada often interact with mainstream Colombian culture, perhaps most notably through a growing system of government-sponsored schools. The complex interrelation between informal cultural activities and formal schooling in these communities provides a unique opportunity to study play and the curriculum in an everchanging society. Drawing from interviews and observations and using narrative descriptions of teaching, this chapter presents the story of educators at one Kogi school as they consider how they can employ play to educate young children to value their traditions but also navigate the world outside those traditions.

CONCEPTUAL FRAMEWORK

Extensive theoretical and empirical work, conducted mostly in Western settings, has argued for the relationship between young children's play and educational and developmental outcomes in a variety of domains, including physical and mental health (e.g., Fjørtoft, 2004; Tremblay et al., 2015), language development (e.g., Toub et al., 2018), and social-emotional regulation (Diamond, Barnett, Thomas, & Munro, 2007; Blair & Raver, 2014). For example, children's play with blocks has been linked to the development of spatial language (Ferrera, Hirsh-Pasek, Newcombe, Golinkoff, & Lam, 2011), mathematics skills and executive functioning (Schmitt, Korucu, Napoli, Bryant, & Purpura, 2018), logico-mathematical knowledge (Kamii, Miyakawa, & Kato, 2004), spatial visualization abilities (Caldera et al., 1999), and math achievement in middle and high school (Wolfgang, Stannard, & Jones, 2001, 2003). What these and myriad other studies supporting the benefits of play suggest is that play is a "laboratory of the possible" (Henricks, 2008, p. 168) where children are free to explore, manipulate, and practice skills that prepare them to navigate and make sense of cognitive and social tasks in the real world (Pellegrini, 2009; Singer, Golinkoff, & Hirsh-Pasek, 2006; Smith, 2010; Zosh et al., 2017). The evidence provides a strong argument for the importance of incorporating play into the curriculum.

That said, if and how play is incorporated into classroom practice and curricula is affected by both teachers' and parents' beliefs about play (Gaskins, Haight, & Lancy, 2007; Kazemeini & Pajoheshgar, 2013), the features of the physical environment, and the stated and unstated goals of education in a particular context (Göncü, Jain, & Tuermer, 2007; Moland, 2017; Roopnarine et.al., 2015). When understood as a phenomenon that is both universal but deeply embedded within children's social and cultural interactions and contexts, studying the role of play in the curriculum requires a lens that accounts for pedagogical as well as contextual influences. And this seems particularly important when considering education in indigenous communities.

As indigenous peoples consider their past, present, and future, and the place that formal education may have in the education of their youth, questions arise as to how play can become a pedagogical approach that honors children's and family's experiences, especially when historically, formal education efforts have done quite the opposite (Ames, 2012; Eisazadeh, Rajendram, Portier, & Peterson, 2017; Peterson, Madsen, San Miguel, & Jang, 2016; Taheri & Chahian, 2015). As a form of cultural learning (Lancy, 2016), however, play can be central to the transmission of knowledge, rituals, and history in communities. For example, in an attempt to re-awaken, maintain, and impart indigenous knowledge in younger generations, the Ewes of Ghana rely on traditional games, dance, and songs to educate and equip children to fulfill the adult roles in the society (Amlor, 2016). Similarly, among the Shona of Zimbabwe, children's games and songs reflect the indigenous knowledge, virtues, and values that are cherished by their society, including discipline, hard work and competitive spirit, dealing with failure, and assuming leadership roles (Mutema, 2013; Nyota & Mapara, 2008). For example, Shona children play the singing game of *Dede zangara uyo mutii*? (What type of tree is that?), in which children are expected to identify different trees and have an understanding of their biophysical environment (Nyota & Mapara, 2008).

Despite the extant examples in the literature of how indigenous communities are defining the role of play in education, more explorations of how this is considered across cultural contexts are needed to inform curricula that are developmentally appropriate and culturally meaningful. In particular, very few studies consider this issue in Latin American indigenous settings as local communities consider their place in a globalized world. The present study explored this question in a Kogi community of the Sierra Nevada de Santa Marta (SNSM), Colombia. As two Kogi teachers, Mr. Joaquín and Mr. Gabriel [Note. Pseudonyms are used throughout the chapter], face the daily challenges of teaching a small group of children in a remote settlement in the Sierra Nevada, they also reflect on how play might help them to foster the skills, values, and dreams that will inspire the next generation of community leaders.

METHODS

The present study draws from data collected in a nine-month ethnographic study of Arhuaco, Kogi, and Wiwa indigenous children's play in the Sierra Nevada de Santa Marta on the Caribbean Coast of Colombia, which is located in the north of the country. Participant observations and interviews took place over nine months from August to November 2015 and February to June 2016 to align with the end and beginning of the school year. Living in remote settlements in the SNSM, the Arhuaco, Kogi, and Wiwa, practice subsistence farming, raise livestock, fish, hunt small game, and sell or trade artisanal crafts, such as hand-woven mochilas, or bags. Settlements are distributed throughout the SNSM, mostly populated by a few dozen extended families each. Although the local language and specific ceremonies and rituals differ across the groups, they have maintained a shared heritage of customs and spiritual beliefs centered on their responsibility for maintaining the balance of the universe (Esmeral Ariza, 2015; Reichel-Dolmatoff, 1982, 1990).

The introduction in recent decades of ethno-education, or formal education for ethnic minorities, supported and funded by the Colombian Ministry of Education, has offered opportunities for social, cultural, and economic development in the indigenous communities of the region. Despite the promise of an integrative ethno-education, however, schooling continues to follow a largely Western model that explicitly and implicitly rejects local knowledge and language (Aikman, 1997; Ferrero Botero, 2015; May & Aikman, 2003). As Ferrero Botero (2015) argues,

> For the state and mainstream Colombian, [ethno-education] means the materialization of the push for modernity and inclusion, as 'other,' of indigenous peoples into a neoliberal multicultural nation. While for indigenous peoples, it is a pivotal mechanism of resistance, based on their struggle to maintain their ethnic identity, seek self-determination, and gain the necessary knowledge to successfully adapt to an intercultural context. (p. 288)

Furthermore, the national political agenda incorporates play as a vital component of the early childhood pedagogical approach to serve the multicultural populations of Colombia (Ministerio de Educación Nacional, 2014), but arguably with little attention to how these ludic practices may be perceived or received by local communities. Thus, tensions arise as children and families access information and resources through formal education yet strive to preserve their local knowledge and practices.

Through naturalistic observations of children's daily activities and interviews with parents, teachers, and community leaders in one settlement from each of the Arhuaco, Kogi, and Wiwa communities, the larger ethnographic study investigated children's play in and out of school; the factors that impact the availability of play resources; and the beliefs that shape play opportunities. The study demonstrated that a complex system of competing priorities and visions of childhood shape when and how children engage in play across the research sites. The present analysis focuses on data from the Kogi community, Ableizhi, given the active role that teachers there took in incorporating play into their curriculum.

Research Site

Ableizhi is located along the Buritaca river basin in the SNSM, and getting there requires a two-hour, off-road drive from the nearest city and a three-hour hike through the sierra. The Kogi ethnic group is known to be the most traditional, secluded, and impenetrable of the ethnic groups in the SNSM. Compared to the other two research sites, Ableizhi has the least regular contact with outsiders. The two-room school was founded in 2004, but at the start of fieldwork in 2015 had been open for only three years after being closed for a few years prior to that. The school is located near a community meeting place; however, children and their families live in smaller compounds at various distances from the school—from a fifteen-minute to an hour-and-a-half walk through the brush. At the start of fieldwork, 40 students were enrolled in preschool through fifth grade, and by the time fieldwork ended, 60 students were enrolled in the school.

Two teachers, who are both Kogi, teach in multi-grade classrooms. Mr. Joaquín teaches preschool through first grade (roughly ages 5–11) and Mr. Gabriel teaches second through fourth grade. Mr. Joaquín and Mr. Gabriel went to school in a neighboring Kogi community and then had the opportunity to complete secondary education in the capital city of Colombia, Bogota. After their education in Bogota, both Mr. Joaquín and Mr. Gabriel sought further pedagogical training. Mr. Gabriel went on to complete college and graduate studies in education and, at the time of the study, Mr. Joaquín was attempting to complete an online college certificate in indigenous education, which was challenging given that he could only access Internet when he traveled to the nearest city.

Procedures

I collected classroom observational fieldnotes and interviews (conducted in Spanish) with the two teachers (both primarily fluent in local Kogi language and also fluent in Spanish) over eight, week-long visits to Ableizhi. These data were analyzed using emic, thematic coding to characterize how play experiences in school were shaped by sociocultural and educational influences, culturally regulated customs, and beliefs about play and education. Ongoing data processing guided fieldwork and data analysis as I tested initial insights, triangulated among different data sources, looked for potentially confirming or disconfirming evidence, and solicited feedback from participants regarding my preliminary understandings (Maxwell, 2005). By identifying emergent patterns in the data, I produced an ethnographic sketch that contextualizes play within the sociocultural milieu of the school and community.

In this account, I draw from the method of portraiture, a qualitative approach that merges systematic, rich description with an attention to the aesthetic whole of the narrative to tell the unique stories and lived experiences of the participants being portrayed (Lawrence-Lightfoot & Davis, 1997). Central to portraiture is the presence of the portraitist-researcher's voice in the narrative and the attention to the relationships she builds with her participant-actors. Thus, this analytical approach was focused on the themes that surfaced as I spent time in communities and shared everyday experiences with children, families, teachers, and other community members (Lawrence-Lightfoot & Davis, 1997). From the perspective of the portraitist-researcher's voice, portraiture allows for actions to be illustrated within the complexity of everyday interactions, which provides a unique approach to look at play in the indigenous educational setting.

What follows is an ethnographic portrait that weaves together the insights gathered from observations and interviews about how teachers negotiate the role of play in educating young children. Mr. Joaquín and Mr. Gabriel explain that they see play and playful forms of learning as culturally relevant and as an opportunity for children to expand their community knowledge. Although their teaching can be marked by typical signs of formal schooling (e.g., whole-group instruction, individual work in notebooks), they also incorporate play and playfulness into their daily classroom activities across the curriculum to engage their learners in thinking about their present and their future. They also negotiate priorities with parents and engage families in the learning process to ensure that education is a communal decision and experience. By describing the efforts of these teachers, I illustrate the approaches that emerge through one indigenous community's attempt to incorporate play into the curriculum, consider the challenges of doing this, and reflect on the opportunities to leverage these efforts to inform the challenge of indigenous education.

PLAY AND THE STRUGGLE
TO EDUCATE THE NEXT GENERATION

Just a few feet downhill from a gathering place, I come to a two-room, concrete school building with tin roof. Just beyond the school, there is a soccer field that ends in a precipice overlooking the Molino River. The school building, which is partially painted white, has exactly two doors and four windows as the only forms of ventilation. The only other structure near the school building is a wooden kitchen shed with a fire pit and two long wood tables, where food is prepared and consumed. This will all change during the time I spend here, with the construction of a concrete kitchen, the addition of a bathroom building a few feet away from the schoolyard, and the planting of a school garden. On a return visit after the completion of the study, a group of non-profit organizations has funded and coordinated the construction of two new classrooms, with a third under construction.

Given its remote location, Ableizhi feels both physically and culturally disconnected from mainstream Colombian society in ways that I do not experience in the other two communities I visit. The arduous trek here makes it almost impenetrable, and a strict stance against tourism imposed by the Kogi communities along this part of the Sierra Nevada make it nearly impossible for outsiders to visit, except for a few, who through close relationships with community members or special permission from leaders, are allowed passage. Although my visits never go unnoticed by members of the community (who often ask my local companions who I am and what I'm doing here), I like to think that over time, the special permission that once gained me entrance to Ableizhi has evolved into close relationships with teachers, children, and their families.

It is through these close interactions that I come to realize that rather than being isolated from outside influences, Ableizhi is daily being confronted by the direct and indirect influences of the world beyond the Sierra Nevada. Teachers are considering what it means to educate children who value their traditions but can also navigate the world outside those traditions; parents are reconciling the generational changes they witness as their children develop and experience things that seem far away from their own experiences as children; and boys and girls are engaging in behaviors and playful educational experiences that deviate from those of their parents when they were young.

The School Day

Children attend school from 7:00 am to noon. The children have a short recess break in the morning, roughly around 9:00 am, when they can have a snack that they either bring from home or they pick from the trees surrounding the school grounds. If there is food for lunch in the kitchen, which is not always the case, children wait around at the end of the school day, playing soccer and gathering in small groups, while the food is prepared by community mothers.

On my first visit, Mr. Joaquín begins class by reading a book in the local language to the whole class. When he finishes the story, he asks first grade students, who can write, to pull out their notebooks to copy and answer the questions on the reading that he has written on the board. Mr. Joaquín then walks over to the younger children and checks the numbers they have written in their notebooks, reading them out loud as a review for students. He then calls preschoolers over to his desk at the front of the classroom in order to write an assignment in their notebooks. He draws large letters, pours glue on them, and then asks children to trace the letters by spreading the glue with their finger. The school has little in terms of available materials and supplies. However, the teachers see the surrounding natural resources as potential materials. On this day, Mr. Joaquín sends a boy outside to collect sand so that the preschoolers can paste it onto the letters they have just traced with the glue. Once the children are done with this activity, they take their notebooks outside to dry.

Most days inside the hot classroom, with only a meager breeze coming through the open windows, follow similar routines. Mr. Joaquín will give students an assignment and then they will spend extended periods of time working in their notebooks. Classroom activities are focused on completing assignments and the teacher either imparting or checking knowledge. However, the luxury of extended time at Ableizhi allows me to see that the school is in a transition toward an educational approach that is open to a diversity of instructional practices, including playful instructional approaches.

Integrating Play into the Curriculum

From talking to teachers and parents, and observing classroom activities over time, I begin to gather that the school at Ableizhi is trying to develop an educational approach that deviates from things-as-usual in the Sierra Nevada indigenous education context to foster "creativity and innovation" in students, as Mr. Joaquín puts it [Note. Direct quotations are translated from Spanish to English.] Although much of their teaching still entails typical educational approaches, like teacher-focused lecturing and planas—rows of practiced writing—Mr. Joaquín and Mr. Gabriel also employ diverse instructional practices—working in groups, building replicas and models, and dramatizing learning—that they believe provide children with experiences that can foster motivation, creativity, and teamwork. It is not necessarily that there is a coordinated set of approaches they implement or a clearly defined curriculum, but rather a commitment to incorporate different ways of teaching and learning as the teachers receive further training.

Mr. Joaquín and Mr. Gabriel both tell me they consider play and playful forms of learning as culturally relevant and as an opportunity for children to expand their community knowledge. They plan for activities in the classroom with an educational goal in mind but allow children to participate in flexible, enjoyable, active learning ways. Much of the playful forms of learning I observe reflect the skills and activities that are typical of this community and this region, such as cooking on the fire, using weaving tools, and utilizing natural materials to build, with the purpose of tapping into students' existing knowledge but also encouraging them to think beyond their current experience.

Mr. Gabriel tells me that "play is important because children learn and form ideas about things they need to know in this world." He says that he includes dramatizations in his instructional practice "to help children envision what they are preparing for in life." Mr. Joaquín is concerned about students' participation in class. Prior to attending school, children have learned to be still and silent during social gatherings and interactions with adults; once they attend school, it is hard to get them to participate in classroom activities. He sees play as a way of drawing students out to share their thinking during instruction and encouraging them to think creatively for their sake and their community's sake. He explains, "What I see is that [students] need to be more dynamic, creative people. People who know how to do many things. For what? So that each of them can also participate and be more creative in their community."

I observe Mr. Joaquín closely as he incorporates play opportunities in his instruction with the younger students in the school. Sometimes they are subtle instructional moves; other times they are full blown, planned activities. For example, he has children collect natural specimens to illustrate concepts and use as manipulatives, he brings in objects that children can play with during class to learn a given concept and incorporates dramatization and games into his lessons. Mr. Joaquín will ask children to go out to the forest surrounding the school to collect leaves, dirt, stones, or fruits to incorporate into the day's lesson. One morning, he sends children outside to look for examples of small and large rocks to help illustrate the mathematical concept of larger/smaller. He sends out groups of four or five children at a time, and they gleefully go out exploring their surroundings for rock samples. One child comes upon a large pile of rocks that have been amassed for the kitchen renovation project, and soon a group of children gathers around him, squatting and picking rocks to take back to the classroom. Once all the children have returned to the classroom with their collections, Mr. Joaquín places all the rocks into a black plastic bowl and invites students to hold, touch, examine, and organize them from smallest to largest, asking questions about students' understanding of the concept. Finding rocks on the ground is perhaps not new for children, but by having them scavenge for them, examine them closely, and utilize them as manipulatives, he has transformed a mundane experience into an enjoyable, active, participatory math lesson.

Early one day, Mr. Joaquín sends the preschool children to the yard to build models of huts of different shapes (round, square, rectangular) with the natural materials around them. Mr. Joaquín explains to me that he thinks of this project as introducing children to mathematical and engineering concepts involved in building but also social studies topics of diversity and plurality. The different ethnic groups of the Sierra Nevada can largely be identified by the shapes of the homes they build, and Mr. Joaquín wants children to consider the cultural diversity that determines people's choices and practices, including how they build their homes. Mr. Joaquín has to attend to other students' needs and join a parent meeting while the younger children are outside building; and, the children are free to organize themselves and their strategy for building their models, choose their building materials, and enjoy the time outdoors. The groups of three or four children gather leaves and cut wooden sticks with machetes to build their structures. They sit on the ground around their structures, tying sticks together with organic fibers and making roofs out of large, green leaves. Midmorning, the children break for a snack and afterward return to the classroom with their models in hand to present to the entire class. As children share the structures they have built, Mr. Joaquín engages the class in a conversation about the different types of homes and how they represent cultural differences.

Sometimes Mr. Joaquín is the one who introduces new materials. In the classroom there are two mochilas, hand-woven bags, with objects Mr. Joaquín has collected for children to use. One bag has marbles that Mr. Joaquín gives students to help them count or solve math problems. The other bag contains a collection of contraptions that the children have built with wood and large, round, smooth seeds to resemble the tool that adults use to "hilar," or spin, the yarn that they use to make mochilas. Mr. Joaquín tells me that the purpose of these creations is to help children learn about their traditional crafts but also learn to innovate on the traditional tools and activities of their community. This is the first step in a multi-step creation process in which the children will eventually make real tools. He says he wants children to make their own tools to learn the craft and then invent new ways of doing this task that has been part of the community's daily life for generations.

One morning I walk into the classroom and find two groups of the preschool children sitting in circles on the floor around colorful objects. Mr. Joaquín purchased the manipulatives for his five-year-old son, Andres, who is not yet enrolled in school but brought them to school for the math lessons with the preschoolers. One group of three boys and three girls is building with large plastic building blocks. They build towers by connecting one with another and then use pieces with wheels on them to make their structures mobile. Mr. Joaquín tells me he wants children to invent something with the blocks and, in the process, learn mathematical concepts, like categorization, size (smaller/bigger), and shapes. The other group of four boys and two girls use colorful tokens and categorize them by color and then stack them on a plastic platform. Mr. Joaquín allows children to manipulate the blocks and tokens by themselves for a few minutes and then comes over to check whether they have been exploring the mathematical concepts he intended by asking them questions to check their understanding. He provides further context for the exploration and then leaves them to continue manipulating the objects independently, for about an hour.

In addition to incorporating the use of objects, manipulatives, and models, the teachers task children with planning and executing skits that represent their learning, drawing out their ability to dramatize and engage in the non-literal, that is, pretend. When I visit the school at the end of the term, I find the children dressed up in feathers, some with bows and arrows made of branches and twine, and others climbing trees. Mr. Joaquín explains that the children are representing lessons about the respect for life, nature, and others that the children learned in ethics class. Over several days, children practice different dramas in groups, dressing up as animals common in the region, building huts with branches and leaves, and acting out farming, hunting, teaching, and ritual scenes, scenarios that they are familiar with in their cultural context. They make their own costumes, create their own props, and practice their dialogues and acting, guided by the teachers. The dramas are then performed at a gathering of the community where children present what they have learned throughout the year. In this way, students and teachers, families and leaders, share in this playful, imaginative way of learning.

Teachers at Ableizhi see education as an important experience that will benefit children and the community as a whole, especially as they interact more and more with mainstream Colombian society. As Mr. Joaquín explains, their goal is to prepare children to innovate and improve upon existing traditional practices. Mr. Joaquín and Mr. Gabriel embrace the challenge of educating children to know their own cultural values and practices and also know and understand the diverse values of other people outside their community.

Saber Propio y Saber Universal

When I speak to parents at Ableizhi, they seem satisfied with the work that Mr. Joaquín and Mr. Gabriel are doing and are supportive of their approaches to teaching, despite their reservations about children's participation in play. Although parents seem perfectly comfortable with, and even open to, the kinds of play that occur at school, when I ask them more generally about their beliefs about play, one type of response illustrates the continued generational and cultural tensions that permeate parents' attitudes about play: Parents bemoan the fact that childhood today seems different from what it was when they were growing up. Milena, one of the mothers I interviewed, explains,

"Our mothers taught us that [children should not play] but today, children are different. They play. I tell my daughter, don't do that, but she doesn't listen, she doesn't understand."

Parents recount the negatives they see in play—they believe it is a waste of time, or fear that children will be physically harmed, or believe that it disrupts the spiritual order in the world. Milena continues discussing the concerns about play disrupting spiritual order,

> Our ancestors tell us that we shouldn't play, we shouldn't dance, we shouldn't jump, do these things. It is better not to play and instead be quiet so there is not a change in the world. We need to be still so the world is still. That is, the equilibrium.

And Verónica, another community mother, explains her concerns about safety,

> Not all games are bad, but I have to correct, I only have to guide them to what game is good and what game is bad. Because there are games, like swinging on the side of the river, or jumping in the river, because what if they are playing in the river and they slip on a rock and the blow can be hard.

Despite their concerns about play, I suspect parents trust Mr. Joaquín's and Mr. Gabriel's approaches for at least two reasons: first, they are both Kogi and are able to communicate to community members and leaders as respected insiders; second, they both invest a lot of time and energy in communicating with parents, informing them about educational methods, and including them in the decisions that affect the school and the students. When I first entered the community, Mr. Joaquín and Mr. Gabriel told me that they welcomed my research but that it would be the parents' ultimate decision whether I was allowed access or not. One morning early in the project, they arrange one of their usual parent meetings and invite me to share my research and purposes with parents. About 20 mothers, fathers, and community leaders gather in one of the classrooms—sitting in the same desks that their children sit in— and ask me about my intentions, whether I will return to their community (as opposed to leaving after one visit, as they have experienced before), and whether I will contribute to the school in some capacity. Mr. Joaquín and Mr. Gabriel facilitate my conversation with parents, interpreting and explaining as I talk research, play, learning, and child development.

Several times during my visits, I watch the teachers as they lead similar parent gatherings to discuss issues related to the activities that take place in the classroom, school construction projects, and the future of education in the community. It is this attention to the communication with parents that

I surmise allows Mr. Joaquín and Mr. Gabriel to employ playful pedagogical approaches in their teaching, without resistance from families; and even encourage their indirect participation as they witness children distill their learning in playful ways. Parents trust what is happening in the classroom and let the teachers make decisions about what children should be doing there. I suspect that it is the teachers' quiet, empathetic, and wise leadership and their vision of what is possible for the school and their community—a commitment to their own ways of knowing yet an informed understanding of cross-cultural interactions that can lead to a thriving future—that open the school doors to play.

Both Mr. Joaquín and Mr. Gabriel refer to this as "saber propio y saber universal," meaning "own knowledge and universal knowledge," to indicate that their goal is to create an educational experience that will help children become proficient in the knowledge that is important to their community (own knowledge) and the non-indigenous knowledge that is important to interact productively outside their community (universal knowledge). Play is one way they try to achieve this. Mr. Gabriel tells me,

> I think that what we should take into account, nowadays, about play, is to understand what is interculturality. Not only should the indigenous students know their sports, their games, but they should also know the sports or games of other cultures. For that reason, it is very important for me that in each [indigenous] institution they also know about foreign games, and that they also know their own games. That is what we are looking for, not to ignore foreign games, not to say that foreign games should not be known. No. For me, games that are from outside are also very important, we must know our games in the same way, we have to know others' games. To talk about interculturality we have to talk about this.

The difficulty they acknowledge is that lessons from formal schooling sometimes overshadow traditional teachings from home. Their responsibility, as they identify it, is to teach students to honor the hard work required to survive in a physical setting like the SNSM and respect their spiritual traditions of honoring the Earth, while gaining new skills and knowledge that may change the economic and cultural structure of their community. They see incorporating play into their curriculum as a way of achieving this goal.

DISCUSSION

The story of incorporating play into the teaching and learning taking place at Ableizhi is a developing one. The above portrait captures a dynamic community that is negotiating its approaches and priorities for educating children.

The way that Mr. Joaquín and Mr. Gabriel bring play and playfulness into their lessons is not extremely different from what may be observed in early childhood environments typically represented in the literature; however, in their context, it is a revolutionary approach within the fraught indigenous education system in Colombia and within a cultural context where adults are skeptical, at best, about the role of play in children's learning and development. It represents an attempt to inject their teaching with experiences that will foster children's ownership, curiosity, and enjoyment (Solis, Khumalo, Nowack, Blythe-Davidson, & Mardell, 2019) and will prepare them to face the challenges of a changing world while leveraging their local and universal knowledge.

The depiction of Mr. Joaquín's and Mr. Gabriel's ways of incorporating play into their teaching is neither entirely unique nor universally representative. And this by no means is the aim of the present ethnographic study. Rather, it is an attempt to make visible the daily experiences of indigenous teachers, children, and families in the SNSM to shed light on how one small school and community is grappling with the tensions that arise when considering play as part of the curriculum. Given the extensive nature of the larger ethnographic study, this chapter offers only a snapshot of the school and community, constrained by the limitations of the qualitative method, which centers texture and detail, and the researcher who, although immersed in the community for an extended period of time, is an outsider with her own cultural and academic worldview that colors her interpretations. That said, insights were shared with participants and data were triangulated along the way to verify the validity of preliminary findings and themes that informed the final portrait. Although the experiences described in this chapter may not represent all similar approaches to incorporate play into indigenous educational settings, it does provide meaningful implications for policy and practice.

Teachers like Mr. Joaquín and Mr. Gabriel need systemic supports to continue to incorporate play into their practices effectively. Governments across the world identify child-centered, play-based, holistic approaches as essential in education. However, few provide pedagogical and technical support to equip teachers with the expertise and skills to facilitate and foster play in their classrooms. Given the structural challenges that indigenous teachers face, in addition to the paradoxes that often arise between play and school (Mardell et al., 2016), a commitment to playful pedagogy from government- and school-level leadership is required. This includes, incorporating playful pedagogy and curricular approaches into pre-service teacher training for teachers working with indigenous populations; adapting curricular materials to specifically identify opportunities for play and playfulness across content areas that draw from local cultural knowledge and practices; training practicing teachers in the facilitation and documentation of play from a sociocultural perspective; creating networks of teachers to support one another in exploring the challenges of incorporating play into the curriculum in indigenous settings; and supporting teachers in communicating their play-based approaches to families in ways that are respectful and accessible.

Importantly, much innovation happens in real time, as teachers make choices in planning and adapting their curriculum to meet the learning objectives and the needs of their students. As they follow children's interests and build on their natural propensity to play, teachers must also consider their educational goals and available materials. In order to achieve this fine balance, they need a level of trust and flexibility from their schools and education ministries to try things out in their classrooms. In indigenous settings this takes on an urgent tone, given that teachers, students, and families in these contexts are often forgotten by researchers and policymakers. When we observe and listen closely to teachers like Mr. Joaquín and Mr. Gabriel, we are better positioned to support them in their pedagogy and their important call to help prepare children to face the challenges and responsibilities of an uncertain tomorrow.

REFERENCES

Aikman, S. (1997). Interculturality and intercultural education: A challenge for democracy. International Review of Education, 43(5–6), 463–479.

Ames, P. (2012). Language, culture and identity in the transition to primary school: Challenges to indigenous children's rights to education in Peru. International Journal of Educational Development, 32, 454–462.

Amlor, M. Q. (2016). Imparting indigenous knowledge through traditional forms of entertainment: The role of ewe play games. World Journal of Social Science, 3(2), 63–74.

Blair, C., & Raver, C.C. (2014). Closing the achievement gap through modification of neurocognitive and neuroendocrine function: Results from a cluster randomized controlled trial of an innovative approach to the education of children in kindergarten. PLOS ONE, 9(11), e112393.

Boyette, A. H. (2016). Children's play and culture learning in an egalitarian foraging society. Child Development, 87(3), 759–769.

Caldera, Y. M., Culp, A. M., O'Brian, M., Truglio, R. T., Alvarez, M., & Huston, A. C. (1999). Children's play preferences, construction play with blocks, and visual-spatial skills: Are they related? International Journal of Behavioral Development, 23(4), 855–872.

Dender, A., & Stagnitti, K. (2011). Development of the indigenous child-initiated pretend play assessment: Selection of play materials and administration. Australian Occupational Therapy Journal, 58(1), 34–42.

Diamond, A., Barnett, W. S., Thomas, J., & Munro, S. (2007). Preschool program improves cognitive control. Science, 318(5855), 1387–1388.

Eisazadeh, N., Rajendram, S., Portier, Christine, & Peterson, S.S. (2017). Indigenous children's use of language during play in language during play in rural Northern Canadian kindergarten classrooms. Literacy Research: Theory, Methods, and Practice, 66, 293–308.

Esmeral Ariza, S. J. (2015). La educación en comunidades indígenas frente a sus proyectos de vida y las relaciones interculturales. Santa Marta: Editorial Unimagdalena.

Ferrera, K., Hirsh-Pasek, K., Newcombe, N. S., Golinkoff, R. M., & Lam, W. S. (2011). Block talk: Spatial language during block play. Mind, Brain, and Education, 5(3), 143–151.

Ferrero Botero, E. (2015). Ethno-education (etnoeducación) in la guajira, colombia: Shaping indigenous subjectivities within modernity, neoliberal multiculturalism, and the indigenous struggle. Latin American and Caribbean Ethnic Studies, 10(3), 288–314.

Fjørtoft, I. (2004). Landscape as playscape: The effects of natural environments on children's play and motor development. Children Youth and Environments, 14(2), 21–44.

Gaskins, S. (1999). Children's daily lives in a Mayan village: A case study of culturally constructed roles and activities. In A. Göncü (Ed.), Children's engagement in the world: Sociocultural perspectives (pp. 25–61). New York, NY: Cambridge University Press.

Gaskins, S., Haight, W., & Lancy, D. F. (2007). The cultural construction of play. In A. Göncü & S. Gaskins (Eds.), Play and development: Evolutionary, sociocultural, and functional perspectives (pp. 179–202). Mahwah, N.J.: Lawrence Erlbaum Associates, Inc.

Göncü, A., Jain, J., & Tuermer, U. (2007). Children's play as cultural interpretation. In A. Göncü & S. Gaskins (Eds.), Play and development: Evolutionary, sociocultural, and functional perspectives (pp. 155–178). Mahwah, N.J.: Lawrence Erlbaum Associates, Inc.

Henricks, T. (2008). The nature of play. American Journal of Play, 1(2), 157–180.

Kamii, C., Miyakawa, Y., & Kato, Y. (2004). The development of logico-mathematical knowledge in a block-building activity at ages 1–4. Journal of Research in Childhood Education, 19(1), 44–57.

Kazemeini, T., & Pajoheshgar, M. (2013). Children's play in the context of culture: Parental ethnotheories. Journal of Science and Today's World, 2(3), 265–281.

Lancy, D. F. (2016). Ethnographic perspectives on culture acquisition. In C. L. Mehan & A. Crittenden (Eds.), Childhood: Origins, evolution, and implications (pp. 173–196). Albuquerque, NM: University of New Mexico Press.

Lawrence-Lightfoot, S., & Davis, J. H. (1997). The art and science of portraiture. San Francisco, CA: Jossey-Bass.

Ministerio de Educación Nacional (2014). El juego en la educación inicial. Bogota, Colombia.Retrieved from http://www.deceroasiempre.gov.co/Prensa/CDocumentacionDocs/Documento-N22-juego-educacion-inicial.pdf.

Mardell, B., Wilson, D., Ryan, J., Ertel, K., Krechevsky, M., & Baker, M. (2016). Towards pedagogy of play. A Project Zero working paper. Retrieved from http://www.pz.harvard.edu/resources/towards-a-pedagogy-of-play.

Maxwell, J. A. (2005). Qualitative research design: An interactive approach. Thousand Oaks, CA: SAGE Publications, Inc.

May, S., & Aikman, S. (2003). Indigenous education: Addressing current issues and developments. Comparative Education, 39(2), 139–145.

Moland, N. A. (2017). Localizing play-based pedagogy: Nigerian educators' appropriation of sesame classroom materials. Global Education Review, 4(3), 17–36.

Mutema, F. (2013). Shona traditional children's games and songs as a form of indigenous knowledge: An endangered genre. IOSR Journal of Humanities and Social Science, 15(3), 59–64.

Nyota, S., & Mapara, J. (2008). Shona traditional children's games and play: Songs as indigenous ways of knowing. The Journal of Pan African Studies, 12(4), 189–202.

Pellegrini, A. D. (2009). The role of play in human development. New York, NY: Oxford University Press.

Peterson, S. S., Madsen, A., San Miguel, J., & Jang, S.Y. (2016). Children's rough and tumble play: Perspectives of teachers in northern Canadian Indigenous communities. Early Years, 38(1), 53–67.

Reichel-Dolmatoff, G. (1982). Cultural change and environmental awareness: A case study of the Sierra Nevada de Santa Marta, Colombia. Mountain Research and Development, 2(3), 289–298.

Reichel-Dolmatoff, G. (1990). The sacred mountain of Colombia's Kogi Indians. Leiden, Netherlands: E.J. Brill.

Romero-Little, M. E. (2010). How should young indigenous children be prepared for learning? A vision of early childhood education for indigenous children. Journal of American Indian Education, 49(1/2), 7–27.

Roopnarine, J. L., Patte, M., Johnson, J. E., & Kuschner, D. (Eds.). (2015). International perspectives on children's play. New York, NY: Open University Press.

Schmitt, S. A., Korucu, I., Napoli, A. R., Bryant, L. M., & Purpura, D. J. (2018). Using block play to enhance preschool children's mathematics and executive functioning: A randomized controlled trial. *Early Childhood Research Quarterly, 44*, 181–191.

Singer, D. G., Golinkoff, R. M., & Hirsh-Pasek, K. (2006). *Play-learning: How play motivates and enhances children's cognitive and social emotional growth.* New York, NY: Oxford University Press.

Smith, P. K. (2010). Children and play. Malden, MA: Wiley-Blackwell.

Solis, S. L., Khumalo, K., Nowack, S., Blythe-Davidson, E., & Mardell, B. (2019). Towards a South African pedagogy of play. A Pedagogy of Play working paper. http://www.pz.harvard.edu/resources/toward-a-south-african-pedagogy-of-play

Taheri, L., & Chahian, G. (2015). Restoration of traditional children's play in Iranian nomadic societies (case study of Kohgilouyeh and Boyer Ahmad). Children (Basel), 2(2), 211-227.

Toub, T.S., Hassinger-Das, B., Nesbitt, K. T., Ilgaz, H., Weisberg, D. S., Hirsh-Pasek, K., . . . & Dickinson, D.K. (2018). The language of play: Developing preschool vocabulary through play following shared book-reading. Early Childhood Research Quarterly, 45(4th Quarter), 1–17.

Tremblay, M.S., Gray, C., Babcock, S., Barnes, J., Bradstreet, C. C., Carr, D., . . . & Brussoni, M. (2015). Position statement on active outdoor play. International Journal Environmental Research Public Health, 12(6), 6475–6505.

Wolfgang, C. H., Stannard, L. L., & Jones, I. (2001). Block play performance among preschoolers as a predictor of later school achievement in mathematics. Journal of Research in Childhood Education, 15(2), 173–180.

Wolfgang, C. H., Stannard, L. L., & Jones, I. (2003). Advanced constructional play with LEGOs among preschoolers as a predictor of later school achievement in mathematics. Early Child Development and Care, 173(5), 467–475.

Zosh, J. M., Hopkins, E. J., Jensen, H., Liu, C., Neale, D., Hirsh-Pasek, K., . . . & Whitebread, D. (2017). Learning through play: a review of the evidence (white paper). The LEGO Foundation, DK. http://www.legofoundation.com/da-dk/research-and-learning/foundation-research

Chapter Two

A Case Study of a New York City Elementary School's Adoption of the Playworld Activity

Beth Ferholt

Within early childhood care and education (ECEC) in the United States, we often find ourselves with promising play pedagogies from other countries, or even from other decades in our own countries' history of developing systems and institutions of ECEC; and with colleagues, including teachers, researchers and children, who are eager to experiment with making these pedagogies their own. However, ECEC is an increasingly hostile environment for such ventures. The 'Position paper about the role of play in early childhood education and care' (2017) by the 'Rethinking Play' special interest group of the European Early Childhood Education Research Association states the problem concisely (and we can simply expand their conclusions to the U.S. for our purposes here): ". . . the value attributed to children's play by policy makers in early schooling is linked to concrete (cognitive) learning outcomes rather than a holistic perspective of children's development, leading to an instrumentalisation and regulation of play and a 'schoolification' of ECEC(Hännikäinen, Singer, & van Oers, 2013. p. 165) . . ."

This chapter presents a case study of the efforts of twenty-five young children, four kindergarten teachers, one teaching artist and one university-based researcher to transform the early childhood curriculum of a New York City public elementary school through their collaborative work with a Swedish preschool play activity over the course of one school year. One of the teachers' primary goals was to create an environment that was less likely to instrumentalize and regulate play. Specifically, the teachers decided to adapt the *playworld* activity, a play activity that is a part of the Swedish scholar, Gunilla Lindqvist's, *Creative Pedagogy of Play* (Lindqvist, 1995), to their various pressing needs in a U.S. ECEC setting, today. Lindqvist's (1995) pedagogy is based in Vygotsky's (1971, 1978, 1987, 2004) theories of play, art, creativity and imagination. This chapter presents several ways that the multigenerational team of this study made use of Vygotsky's understanding of the creative potential of children's play and of art to counter schoolification in their early childhood curricula.

Playworlds can be described as combinations of adults' forms of creative imagination, which require extensive experience (e.g., art, science), with children's forms of creative imagination (e.g., play), which require the embodiment of ideas and emotions in the material world. The development of both children and adults in this intergenerational, hybrid form of play has been of central interest to playworld researchers in part because, unlike many intergenerational activities, playworlds allow children as well as adults to take the position of expert. Findings of this study include the unexpected supposition that it was the leadership of one child, whose voice was rarely heard in the classroom until the playworld was near its end, which played a key role in the playworld activity being championed by participating teachers, which in turn played a key role in the playworld activity being adopted, rather than tried and discarded, by the school in which it was being created.

In *Play & Culture Studies, v. 11* (Marjanovic-Shane et al., 2011), a group of playworld scholars from Sweden, Finland, Serbia and the United States, including the author of this paper, discussed this relatively new form of play activity. We were inspired by the arrival of playworlds in the U.S. in 2003 and our recent formation of the International Playworld Network at the Laboratory of Comparative Human Cognition (LCHC) at the University of California, San Diego. However, while playworlds proliferated internationally, playworlds were not created in any early childhood classrooms in the U.S., aside from those few classrooms originally connected to LCHC, until the playworld of this study took place in 2017–2018.

This chapter presents findings from a case study of the first U.S. playworld to be adopted by–rather than simply housed in—a U.S. school or preschool. This study was not designed to produce findings that could be formulated as practice or policy recommendations. Rather, this study was designed to highlight underappreciated or little understood aspects of this playworld while supporting the teachers in their efforts to sustain their playworld work by achieving the adoption of the playworld activity by their school, i.e., having their school reorganizing itself to support the playworld activity.

Through this study, several areas of focus emerged that may be of interest to U.S. early childhood teachers who want to undertake creating playworlds, as well to playworld scholars thinking about the lack of proliferation of playworlds in the U.S. These include: time (on two scales), solidarity in resistance (of early childhood teachers and their administrators to restraints that the teachers feel are imposed upon them in their work with young children), artists working with teachers, trust and collaboration between teachers, and the afore-mentioned potentially effective power of young children's voices.

This chapter will first present the playworld activity's theoretical underpinnings and contributions from playworld studies that have been undertaken in several different countries. Next the chapter will describe the study methods and the process of creating this particular playworld at this particular school in the U.S. The chapter will conclude with a discussion of the aspects of this process that our analysis indicated were particularly significant in the process of the school moving from simply housing the playworld activity to reorganizing itself, to some degree, to support the playworld activity.

PLAYWORLDS

Playworlds are grounded in the theories of L. S. Vygotsky (1971, 1978, 1987, 2004) and the internationally known work of Gunilla Lindqvist of Sweden (1995, 2001, 2003) and Pentti Hakkarainen of Finland (2004), as well as in the work of less widely known theorists and various local pedagogies. Lindqvist (1995, 2001, 2003) interprets Vygotsky's theory of play through his *Psychology of Art* (1971), and through a reading of *Imagination and Creativity in Childhood* (Vygotsky, 2004) that focuses on Vygotsky's assertion that children's play is a creative cultural manifestation in humans. In *The Role of Play in Development,* Vygotsky (1978) states: "Only theories which maintain that a child does not have to satisfy the basic requirements of life but can live in search of pleasure could possibly suggest that a child's world is a play world (p.102)". Instead, a child's world is as "real" as our own. Adults are always a part of children's "real" lives, and thus a part of children's play; and therefore, designing a play pedagogy involves deciding *upon the ways that* adults will join children in play, not whether adults will enter children's play at all. It is Vygotsky's (1978) insistence that a child's world is not a play world, separate from and less real than the adult's world, which supports Lindqvist's conviction that children are never alone in play.

In playworlds that are directly inspired by Lindqvist's work, such as the playworld of this study, interactions between adults and children are structured around a piece of children's literature or another work of art, such as an oral folk tale. The adults and children work together to "bring the literature to life" (Lindqvist, 1995, p.72) through drama (or, in some cases, dance, although we will here discuss the dramatic playworlds). The participants assume roles, characters from the literary piece, and "make use of the intrinsic dynamism between world, action and character in drama and play" (1995, p.72). The children and adults transform their classroom into the imaginary world of the chosen narrative through joint scripted and improvisational acting, as well as through joint production of props and sets. The common fiction of playworlds becomes a common context for adults and children in which all participants are able to find the potential to "provide our existence with meaning" (1995, p.203). (For a more in-depth discussion of playworld origins in theory and practice please see Nilsson & Ferholt, 2014.)

Playworlds and playworld studies continue to be created and their findings discussed in new publications. A resource for learning about recent playworld work that is or has been connected to LCHC is the playworld section of *The Story of LCHC: A Polyphonic Autobiography* (available at http://lchcautobio.ucsd.edu/), a living electronic document. The following summary of playworld studies that most closely resemble the playworld of this study in several structural regards, is elaborated upon in this electronic document, where one can find links to playworld work in Finland, Sweden, Japan and other countries.

Playworld research in Finland has focused on the psychological effects of adult-child joint play on children's development and general abilities, such as school readiness (Bredikyte & Hakkarainen, 2011; Hakkarainen, 1999; 2004; 2006; 2008; Hakkarainen et al., 2013.). Finnish playworld research has also applied a socio-culturally oriented critical research tradition to the study of adult-child interaction in playworlds (Rainio, 2010), with a focus on the development and manifestations of children's agency and voice in playworld activities (Hofmann & Rainio, 2007; Rainio, 2007, 2008a) on the challenges occurring in playworld classrooms based on the contradictory relationship between teacher control and management and student agency (Rainio, 2008b; 2010); and on gender from a critical gender perspective by Rainio (2009).

Recent research examining playworld projects in Swedish preschools has shown how teacher's participation in these projects transforms their relational competence (Ferholt et al., 2018). Observations from this research have also formed the basis for critiques of the dichotomization of play and learning that often shape the pedagogical and policy agendas of early childhood education internationally (Ferholt & Nilsson, 2017a; Nilsson et al., 2017); discussions of the aesthetics of play (Ferholt & Nilsson, 2016c; Ferholt & Nilsson, 2017b); and arguments concerning creativity in the field of early childhood education (Ferholt et al., 2014; 2016).

Recent playworlds research in Sweden has also focused on methodological contributions. A book written by and for researchers and preschool teachers, *Play, learning and happiness!–Playing and exploring in preschool* (Nilsson et al., 2018), describes a framework for future research studies that is called *early childhood education research from within*. Cross-cultural playworld analyses has been used to study imagination and the use of psychological tools (Hakkarainen & Ferholt, 2013) as well as agency, engagement and ambivalence (Ferholt & Rainio, 2016).

In the U.S., playworld research has combined quasi-experimental work with deep ethnographic analyses of adult-child participation. This work has shown that participation in a playworld improves children's narrative and literacy skills (Baumer et al., 2005) and that playworlds can lead to the mutual socio-emotional development of both adults and children (Ferholt, 2009; Ferholt & Lecusay, 2010). U.S. playworlds have also provided unique evidence of the synergy between emotion and cognition, a notoriously difficult process to study, but also one recognized to be of central importance to cognitive and social development, through the study of *perezhivanie* (or intensely-emotional-lived-through-experience) (Ferholt, 2009; Ferholt, 2010; Ferholt, 2015; Ferholt & Nilsson, 2016a, 2016b). And analysis of U.S. playworlds has been used to expand Vygotsky's concept of the zone of proximal development (ZPD) through the study of the development in both adult and child playworld participants (Ferholt & Lecusay, 2010).

METHODS

Design

Lindqvist fully appreciated that the confrontation of theory with practice is a powerful source of theoretical development. Lindqvist (1995, 2001, 2003) designed and implemented her creative pedagogy of play to further her reinterpretation of Vygotsky's (1987, 2004) theory of play. Although Lindqvist did not use the term, many of the playworld studies mentioned above, Lindqvist's own playworld studies and the study of this chapter can be described as 'formative interventions' (Engeström, 2008).

Engeström describes formative interventions by contrasting formative interventions with "the linear interventions advocated [. . .] by the literature on design experiments" (Engström, 2008, p. 15). He states that the crucial differences between the two are as follows: "In formative interventions, the subjects (whether children or adult practitioners) construct a novel solution or novel concept the contents of which are not known ahead of time to the researchers"; "In formative interventions, the contents and course of the intervention are subject to negotiation and the shape of the intervention is eventually up to the subjects"; and, "the aim is to generate intermediate concepts and solutions that can be used in other settings as tools in the design on locally appropriate new solutions" (Engeström, 2008, p. 15–16).

Participants

The participants in the playworld of this chapter included the entire class of 25 children aged 4–6 at the start of the year and 5–7 after December, the teacher of this class, and three teachers from two of the three other kindergarten classes in the building. All of these participants were based in a public elementary school in New York City that offers priority to children who qualify for free or reduced lunch. The other two central participants in this playworld were one freelance teaching artist and one university-based researcher (the author). Also present were one first grade teacher, one paraprofessional, several high school student helpers, several "push-in" "specials" teachers (science, gym, and library teachers), one volunteering retired teacher and several student teachers, including one teacher in training from Sweden. All were present for one or more playworld sessions and contributed notes, verbal insights and photographs to the pedagogical documentation (Alnervik, 2013) process. Two visual artists also contributed their photographs and video footage of the playworld on three separate occasions. The teachers who entered the playworld in role were both senior teachers, one having taught for 17 years and one, the classroom teacher who hosted the playworld, having taught for 19 years.

Ethnographic Data

The Pedagogy of listening and exploratory learning approach are inspired by the Reggio Emilia preschools of the Northern Italy (Reggio Children and Project Zero, 2001). Loris Malaguzzi is the person most famously associated with this pedagogy whose significant concepts include a) pedagogical documentation, which is a tool and an approach which makes children's interests, questions and hypotheses about phenomena and relationships in the world visible, and b) the organization of pedagogical work in the preschool into yearlong exploratory projects. As the playworld was conceived as a yearlong project that was being created using pedagogical documentation, as well as a project designed to teach the teachers how to practice pedagogical documentation (as discussed below), materials generated for and through the pedagogical documentation process constituted the ethnographic data for this study.

Field notes; written records of children's words; audio recordings of teachers' meetings and devising/rehearsals with the teaching artist; photographs and video recordings of playworld sessions, including art production and reflection, and of class meetings, were produced by all participants and were incorporated into the pedagogical documentation practice. Preliminary analysis took place during these nearly weekly pedagogical documentation meetings over the course of the playworld's duration, such that teachers and the university-based researcher engaged in the first stages of analysis together and with a primary concern for the development of the playworld itself (see Ferholt, 2010).

Pedagogical documentation involves children in documentation and reflection, so that child participants were also involved in preliminary analysis, although less explicitly than were adult participants. Between playworld sessions the children viewed and discussed relevant videos, photographs and their own, transcribed words. Further analysis was guided by this initial analysis: The field notes made by several different participants and the teachers' discussions at what appeared to be points of tension,. rapid development or reflection in the playworld process, were analyzed in greatest detail during this second stage of analysis.

The Trolls' Playworld

The U.S. Trolls' playworld was a result of seven years of collaboration between the university and this public elementary school. When working on a playworld research project with preschools in Sweden, and living in Sweden, I hosted the principal of the school, a former student of mine who was then a paraprofessional at the school, Rick (all names are pseudonyms), and a fifth grade teacher at the school. During the visit the school principal expressed her sense of a kinship between her own Dewey-inspired elementary school and the three Swedish preschools with which I was working, including their instantiations of the playworld pedagogy. Thus, the principal of the school was not only supportive of some aspects of the Swedish preschools and the playworld activity influencing her school, she actually initiated this influence after her visit to Sweden by inviting me to keep working with her school in relation to Swedish EDUCARE and by sending many of her teachers to visit the three Swedish preschools.

These Swedish preschools' former pedagogista (master teacher), Tove, an internationally known master teacher and scholar of pedagogical documentation, as well as the director of the three Swedish preschools, Anders, offered to meet with several teachers at the school to help these teachers learn more about the aspect of the Swedish preschools that interested them most: pedagogical documentation. Tove had recently found that the playworld pedagogy was useful in helping novice teachers to avoid being shy when they were documenting their own work with the children. As Tove explained to the teachers, to listen in the pedagogy of listening you need to see yourself and ask how you are thinking about children and childhood. We New York City residents understood Tove to mean that the pedagogy of listening helps teachers to listen in new ways, but that this requires exploring and reflecting upon one's own teaching process. The New York City teachers immediately responded to Tove's suggestion concerning the playworld pedagogy, saying that they could imagine it would be much easier to document themselves playing than to document themselves teaching. As attempts at pedagogical documentation during the spring before the Troll's playworld had been focused on the work related to the kindergarten classes' shore study, the burgeoning playworld work was also focused on the shore.

The summer preceding the classroom work on the Troll's playworld, the work on the Troll's playworld proper can be said to have begun. Several meetings with different combinations of teachers were held this summer, always including Sarafina (a senior teacher who would participate in role–as a character in the playworld—and whose class would participate) and Gaby (another senior teacher who would also participate in role), and sometimes including Rick (who had completed his degree and been hired as a teacher at the school). One of these meetings included the teaching artist, Olivia, and Sarafina and Gaby immediately identified Olivia's coaching as key to their becoming participants in role in the playworld. As Olivia explained, the acting sessions would prepare the teachers to enter the playworld in role and so to play together with the children. These sessions would consist of activities designed to help teachers to improvise and play, to develop the characters that the teachers would play, and to collaboratively devise performances of scenes from the book upon which the playworld would be based.

In these summer meetings the teachers chose a version of the folk tale, The Three Billy Goat's Gruff. Part of the story's appeal for the teachers was that this book included a bridge over water and this was a part of the shore landscape that the class would visit weekly through their shore curriculum. Another part of the story's appeal was that Sarafina wanted to be the Troll. Sarafina began the playworld once her class was somewhat settled into the year's routine's by reading the book out loud to her class. However, despite having the funding for substitute teachers, it was nearly impossible to schedule times for all four teachers or even two or three teachers to meet for pedagogical documentation, times to meet with Olivia, or times when Sarafina's class could work on playworlds and have enough adults in the room for documentation to take place. As is the case for most public elementary school teachers in the U.S., these teachers' days were filled with many unexpected and urgent tasks, most of which were caused by lack of funding and staffing for public schools. Also, when the playworld sessions with the children did take place, while an hour and a half after school sufficed for a meeting, the 40 minute periods allotted during the school day felt, the teachers agreed, too short by at least half: Just when a playworld session with the children got started it had to be cleaned up.

Despite these difficulties, Sarafina gradually moved to adding sounds to the story readings and then to having the children represent aspects of the story and their thoughts about the story in small group work with clay, various visual media, blocks, sound making instruments along with children reading and retelling the story, and in the dramatic play area. These representations and reflections and the processes of creating them were documented by whoever could be in the room at the time with Sarafina, and the teachers started to collect some of these documentations in power point documents (following the Swedish pedagogista's model) during their pedagogical documentation meetings. In order to speed up the process, I would do the actual pasting into a power point of the objects and text that the teachers chose and dictated, both during and after their meetings. By the winter break in December, through their few workshops with Olivia, Gaby and Sarafina had also strengthened their resolve to act in the playworld.

Due, we suspect, to Sarafina's anticipation of the creation of the playworld, her classroom had also come to be frequently visited by the trolls or a troll without her initiating or even expecting this to happen. These visits became apparent to the teachers through the listening to the children that the pedagogical documentation practice enhanced. The children had begun to bring the story into other media, often three dimensional media, and they soon found some of the troll's hair at the shore, then more in the classroom; and they also explained that what Sarafina had thought was a problem with the lights in her room was actually the troll or trolls turning the lights on and off.

By winter break Gaby and Sarafina had made a decision that allowed them to enter the playworld in role and they began, over break, to rehearse their January arrival in the classroom. Because Sarafina expressed more discomfort with participating in role than did Gaby, Serafina and Gaby decided they would be sister trolls in the playworld, with Gaby caring for Sarafina. Sarafina would be losing her hair from stress, particularly stress from the loud noise of the goats clip-clopping over the bridge, and would thus be mute, requiring Gaby to translate for her as well as to for her. This put Sarafina sufficiently at ease to enter the playworld in role. Gaby would also enter the playworld in role through work around voice, particularly through her use of a hockey mouth guard on her teeth, which would make it difficult for her to articulate her words (making her sound more troll-like).

After winter break the two trolls entered the classroom for a short time. They had difficulty staying in role and did not interact with the children but they managed to make a powerful impression. The pedagogical documentation highlighted the children's interest in bridges during the fall and into the winter and at this time time machines, designed to take the trolls home so that they could avoid loud noises (such as clip-clopping over their heads) were carefully planned and built in small groups using cardboard boxes, a great deal of tape and other materials. These time machines were built over the course of many months and had many details, scales and foci, but the theme of "returning to family" appeared to the adult participants to emerge more frequently in tandem with the increase in news coverage of immigrant children separated from their families at the U.S. border.

These time machines next moved to an extra room downstairs after much discussion amongst the teachers about the best location for a longer play-world session with the adults in role. The teachers also decided to include Olivia, the teaching artist, in role as a goat during this session, setting the scene while they waited to appear, hiding from the children's sight, under the bridge (a table with a cloth over it). When the two trolls came out from under the bridge the children remained seated as the audience but engaged verbally with the trolls, explaining to them how their time machines worked, before the trolls and then the children left the extra room.

The time machines then returned to the classroom and were all connected through a button, so that they were all coordinated even though they were not yet ready for the big day when the trolls would use them to return to their families. Working on the time machines remained one of the favorite activities of most of the children and the work generated endless class and small group discussions about everything from whether or not time machines were best powered by LED batteries to whether or not time machines should carry milk in them in case the trolls' dogs wanted milk in their cereal.

During Sarafina's class's almost-frenzied post-downstairs performance months, during which time they were constructing their time machines, the trolls visited several more times and a pattern emerged. Instead of engaging the trolls in enacting the original story as it had been evolving through the children's various retellings between playworld sessions, as the adults expected the children to do, the children took the trolls by their hands and showed them the classroom, toys and books from home, how to eat food, loose teeth, etc. The trolls were now, it seemed, visitors who would soon be sent back "home" and they needed lots of feeding and petting, as well as snuggling and "hanging out" with their new friends, the children.

Then, before the teachers knew it, the end of the school year was upon them all. The teachers had not yet begun their role-play in the story with the children, rather than just interacting with the children while in role but when the story was not unfolding. However, role-play in the story with the children was what the teachers understood to be the heart of a playworld and was what they wanted to achieve.

In response to this dilemma Sarafina led her class in planning a final party with the trolls and when the assigned day arrived they all danced together under a miniature disco ball. Then the trolls left to join their families through the time machines, which had been moved in front of the door and configured into a sort of tunnel. Because dance parties were a part of the non-playworld classroom routine and the trolls' joining their families was a part of the playworld story, this final playworld session moved the playworld into adult-child joint role-play in the playworld story.

The trolls actually left the classroom and the school as well as the disco party and they then waved to the children from across the street. The children were gathered at the window waving back. When Sarafina returned to the class a little while later, a basket of rolled notes thanking the children had been found in the classroom. Sarafina read the notes and distributed them, one to each child. In the final class discussion that ensued, the children decided that the trolls were "safe with their families," "where they belonged," but that they "must have loved us" because they had spent so much of their time in the classroom.

Finally, over the summer the teachers reflected upon their yearlong playworld and made a scheduling request, which the principal of the school granted. The next year they would have a set "joint prep" period every week. This would be a time when all three kindergarten classes would be with gym, art or music teachers. Sarafina's classroom would be empty at this time, ready to host any number or combination of students as they created a playworld with all four classroom teachers, and this classroom was a space where playworld sets and props could remain set up for as long as needed. Furthermore, this joint prep period would come before recess and lunch and would, thus, allow playworld activities to continue for up to two periods if lunches were eaten in the classroom (a logistical feat, but possible).

AREAS OF FOCUS

Time

The forms of collaboration that led to the Troll's playworld and subsequent changing of one school's schedule to accommodate the playworld activity were complex and multifaceted, required many resources and much chance, and took place with the input of scores of people over seven years. A play activity that is popular in a country with the most famous early childhood education and care system in the world, that has been shown to promote early literacy skills, and whose less popular benefits are important and well documented, would, one might assume, be easily and quickly adopted. However, this activity was not adopted without a significant and very long struggle, even by a school with a play-welcoming teaching body and administration. This is an aspect of this area of focus that concerns time across years, while the following concerns time across weeks and hours.

The first thing that the teachers in the Trolls' playworld asked was support for the playworld activity in this school related to the weekly schedule. The teachers decided that they did not want to ask for supplies or extra pay for their hundreds of hours of extra work, or even for funds to pay Olivia's salary, but rather that what they wanted first and foremost was to all four be free at the same time to create playworlds with a small group of children once a week; and to work for two periods at once, not one, if needed. This area of focus appeared early in the Trolls' playworld when Gaby described the Reggio Emilia preschools as being inspirational to her not primarily because of the artworks they produce, but because they are concerned with giving creative activities enough time to develop.

Solidarity in Resistance

A recurring theme that the teachers raised in their pedagogical and planning meetings was that the playworld activity could possibly be adopted by their school because the school, including teachers, parents and administrators, has a long history and strong present of resisting policies and practices that the school believes are not in the best interests of the children. The school resists a variety of policies and practices that are now common in early childhood and childhood education and has actively supported free play in kindergarten for several decades. Gaby expressed a strong commitment to being with students 'how they want to be, how they need' in the current climate (of schoolification), while Sarafina, who is one of the founders of the school, often stated that the school has always had a strong commitment to children learning through play and currently pushes back against kindergarten becoming a 'new first grade.'

Artists Working with Teachers

Gaby and Sarafina repeatedly allocated most of the funds for the project to pay for yet another session with Olivia. At several points when I suggested that they did not need another session with Olivia, they forcefully disagreed with me. It was rare for the two of them to insist with such force that we do anything that depleted our meager resources.

Trust and Collaboration between Teachers

A running observation by the teachers throughout the Troll's playworld was that the playworld work that consisted of collaborating with fellow teachers in the playworld preparation, reflection and performances, and especially those few moments of preparation before performances when the teachers were helping each other to enter their roles, were very important for the teachers in several ways. Gaby said at the start of the playworld work that working together with Sarafina had been a goal of hers for years, and at the end of the Troll's playworld she said: 'When we are working together it is so clear to me that this is the most important thing we can do . . . Then tomorrow comes . . . But I know all will be OK when I am here (working together on playworlds).' And in one teacher reflection and planning meeting, Gaby said that one of the things she had learned this year, in part through her work in the playworld with Sarafina, was that she did not want to teach alone ever again. For her part, Sarafina stated during a later reflection that she wanted to work with Gaby again in playworlds next year because "we both need each other."

The Potentially Effective Power of Young Children's Voices

One of the children in the class was having such a difficult time that he had a paraprofessional assigned to him to keep him from disrupting the class or hurting himself, and he was often not participating in the playworld activity, either because he had been taken out of the room by his paraprofessional for some reason or other or because he chose not to join the activity. However, during one class discussion that took place shortly before the last playworld session with teachers in role, it became clear that this child had been quite engaged with the playworld activity for some time. He had been lying on Sarafina's lap and wiggling about, barely able to remain in the meeting, when suddenly he raised his hand, sat on a chair, and gave a long explanation about an aspect of the playworld that seemed to be about hiding, fear and death.

As the children were apt to do in this playworld, a philosophical discussion about some issues of importance was taking place in a whole class circle with Sarafina helping the children to take turns speaking and asking an occasional question to clarify what someone was saying. These conversations were often about some detail in the playworld and this particular conversation was, in part, about ghosts. The child whom we had thought was not following the playworld activity very closely over the course of the year, was now explaining to his classmates that he had been hiding behind a copy machine in the hall many days and that he had very strong ears so he always heard the trolls arriving even if he was not in the room for a playwolrd session. Then this child offered a great deal of information to his classmates about ghosts and other issues at hand.

I found the discussion a little hard to follow but the other children began asking questions of this child. They appeared to understand every word and asked the child to call on them, to answer their questions and to explain things to them. In one moment this child moved from being severely disruptive of the playworld activity and other activities in the room to being the agreed-upon playworld authority, and he was still leading the discussion after thirteen minutes, when it was time to end the conversation for lunch.

For Sarafina this was the moment that made the struggles to sustain the playworld activity 'all worthwhile.' She called it a 'transformation from start to end,' and saw similar if less extreme rapid development of many of the children over the course of the Troll's playworld. She also often attributed this one child's leaps in development, which continued into the following year, directly to the playworld. Sarafina said of this child: 'So amazing. How they articulated themselves and spoke to each other with such inference and depth. Unbelievable, incredible, magical. The miracle of (child's name).'

Rick attributed this rapid and unexpected development in part to "the immediacy of their (the children's) buy in. Like they were waiting for adults to do this at school." Rick said that it was as if the children were saying of their teachers in role: "They are doing this! They are breaking down concepts already fossilized in 4 and 5-year olds in school. Not doing the boring thing, school, the predictable. Look, is this really happening? It is! In my school. It is really happening." (direct quote, February 1, 2019, playworld meeting)

Sarafina attributed this "miracle" in part to chaos. She said she could see the interweaving of fantasy and reality by the children in her class when she was in role. The children were mischievous but she couldn't leave her place to do anything when she was stuck in her role. She said she always says "Chaos is learning," quoting Mahatma Gandhi, when people visit her class, but now she had to remind herself of this very truth: "They needed the chaos to learn. Being in character made me say it to myself. I could not come out of character to calm the chaos, but it was OK." (direct quote, February 1, 2019, playworld meeting)

For Sarafina this one child's voice was raised and heard by his classmates due to an interweaving of fantasy and reality in chaos. This is what can happen in playworlds, as we know from studies of playworlds in many countries. And this one child's raised and heard voice, after his extended silence, is, in good part, what motivated Sarafina, Gaby, Rick and Fay (Gaby's co-teacher) to ask–in such a way that they made a strong case in favor of their request—for their school to adopt the playworld activity.

CONCLUSION

This study does not provide an answer to the question of how the playworld practice can secure the ongoing support of the institution in which it is housed. We cannot discover through this study how or why this particular school moved from simply housing playworlds to reorganizing itself, to some degree, to support playworlds. We certainly cannot use this study to speculate about playworld adoption in other schools, nonetheless in preschools.

However, at the start of the process of creating this playworld, in August before the Trolls' playworld began, Gaby said that 'come hell or high water' she and her fellow teachers would create a playworld at their school in the coming year. Some things then contributed more than others towards the teachers knowing what they wanted to ask of their principal such that the school could and might support the continuation of their work with playworlds; and some things contributed more than others towards the teachers having the motivation to ask for what they wanted and to ask for what they wanted with the necessary conviction. The above-discussed five areas of focus, which emerged from this case study, are the areas that appeared most likely to be of interest to U.S. early childhood teachers who want to undertake creating playworlds and of interest to playworld scholars who are thinking about the lack of proliferation of playworlds in the U.S.

Unfortunately, of course, long-term engagement of schools and preschools with many different community members and institutions; teacher control of school and preschool day schedules; solidarity in resistance to externally-imposed policies and practices that the school or preschool believes are not in the best interests of the children; artists working in schools and preschools with teachers; activities that support the development of teacher trust and collaboration; and the amplification of unexpectedly powerful children's voices, are not easy to come by in ECEC in the U.S. at this time. And it is far from clear that further study could impact this reality. Still, Sarafina, Gaby, Rick and Fay will continue to imagine and create playworlds with their students thanks, at least in part, to their school's adoption of the playworld activity.

ACKNOWLEDGMENT

This study was completed in part with the support of the Lester and Alice Crow Professorship in Education.

REFERENCES

Alnervik, K. (2013). *"Men så kan man ju också tänka!" Pedagogisk dokumentation som förändringverktyg i förskolan.* Retrieved from http://hj.divaportal.org/smash/record.jsf?pid=diva2:659182

Baumer, S., Ferholt, B., & Lecusay, R. (2005). Promoting narrative competence through adult-child joint pretense: Lessons from the Scandinavian educational practice of playworld. *Cognitive Development*, 20, 576–590.

Bredikyte, M., Hakkarainen, P. (2011). Play intervention and play development. In C. Lobman & B. O'Neill (Eds.), *Play and Culture. Play and Culture Studies, Vol. 11* (pp. 59–83). Maryland: University Press of America.

Engeström, Y. (2008). *The Future of Activity Theory*. Paper presented at the Second Congress of the International Society for Cultural and Activity Research. San Diego, CA.

European Early Childhood Education Research Association, the 'Rethinking Play' specialinterest group. (2017). Position paper about the role of play in early childhood education and care. Available at www.eecera.org/custom/uploads/2017/01/POSITION-PAPER-SIG-RETHINKING-PLAY.pdf.

Ferholt, B. (2009). *Adult and Child Development in Adult-Child Joint Play: the Development of Cognition, Emotion, Imagination and Creativity in Playworlds*. University of California, San Diego.

Ferholt, B. (2010). A multiperspectival analysis of creative imagining: Applying Vygotsky's method of literary analysis to a playworld. In C. Connery, V. John-Steiner and A. Marjanovic-Shane (Eds.), *Vygotsky and Creativity: A Cultural-Historical Approach to Play, Meaning-Making and the Arts*. New York: Peter Lang.

Ferholt, B. (2015). Perezhivanie in Researching Playworlds: Applying the Concept of Perezhivanie in the Study of Play. In S. Davis, Ferholt, B., Grainger-Clemson, H., Jansson, Satu-Marie and Marjanovic-Shane, Ana (Eds.) *Dramatic Interactions in Education: Vygotskian and Socio-Cultural Approaches to Drama, Education and Research*. London: Bloomsbury.

Ferholt, B., and Lecusay, R. (2010). Adult and child development in the zone of proximal development: Socratic dialogue in a Playworld. *Mind Culture and Activity*, 17:1, 59–83.

Ferholt B, Lecusay R and Nilsson M (2018) Adult and child learning in playworlds. In: Smith P (ed.) *The Cambridge Handbook of Play: Developmental and Disciplinary Perspectives*.Cambridge: Cambridge University Press.

Ferholt, B., & Nilsson, M. (2016a). Early Childhood Perezhivaniya. *Mind Culture and Activity*, Published online: 21 Jul 2016, pp. 1–3. Philadelphia: Taylor and Francis Publisher.

Ferholt, B., & Nilsson, M. (2016b). Perezhivaniya as a Means of Creating the Aesthetic Form of Consciousness. *Mind Culture and Activity*, Published online: 21 Jul 2016, pp.1–11. Philadelphia: Taylor and Francis Publisher.

Ferholt, B. & Nilsson, M. (2016c). Play: Aesthetics and the Ambiguity of Play in Early Childhood. In *The Encyclopedia of Educational Philosophy and Theory* (pp. 1–5). New York: Springer Publishing Company.

Ferholt, B., & Nilsson, M. (2017a). Aesthetics of Play and Joint Playworlds. In T. Bruce, M. Bredikyte, P. Hakkarainen (Eds.) *The Routledge International Handbook of Early Childhood Play*. (pp. 58–69). London: Routledge.

Ferholt, B., & Nilsson, M. (2017b). Playworlds and the Pedagogy of Listening. In Tina Bruce, Milda Bredikyte, Pentti Hakkarainen, (Eds.). *The Routledge International Handbook of Early Childhood Play*. (pp. 261–273). London: Routledge.

Ferholt, B., Nilsson, M., Jansson, A. & Alnervik. K. (2014). Creativity in education: Play and exploratory learning. In Thomas Hansson (Ed.). *Contemporary Approaches toActivity Theory.* Hershey, Pennsylvania: IGI Global.

Ferholt, B., Nilsson, M., Jansson, A. & Alnervik. K. (2016). Current playworld research in Sweden: Rethinking the role of young children and their teacher in the design and execution of early childhood research. In Iorio, J. M. & Parnell, W. (Eds.). *Disrupting Early Childhood Education Research: Imagining New Possibilities.* New York: Routledge.

Ferholt, B. & Rainio, A. P. (2016). Teacher support of student engagement in early childhood: embracing ambivalence through playworlds. *Early Years*, 36:4, 413–425.

Hakkarainen, P. (1999). Play and motivation. In Y. Engestro˙m, R. Miettinen, & R. Punama˙ki (Eds.), *Aspects on activity theory* (pp. 231–249). Cambridge University Press.

Hakkarainen, P. (2004). Narrative learning in the fifth dimension. *Outlines: critical social studies, Copenhagen*, v. 6, n. 1, 5–20.

Hakkarainen, P. (2006). Learning and development in play In Einarsdottir, J., Wagner, J. (Eds.) *Nordic Childhoods and Early Education*. 183–222. Conneticut: Information Age Publishing.

Hakkarainen, P. (2008). The challenges and possibilities of a narrative learning approach in the Finnish early childhood education system. *International Journal of Educational Research* 47, 292–300

Hakkarainen, P., Bredikyte, M., Jakkula, K.& Munter, H. (2013). Adult play guidance and children's play development in a narrative play-world. European Early Childhood Education Research Journal 21: 2, 213–225.

Hakkarainen, P. and Ferholt, B. (2013). Creative Imagination in Play-Worlds: Wonder-Full Early Childhood Education in Finland and the United States. In K. Egan, A. Cant and G. Judson, (Eds.), *Wonder-full Education: The Centrality of Wonder in Teaching and Learning Across the Curriculum*. New York: Routledge.

Hoffman, R. R., & Rainio, A. P. (2007). It doesn't matter what part you play, it just matters that you're there. In R. Alanen & S. Pöyhönen (Eds.), *Language in action. Vygotsky and Leontievian legacy today*. Newcastle-upon-Tyne: Cambridge Scholars Publishing.

Lindqvist, G., (1995). Lekens estetik. En didaktisk studie om lek och kultur i förskolan. Forskningsrapport 95: 12, SKOBA, Högskolan i Karlstad. (The Aesthetics of Play. A Didactic Study of Play and Culture in Preschools. Acta Universitatis Upsaliensis. Uppsala studies in Education 62. Stockholm/Sweden: Almqvist & Wiksell International)

Lindqvist, G., (2001). When small children play: How adults dramatize and children create meaning. *Early Years*, 21 (1), 7–14.

Lindqvist, G., (2003). Vygotsky's theory of creativity. *Creativity Research Journal*, 15(4), 245–251.

Marjanovic-Shane, A., Ferholt, B., Miyazaki, K., Nilsson, M., Rainio, A. P., Pesic, M. & Beljanski Ristic, L. (2011). Playworlds: An Art of development. In C. Lobman & B.O'Neill (Eds.), *Play and Culture. Play and Culture Studies, Vol. 11* (pp. 3–31). Maryland: University Press of America.

Nilsson, M. & Ferholt, B. (2014). Vygotsky's theories of play, imagination and creativity in current practice: Gunilla Lindqvist's "creative pedagogy of play" in U. S. kindergartens and Swedish Reggio-Emilia inspired preschools. *Perspectiva,* 32:1, 919–950.

Nilsson, M., Ferholt, B., Lecusay, R. (2017). 'The Playing-Exploring Child': Reconceptualizing the Relationship between Play and Learning in Early Childhood Education. *Contemporary Issues in Early Childhood*, 18(3), pp. 1–15. Los Angeles, London: SAGE Publications.

Nilsson, M., Grankvist, A-K., Johansson, E. & Thure, J. Ferholt, B. (2018). *Lek, lärande och lycka: Lekande och utforskande i forskolan (Play, learning and joy: Playing and exploring in preschool).* Malmo: Gleerups.

Rainio, A. P. (2007). Ghosts, bodyguards and fighting fillies: Manifestations of pupil agency in play pedagogy. ACTIO: *International Journal for Human Activity Theory*, 1, 149–160.

Rainio, A. P. (2008a). Developing the classroom as a figured world. *Journal of Educational Change*, 9(4), 357–364.

Rainio, A. P. (2008b). From resistance to involvement: Examining agency and control in a playworld activity. *Mind, Culture and Activity,* 15(2), 115–140.

Rainio, A. P. (2009). Horses, girls, and agency. Gender in play pedagogy. *Outlines - Critical Practice Studies*, 1, 27–44.

Rainio, A. P. (2010). *Lionhearts of the Playworld: An Ethnographic Case Study of the Development of Agency in Play Pedagogy.* University of Helsinki, Finland, Helsinki.

Reggio Children and Project Zero. (2001). *Making learning visible: Children as individual and group learners.* Reggio Emilia, Italy: Reggio Children and Project Zero.

Vygotsky, L. S. (1971). *The psychology of art.* Cambridge, MA: M.I.T. Press.

Vygotsky, L. S. (1978). *Mind in society: The development of higher psychological processes.* Cambridge, MA: Harvard University Press.

Vygotsky, L. S. (1987). Imagination and its Development in Childhood. In *The collected works of L. S. Vygotsky.* New York: Plenum Press.

Vygotsky, L. S. (2004). Imagination and creativity in childhood. *Journal of Russian and East European Psychology*, 42(1), 7–97.

Chapter Three

Home-Based Child Care Providers' Perspectives about Play, Curriculum, and Quality Improvement Initiatives

Alison Hooper, Juana Gaviria-Loaiza, and Cailin Kerch

Children's opportunities to play are crucial to their early education. However, opportunities for play have been decreasing, especially in educational settings. One setting where little is known about play opportunities is home-based child care (HBCC). HBCC is generally defined as any non-parental child care that takes place in a residential setting. This includes both in-home child care programs that are regulated by the state and those that are unregulated, such as grandparents caring for grandchildren while parents work. Although many children attend HBCC, there is little research about this child care context. Many HBCC providers have low levels of formal education to prepare them to support children's learning through play. However, HBCC providers often are subject to fewer external regulations that can serve to restrict opportunities for play.

Although characteristics of HBCC may promote playful learning, such as the small group sizes and multi-age enrollment, research has not examined how HBCC providers describe their play practices and how they integrate play and curriculum. Additionally, there are growing opportunities for HBCC providers to participate in quality improvement (QI) initiatives, some of which have primarily included classroom-based teachers. These initiatives may encourage or require HBCC providers to implement certain practices related to curriculum that may in turn limit or enhance opportunities to play. In this chapter, we describe research that explored how HBCC providers describe their practices and beliefs related to play and curriculum, as well as their participation with QI initiatives that may influence these beliefs and practices.

PLAY

Play is an important aspect of childhood that comprises most of children's time. Play enhances children's development and learning across domains, including language, emotion regulation, and executive function (Cabrera, Karberg, Malin, & Aldoney, 2017). Play has been used and defined in multiple ways within the literature. It is an action that is recognized when observed but that is difficult to define (Lillard et al., 2013). Authors usually refer to the play characteristics to describe it, which include free choice, positive affect, and nonliterality, among others (Johnson, Christie & Wardle, 2005).

Children's play is often described in the ECE literature within two main categories: free play and guided or educational play. Free play is an unstructured type of play in which children have the possibility to choose what, where, with whom, and/or when to play (Johnson et al., 2005). Educational play refers play with more structure that is often guided by an adult with academic or learning purposes in mind. Wood (2014) describes three modes of educational play that help delineate how play and education are interrelated in practice. In *child-initiated* play, practitioners make their curriculum decisions based on children's interests and activities and are supportive and responsive of their needs. In *adult-guided* play, children's free activities are fundamental, but structured play is also valuable to enhance learning. Therefore, in this mode practitioners have certain curriculum goals in mind when playfully interacting with children while being receptive to children's interests. *Technicist* play is driven by policy or curricular models in which play is expected to elicit specific outcomes based on previously formulated goals that support school readiness. The play may quickly become overtly adult-led, with children's play interests being diminished.

PLAY IN EARLY CHILDHOOD SETTINGS

Young children spend the majority of their time either at home or in some form of non-parental child care. It is important then to explore the different play exposure that they may experience within these settings.

Play at Home. Many features of the home environment lend themselves to free play experiences. Children often have the flexibility to choose among different resources available, as well as family members to engage with, including siblings and parents. Studies exploring play at home have usually focused on the resources and opportunities available for children and on interactions with parents (Tamis-Lemonda, Shannon, Cabrera, & Lamb, 2004).

Parental involvement in children's play seems to be important to supporting children's outcomes. For instance, parent participation in children's play supports literacy development (Cabrera et al., 2017; Tamis-Lemonda et al., 2004). Playing with siblings also seems to benefit children's development. For instance, children with siblings engage in pretend play more often than do children without siblings (McAlister & Peterson, 2007). Further, older siblings may serve as role models in literacy activities and support children's language skills through their play interactions (Williams & Rask, 2003).

Play in Early Childhood Classrooms. In recent years, the role of play in ECE classrooms has been hotly debated. Due to a push towards more academic-focused curricula to ensure school readiness, time allocated for play has decreased in many classrooms (Miller & Almon, 2009). Despite the evidence of links between play and school readiness, many schools have narrowly focused on teaching academic skills through whole-group direct instruction and teacher-directed small group activities. This is mainly due to policy initiatives focused on meeting academic standards (Vu, Han, & Buell, 2012), which has led to a troubling lack of play experiences in many ECE classrooms.

In a play-based classroom, educators support play through guided instruction, materials, and peer interactions. Teachers often create centers, for example, with specific learning objectives that allow children to play in multiple ways based on their motivation and election. This facilitates learning through educational play without direct instruction (Kotsopoulos, Makosz, Zambrzycka, & McCarthy, 2015). Teacher-child interactions during play also enhance children's learning (Mecham, Vukelich, Han, & Buell, 2013). However, many classrooms have high student-teacher ratios, which can limit the quality and amount of interactions a teacher can have with a particular child.

Free play in ECE can have a laissez-faire connotation and may be less valued due to lack of evidence-based support (Wood & Hedges, 2016). However, child-directed play is considered a fundamental and undeniable right of the child and is important for development (Johnson et al., 2005). Both free and educational play should be embedded within curricular approaches (Copple & Bredekamp, 2009).

Curriculum and Play

The role of play differs within early childhood curricular frameworks, models, and approaches based upon their underlying theoretical components. Curriculum can be defined as the contextual interaction between the teacher and learner. Curriculum content, the *what,* and the pedagogy, the *how,* interplay explicitly or implicitly in a learning environment (Wood, 2014; Roopnarine

& Johnson, 2013). Curriculum in ECE can be an educational program with explicit connection to developmental standards or a set of educational goals implicitly connected to an approach or framework based upon developmental theory (Rooparnine & Johnson, 2013).

Curricular approaches in ECE vary widely from more structured programs with a defined scope and sequence (i.e., Opening the World of Learning, Frog Street) to less structured frameworks or approaches (i.e., HighScope, Reggio Approach). Play is a component of most ECE curricular approaches. However, the frequency and type of play vary widely despite recommendations that play be 'at the center of curriculum' (Van Hoorn, Nourot, Scales, & Alward, 2014).

A child's experience within a classroom is contingent upon an educator's curricular adherence, coherence, and external control. The interactions within a teacher-child dyad may be distinctive to the educator's adherence to the selected curricular approach. Moreover, coherence to curriculum can be deeply intertwined with culture, history, and social complexities. External control includes features like government influences that influence the child's experiences. Curricular adherence, coherence and control all influence the way curriculum is enacted and the way play is valued within an ECE setting (Wood & Hedges, 2016).

HOME-BASED CHILD CARE

Most of the research about play and curriculum in ECE has focused on classroom-based settings and has not included HBCC. Therefore, we know little about how HBCC providers make decisions about curriculum and play. However, seven million children in the United States attend HBCC before kindergarten entry. Of all of the child care arrangements in the United States, 97 percent are home-based (NSECE Project Team, 2015a), meaning that out of 100 child care settings or programs, only 3 would be center-based and 97 would be home-based.

HBCC represents a heterogeneous group of providers. Family child care (FCC) and family, friend, and neighbor care (FFN) are two common subgroups of HBCC. FCC is typically defined as care that is regulated or licensed by the state. FCC providers often care for unrelated children and receive payment (NSECE Project Team, 2015a). FFN providers are unlicensed, and they primarily care for children to whom they are related. Delineating providers as FCC or FFN can be complicated given that licensing regulations vary widely (National Center on Early Childhood Quality Assurance, 2015). This makes it challenging to generalize research findings and draw conclusions about this diverse population.

To address the challenges of categorizing HBCC providers and the variation in licensing requirements, a recent nationally survey of HBCC providers grouped providers as listed, if they appeared on any state or national list, and unlisted. Unlisted providers were further delineated as paid, if they received payment for at least one child in care, and unpaid. The National Survey of Early Care and Education found that listed HBCC providers serve an average of eight children, while unlisted paid providers serve approximately four children and unlisted unpaid providers serve two. Unlisted providers are much more likely to care for children to whom they have a prior relationship. Most HBCC providers care for children in their own home, and many HBCC providers work alone, although 40 percent of listed providers report having at least a part-time paid assistant (NSECE Project Team, 2015a).

FEATURES OF HOME-BASED CHILD CARE

There is wide variation in the typical characteristics of a HBCC setting. Some, most often licensed FCC settings, operate similar to a center-based program and follow a daily schedule very similar to that of a preschool classroom. Other HBCC providers have less structure, and children's daily experiences are more similar to what they would experience in parental care.

Because HBCC takes place in a residential setting, it shares many features with a home environment. Many families select HBCC because they prefer to have their children cared for in a home, because of the opportunities for individual attention that stem from a small group size, and because siblings can receive care together (Porter et al., 2010). These are also reasons why HBCC may be an ideal setting for play. Research has found that in center-based classrooms teachers were less available to offer individual attention (McCabe & Frede, 2007), and children experienced greater stress than did children who received care in a home (Vermeer & van IJzendoorn, 2006).

One common feature of HBCC is mixed-age enrollment. Mixed-age settings provide ideals spaces for children to learn through play with their peers. When children play with mixed-age peers, younger children are gently pushed to play within their zones of proximal development, have models to emulate through their older peers, and enjoy additional sources of care and support (Bailey, Burchinal, & McWilliam, 1993; Gray, 2011). However, children often have few opportunities for mixed-age play, especially in center-based ECE settings. We suggest that HBCC settings, where many children spend time, can serve as spaces for enriching, mixed-age play. However, depending on how curriculum is used mixed-age play experiences will vary and could be reduced.

About 55 percent of HBCC providers nationally who appear on a list, including those who are regulated or licensed, report using a curriculum (NSECE Project Team, 2015b). Little research has explored which curricula providers report using and their training to implement curricula. However, research has found that HBCC providers are less likely than are center-based providers to implement curriculum or receive training on curriculum (Phillips & Morse, 2011).

QUALITY IMPROVEMENT IN HOME-BASED CHILD CARE

For a number of reasons including a concern about program quality and children's school readiness (Bassok, Fitzpatrick, Greenberg, & Loeb, 2016), there has been recent attention to improving quality in HBCC. Quality Rating and Improvement Systems (QRIS) are one strategy for quality improvement (QI), and many states now have QRIS that include HBCC. QRIS have emerged as the primary mechanism for states to measure and improve child care quality. Other QI supports for HBCC include home visiting, play and learn groups, and training (Bromer & Korfmacher, 2017). Providers participating in home visiting displayed increased knowledge of curriculum implementation (Forry et al., 2011). However, little else is known about how QI initiatives may influence how HBCC providers use curriculum and support play.

QRIS offer some guidance related to play and curriculum. Many QRIS use observational measures of quality to determine quality ratings. The most commonly used measure of quality for HBCC is the Family Child Care Environment Rating Scale–Revised (FCCERS; Harms, Cryer, & Clifford, 2007). In order to score highly, providers must provide access to play materials for most of the time that children are awake and able to play. QRIS often have standards related to curriculum that providers must meet in order to earn a higher level ; sometimes a list of pre-approved curricula is specified from which providers must choose. Depending on providers' level of education and experience, they may experience challenges meeting and integrating the requirements related to play as well as those related to curriculum.

Some research has indicated that in child care centers, QRIS may contribute to teachers making substantive changes to quality when they have a lower rating. However, teachers in higher-rated centered-based programs may make only structural or superficial changes (Tarrant & Huerta, 2015). A study of center-based providers' decisions to participate in a QRIS found that participants reported barriers that affected their engagement, including overly strict standards and requirements that were not achievable in mixed-age contexts (Hallam, Hooper, Bargreen, Buell, & Han, 2017). Tonyan, Nuttall, Torres, and Bridgewater (2017) suggest that to increase HBCC providers' engagement in QI, initiatives must ensure they are aligned with the needs and interests of providers, including matches relating to both the content and delivery of initiatives.

Given the limited research literature about HBCC, specifically related to children's play opportunities and curriculum decisions, and the increase in QI initiatives aimed at supporting HBCC, it is important to understand HBCC providers' perspectives related to curriculum, play, and QI. The following questions guided this research: 1) How do HBCC providers describe their curriculum use and play practices?, and 2) What are HBCC providers' perspectives related to QI initiatives, and how do these relate to play and curriculum?

METHODS

State Context

HBCC providers are required to be licensed in the state where this research occurred if they serve one or more children to whom they are not related. Providers may serve up to six children in a licensed FCC program and up to 12 children in a large FCC program, which also requires an assistant. Licensed providers are able to participate in the state's voluntary QRIS, which also serves licensed center-based programs. The QRIS has five quality levels. A observation of program quality is required to achieve a level 3–5. Programs are incentivized to participate through small grants and tiered reimbursement, where providers receive additional funding for serving low-income children who receive child care subsidy depending on their quality level. Previous research has identified that these financial incentives are a primary reason HBCC providers identify joining the QRIS (Hallam et al., 2017). Participating programs also have access to on-site technical assistance and professional development.

Sample

This research was part of a larger mixed methods study of HBCC providers. The sample for this analysis consisted of 29 HBCC providers in one state. We selected these providers from a sample of 252 HBCC providers who responded to a statewide survey. We purposefully selected our sample to represent a broad range of caregiving beliefs and instructional practices based on the results of an earlier phase of the study (Hooper, 2019). The characteristics of the participating programs and their child care programs are displayed in Table 3.1.

Table 3.1.　Characteristics of Home-Based Provider
Participants and Their Programs

Variable	Frequency
Time licensed	
Unlicensed	10.3%
Up to 10 years	34.5%
10 to 20 years	27.6%
More than 20 years	27.6%
Children enrolled	
Less than 5	17.2%
5 to 7	44.8%
8 or more	37.9%
QRIS participation	
Not eligible (unlicensed)	10.3%
Not participating	34.5%
Level 1 or 2	20.7%
Level 3 or 4	27.6%
Level 5	6.9%
Highest level of education	
High school diploma/GED or less	24.1%
Some college credits	44.8%
Associate's degree	10.3%
Bachelor's degree or higher	20.7%
Provider race and ethnicity	
White, non-Hispanic	51.7%
African-American, non-Hispanic	41.4%
Hispanic or Latino	5.7%

Note: N=29

Measures

We used a semi-structured interview protocol that included 12 questions and accompanying prompts related to a variety of topics, including whether providers use curriculum, how they describe a recent activity they did with children, and how they interact with outside systems designed to support them in their work. We piloted the protocol with a HBCC provider not eligible for the sample, and we made minor adjustments to improve clarity. Additionally, we matched interview responses to administrative data from the QRIS to determine who was participating in the QRIS and at what quality level.

Procedures

We contacted selected providers by telephone and invited them to participate in the study. The first author and a research assistant conducted recruitment and data collection. We conducted interviews in person or over the telephone. Interviews were audio-recorded and lasted from 30-90 minutes. Audio recordings of the interviews were transcribed verbatim and imported into NVivo 11 software for analysis.

Analysis

We analyzed transcripts using a combination of a priori coding and thematic analysis with emergent codes. To begin to answer the first research question about providers' play practices, we coded responses about the level of educational play using the levels of play and definitions identified by Wood (2014): child-initiated, adult-guided, and technicist.

To further answer the first research question about curriculum use and play practices and to answer the second question about QI initiatives, we used thematic analysis, which uses open coding to allow main themes to emerge and then organizes themes in a meaningful way. We followed the six steps recommended by Braun and Clarke (2006): 1) familiarization with data, 2) generating initial codes, 3) searching for themes, 4) reviewing themes, 5) defining and naming themes, 6) producing report. The authors thoroughly read each transcript. We generated initial codes separately based upon research questions. Next, we agreed upon and defined a set of initial codes and separately coded the transcripts. For both a priori and open coding, we resolved any disagreement in coding through revisiting the definitions to reach consensus. Through discussion and peer review, we used our codes to search for themes. We developed themes inductively and defined them using support from prior research (Braun & Clarke, 2006; Nowell, Norris, White, & Moules, 2017).

RESULTS

We review results separately for each research question, first presenting the themes related to curriculum and play, and then describing the theme related to participation in QI initiatives. The themes and the codes that comprise them are displayed in Figure 3.1.

Curriculum Use and Play Practices

The first research question addresses how providers describe their curriculum use and play practices. Based on their responses, we identified three themes related to curriculum and play. First, providers make different decisions about whether to use a curriculum. Second, HBCC describe play occurring in a

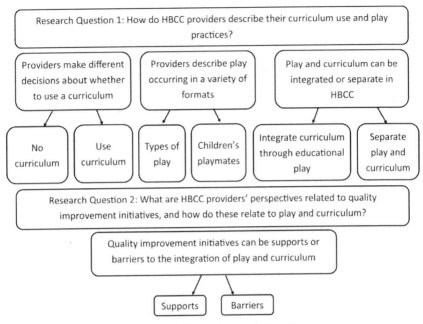

Figure 3.1.   Themes and Codes Relating to Research Questions.

variety of formats. Finally, play and curriculum can be integrated or separate in HBCC. Each theme is described below. The codes related to these themes, their definitions, and their frequencies are found in Table 3.2.

Decisions about Curriculum Use. Participants were asked to describe their process of planning activities for children, and specifically whether they used a curriculum or set of learning activities. If they said yes, they were asked to describe what they used and how they used it. Many providers described using a purchased packaged curriculum or combining two or more of these curricula. The curricula providers mentioned were Funshine Express, Mother Goose Time, Creative Curriculum for Family Child Care, and the Redleaf Family Child Care Curriculum. All are on the list of approved curricula for the state's QRIS and are designed for HBCC contexts. Some providers specifically mentioned modifying these curricula to better meet children's needs: "I gear the lesson plans up and down for my kids based on what they can handle." Others described making modifications based on their own or the families' values: "The things that I feel that are important to me, important to the families, the sign language, and all of that, then I just add that in there."

Almost all providers who did not use a packaged curriculum reported that they did not use any curriculum. Reasons for not using curriculum included

Table 3.2. Codes Relating to Play and Curriculum

Codes and Sub-Codes	Definition	Number of References	Number of Participants
Free Play	Children have freedom to choose what and where to play with objects, materials, or nature	22	12
Free play is main activity	Free play makes up majority of the daily schedule	3	1
Free play is one daily activity	Free play is one of multiple scheduled activities in which children participate	9	7
Educational Play	Activities that integrate educational goals into children's play episodes	33	14
Child-led	Following the child's interest and disposition to plan and implement a curriculum that is responsive to the child's play	9	7
Adult-guided	Provider has some planned curricular goals to implement through play, but these are responsive to the child's interests and choices	4	3
Technicist	Play activities are planned with the provider's goals in mind and are oriented towards curriculum targets; child's play is diminished and structured to achieve educational goals	8	5
Children's Playmates			
Same-Age Peers	Play occurs specifically between same-age peers and not across age groups	2	2
Mixed-Age Play	Play occurs between children of different ages	3	3
Provider as Co-Player	Provider is actively involved as a participant in children's play	11	7
Play vs. Curriculum	Play is and should be a separate activity from teaching	2	2
Curriculum Use			
No curriculum	Provider does not use a curriculum, whether purchased or self-created	25	14
Purchased curricula	Provider names a specific curricular program that can be purchased	16	12
Combination	Provider use more than one purchased curriculum	4	3
Self-created	Provider designs own curriculum; may be based on early learning standards or their own ideas	2	1
Modifications	Modifying a purchased curriculum to adapt it to provider's context or needs of the children	8	7

curriculum not fitting with their beliefs ("I don't really believe in curriculum"), the prohibitive cost ("Curriculums are ridiculously expensive, so that's not feasible for me"), and a lack of time and energy ("I can't get into all of that, because along with teaching these children, I have to change diapers, I have children that I have to feed.").

One provider reported that she used a self-created curriculum. She described developing her curriculum based on her participation in training related to supporting a child with autism: "I develop my own curriculum. . . . We really got a lot of materials during that time, and I developed a lot of the preschool program through those."

Formats of Play. Providers described children participating in both free and educational play. Because we conceptualize educational play as an interaction in which providers may link play and curriculum, we describe those comments later in the results.

Free play. When providers talked about free play, they primarily talked about it as one of the activities in their schedule: "Then after their snack, they get some play time. Then about 11:45 they wash up and we have lunch." They described opportunities for both indoor and outdoor free play. One provider described free play as children's main activity. When asked to describe a recent activity she had planned, she said, "It's really hard to since it's all really just free play." Other providers described free play as a primary activity only during the summer: "Basically for the summer months we're playing. I try to get outside a lot and stay out as much as possible with them."

Children's playmates. Providers described children playing with same-aged peers, mixed-age peers, and with the provider. When providers talked about actively engaging in children's play with children, they described participating in outdoor play and playing on the floor with young children. One provider highlighted the value of being a coplayer in her relationships with children: "The more you play with them, the more they relate to you better. The more they trust you and the more they're happier to be here." Another talked about taking time to engage in play to ensure that each child received individual attention. One provider said that she liked the freedom she had as a HBCC provider, saying, "I like to be able to shut the playroom door, and play with the kids. Get on the floor, 'cause they're young."

Providers talked about children engaging in mixed-age play and the learning that both older and younger children experience through mixed-age play. One said, "The nice thing about a home child care is, you know, you have the older children playing with the infants, and the infants learn from the older children, and it's kind of like scaffolding type thing that you see going on." There were few comments about children specifically engaging in play with same-aged peers. One provider shared how her curriculum provided different activities for different ages of children. Another reported planning different types of experiences depending on children's ages; for infants and toddlers she offered more opportunities for free play, and offered older children more planned curricular experiences.

Relationship of Play with Curriculum

Educational Play. Many providers described engaging children in educational play, which is one way that providers may integrate their curriculum into play. This included general comments about learning through play, such as, "Learning through play I think is very important. I think that's how they learn the most." Other providers were more specific in how they described educational play. In these cases, we coded their level of educational play as child-initiated, adult-guided, or technicist based on the definitions from Wood (2014). Participants provided examples of all three types. For example, for child-led play, a provider said, "I feel as though they learn better through creative play. Sometimes I let them guide me. I find teachable moments. I think that works best."

Some providers made comments about learning through play, but when they described an example, it was of technicist play with providers directing play by imposing their educational goals. For example, "Even if you are sitting on the floor and you are playing with the kids and you wanted them to write their name or whatever, you want everything to be fun for number one. . . . I will use like a cardboard or something and just put flour on the cardboard or salt and they can use their index finger to learn how to write, but they still are playing." However, some providers, including the one who provided this quote, described how this was a shift from their previous practice of doing teacher-directed whole-group instruction. They shared that they had learned to implement hands-on experiences through the QRIS.

Play and Learning Are Separate. Two providers notably described play as something that was separate from teaching or learning. One talked about ensuring the children in her care were prepared for life through giving them opportunities to do more than just play: "It's just not all about playing, you have to learn life skills." The other provider shared how she believed Head Start had become too play-based: "My daughter went to Head Start. . . . I thought it was really good when she went, but a lot of things have changed since then. It was more educational then. I think they go a little overboard with the play nowadays."

Quality Improvement Initiatives

The second research question examined providers' perspectives related to QI initiatives and how experience working with QI initiatives related to their play practices and curriculum. Most providers had experience with some kind of QI initiative. They primarily talked about the QRIS and professional development workshops. Many comments about their practices related to curriculum and play. These codes are presented in Table 3.3. We identified one theme that integrates these codes: QI initiatives can support or inhibit the integration of play and curriculum.

Quality Improvement Initiatives as Supports. One benefit of engaging with QI initiatives was financial incentives that allowed providers to purchase curricula. One provider said, "The curriculum assessment tools, the tools that you get are extremely expensive and they just give them to you if you're [Level] Three or whatever." Another said, "You have to be in the [QRIS] to get some of the grants. Grants like for curriculum. We just did a curriculum grant not too long ago, maybe a couple years ago."

The benefit providers talked about most was one-on-one and group professional development. Many providers shared about their QRIS technical assistant (TA). One provider said about her TA, "They love it when she comes, because she'll sit in there and do the same thing we do. We try to interact with them and play with them." Providers talked about how their TA helped them learn to integrate curriculum and play and offer more hands-on experiences: "I was teaching without [QRIS]. I mean, I did well, but with [QRIS], I think it's more enjoyable for the kids." One provider described how her TA gave her ideas for creative play materials:

"I love the TA. They're so useful. . . . I have a sliding board over here. . . . It's from an old playset that I used to have. I saved the slide, and so we took a walk around. My TA said, 'You know what you can do with this? You can set this up like they do at the [museum], or the [children's museum].'"

Providers talked about the benefits of workshops for helping them learn to implement curricula: "I do like going to the ones where they have about the different curriculum and things like that just for ideas." Another shared how she learned to modify curriculum to meet the children's needs, saying, "I was able to take my curriculum and attach it to my assessments and observations and from there, it kind of like all went together."

Quality Improvement Initiatives as Barriers. Providers also shared barriers they experienced through their participation in QI initiatives. Specifically, they described how initiatives sometimes were not supportive of HBCC, and providers felt pressure to make their program more like a classroom. When

Table 3.3. Codes Relating to Quality Improvement Initiatives

Codes and Sub-Codes	Definition	Number of References	Number of Participants
Challenges			
Not useful	Provider finds an initiative not useful or is unclear about its benefits	2	2
Too much work	Amount of work or requirements is too much; includes taking away from time with children	6	5
Push to formalize	Provider perceives a quality improvement support as trying to make HBCC less home-like and more like school	6	4
Benefits			
Support	Provider receives group or individualized training	27	14
Financial and material	Provider receives a curriculum or training through participation	4	2

describing her decision to stop participating in a QI program, one provider said:

> I don't think that they really appreciate the differences between a center and a family-based program. The beauty of it being in a home, and it feeling like a home, and not like a center classroom. I didn't mind all the work, and it was a lot of work, but I just didn't want to put in all that effort to create a program that I didn't want, so I left.

Other barriers included the general lack of benefits and the amount of work. One provider shared, "They were not very supportive of the providers. I felt like it was taking away from working with the kids, and it was a lot more geared towards paperwork." Another provider described designing her own curriculum and aligning it with early learning standards. However, then QRIS regulations changed. She said, "I started purchasing Mother Goose. I did that mainly so I could get my [Level] 5 because if I did my own lesson plans, I had to tie them back to [standards], and I had done that at one point but then I think some things have changed. And so it was just easier if I bought it."

DISCUSSION

This study provides insight into how one group of HBCC providers describe play and curriculum and the ways in which QI supports may influence them.

Play and Curriculum

In response to the first research question about curriculum use and play practices, providers described different levels of educational play and a range of levels of curriculum implementation. Specifically, the participants highlighted some of the unique aspects of HBCC compared to center-based settings and how those related to play and curriculum implementation.

Participants emphasized the importance of maintaining a home-like environment with time and space for play, rather than operating like a classroom. This aligns with the research reporting that the home-like environment is one reason families select HBCC (Porter, 2010). Providers described giving children experiences playing with mixed-age peers and with the provider as coplayer, both of which are related to children's learning (Gray, 2011; Meacham et al., 2013).

Providers described both free and educational play when discussing their daily activities and their interaction with QI supports. The level of adult involvement in play varied, ranging from child-led to technicist (Wood, 2014).

Some researchers believe that educational play, especially technicist play, may unintentionally dissolve the child's play experience through too much adult interference (Johnson & Wu, 2019; Wood, 2014). In contrast, other researchers note the benefits to children's learning when adults facilitate play in responsive ways (Tamis-Lamonda et al., 2004). Because this study did not include direct observations, it may be that some of the instances of reported educational play that the providers described may have served to limit playfulness rather than facilitate it.

Providers described using a range of packaged curricula, all of which the QRIS endorsed. However, the emphasis on child-led or guided play within their design varies. Additionally, many providers did not seem to be using these with fidelity. Many of the providers using a curriculum also talked about free play, so it does not seem like these are mutually exclusive in HBCC. Those who did not use a curriculum cited the cost, their beliefs, and the time demands as reasons. This is an empirical contribution to the very limited literature about curriculum use in HBCC.

Role of Quality Improvement Initiatives

Our second research question explored HBCC providers' experiences with QI initiatives and how interfacing with QI initiatives may related to play and curriculum. Providers described the financial and professional learning benefits of QI initiatives, coupled with challenges related to standards that they believed did not truly fit a HBCC environment (Hallam et al., 2017). Participants' descriptions of supports and barriers reveal an interesting pattern in the way these initiatives may relate to curriculum and play. Using the matrix considering the level of child and teacher input in play outlined in Miller and Almon's (2009) *Crisis in the Kindergarten*, our findings suggest that where there is low child initiative and/or low teacher input, engaging with a QI support may help HBCC providers better integrate play and curriculum. We found examples of this with providers who reported previously doing primarily didactic teaching and with those who reported previously having a laissez-faire, even chaotic, environment. Through QI supports, these providers learned to better integrate their curricular goals with play. However, in programs where there was high teacher input and high child initiative, QI supports did not seem to support practices related to play and curriculum and even acted as a barrier. These providers may adopt a packaged curriculum in order to advance in the QRIS, which could lead to reduced play opportunities, especially given the lack of research about the quality of these curricula.

This mirrors Tarrant and Huerta's (2015) findings that lower-rated center-based programs in a QRIS were the ones who tended to make meaningful changes to their practices, while those who were higher-rated made more structural changes. We saw examples of both in this study. For example, one provider described purchasing a packaged curriculum to ensure she met a QRIS standard and then switching back to her self-created curriculum. In contrast, lower-rated providers talked about more substantive changes to their practices, like beginning to support learning in more playful ways.

The characteristics of the QI staff who interact with providers may also be important. For example, when providers work with a coach who builds trust and models play-based learning facilitation, they may learn to better support children's learning through play. Providers who work with a coach who focuses on more structural aspects of quality and does not engage in relationship-based strategies may not experience the same benefits (Bromer & Korfmacher, 2017).

LIMITATIONS

A limitation of this study is that we conducted secondary analysis of interviews. Because we did not specifically ask about providers' play beliefs and practices, there are likely perceptions about play that we did not capture. Additionally, these providers are all from one state. Most are licensed, and the remaining providers are on a state list because they receive some state funding. Therefore, they may not represent the perspectives of the much larger group of unpaid, unregulated HBCC providers. The experiences with QI initiatives may not be generalizable to HBCC providers in other states, given the wide variation in systems like QRIS.

IMPLICATIONS AND DIRECTIONS FOR FUTURE RESEARCH

As many QRIS continue to revise their quality standards, it is important to be aware of the unintended consequences that may result from requiring HBCC providers to use a specific packaged curriculum, especially given the lack of evidence base around the effectiveness of these curricula. Although requiring a specific curriculum is easier to measure and regulate, it may serve to limit providers' creativity and, depending on their level of implementation, opportunities for play. Further, if HBCC providers do not philosophically agree with the curriculum's approach and content, the providers may adopt it only to meet a standard and then revert to their previous practices.

Providers recognized the underlying tension they felt from QI initiatives, whether explicit or implicit, to make their program more like a classroom and less like a home (Hallam et al., 2017). Some chose to actively work against this by ending their participation in the QRIS. Others chose to remain engaged but to, as one provider said, "shut the playroom door," and continue to enjoy the role of a coplayer. This highlights the importance of utilizing best practices for supporting HBCC providers in QI initiatives (Bromer & Korfmacher, 2017; Tonyan et al., 2017).

Future research should intentionally examine HBCC providers' beliefs and practices related to play. This could occur through soliciting providers' perspectives and conducting direct observations. It is important to gain a better understanding of the ways in which HBCC providers' beliefs and practices are shaped through their interactions with QI initiatives and the ways this affects children's experiences related to play. These interviews highlight the potential for positive changes in practices, along with unintended consequences that may limit children's play experiences. The specific practices coaches and trainers use may be one factor in whether QI supports encourage or limit play.

Overall, many of the features of HBCC make it a context that can promote rich play, including small group sizes, a flexible and home-like environment, mixed-age groupings, and relatively few requirements related to instruction. Given the large number of children attending HBCC, we want children attending these settings have meaningful, playful experiences that prepare them for later learning. Helping HBCC providers who currently have didactic or laissez-faire practices shift to using a curriculum may be one way to do this. However, the way in which providers are supported in implementing their curriculum is crucial to consider moving forward to ensure that the HBCC can remain a positive context for play.

REFERENCES

Bailey, D. B., Burchinal, M. R., & McWilliam, R. A. (1993). Age of peers and early childhood development. *Child Development, 64*(3), 848–862.

Bassok, D., Fitzpatrick, M., Greenberg, E., & Loeb, S. (2016). Within- and between-sector quality differences in early childhood education and care. *Child Development, 87*(5), 1627–1645.

Braun, V., & Clarke, V. (2006). Using thematic analysis in psychology. *Qualitative Research in Psychology, 3*(2), 77–101.

Bromer, J., & Korfmacher, J. (2017). Providing high-quality support services to home-based child care: A conceptual model and literature review. *Early Education and Development, 28*(6), 745–772.

Cabrera, N. J., Karberg, E., Malin, J. L., & Aldoney, D. (2017). The magic of play: Low-income mothers' and fathers' playfulness and children's emotion regulation and vocabulary skills. *Infant Mental Health Journal, 38*(6), 757–771.

Copple, C., & Bredekamp, S. (2009). *Developmentally appropriate practice in early childhood programs serving children from birth through age 8.* (3rd ed.). Washington, D.C.: National Association for the Education of Young Children.

Forry, N., Anderson, R., Zaslow, M., Chrisler, A., Banghart, P., & Kreader, J. L. (2011). *Linking home-based child care and state-funded preschool: The community connections preschool program (Illinois Action for Children). Evaluation phase 1-implementation study.* Chicago, IL: Illinois Action for Children.

Gray, P. (2011). The special value of children's age-mixed play. *American Journal of Play*, *3*(4), 500–522.

Hallam, R., Hooper, A., Bargreen, K., Buell, M., & Han, M. (2017). A two-state study of family child care engagement in Quality Rating and Improvement Systems: A mixed-methods analysis. *Early Education and Development*, 28(6), 699–683.

Harms, T., Cryer, D., & Clifford, R. M. (2007). *Family Child Care Environment Rating Scale Revised Edition*. New York, NY: Teachers College Press.

Hooper, A. (2019). Classifying home-based child care providers: Validating a typology of providers' beliefs and self-reported practices. *Early Childhood Education Journal*, 47(3), 275–285.

Johnson, J. E., Christie, J. F., & Wardle, F. (2005). *Play, development and early education.* Boston: Pearson/Allyn and Bacon.

Johnson, J. & Wu, M. (2019). Play. In Brown, Benson, McMullen, File (Ed.). *Handbook of Early Childhood Care and Education.* (pp. 79–98).

Kotsopoulos, D., Makosz, S., Zambrzycka, J., & McCarthy, K. (2015).The effects of different pedagogical approaches on the learning of length measurement in kindergarten. *Early Childhood Education Journal, 43,* 531–539.

Lillard, A. D., Lerner, M. D., Hopkins, E. J., Dore, R. A., Smith, E. D., & Palmquist, C. M. (2013). The impact of pretend play on children's development: A review of the evidence. *Psychological Bulletin, 139*(1), 1–34.

McAlister, A., & Peterson, C. (2007). A longitudinal study of child siblings and theory of mind development. *Cognitive Development*, *22*(2), 258–270.

McCabe, L. A., & Frede, E. C. (2007). Challenging behaviors and the role of preschool education. *National Institute for Early Education Research. Preschool Policy Brief*, 16.

Meacham, S., Vukelich, C., Han, M., & Buell, M. (2013). Preschool teachers' language use during dramatic play. *European Early Childhood Education Research Journal, 22* (5), 250–267.

Miller, E., & Almon, J. (2009). Crisis in the kindergarten: Why children need to play in school. *Alliance for Childhood.*

National Center on Early Childhood Quality Assurance. (2015). *Research brief #2: Trends in family child care home licensing regulations and policies for 2014.* Washington DC: Office of Child Care, Administration for Children and Families, U.S. Department of Health and Human Services.

National Survey of Early Care and Education Project Team (2015a). *Fact Sheet: Who is providing home-based early care and education?* OPRE Report No. 2015–43, Washington DC: Office of Planning, Research and Evaluation, Administration for Children and Families, U.S. Department of Health and Human Services.

National Survey of Early Care and Education Project Team (2015b). *Measuring predictors of quality in early care and education settings in the National Survey of Early Care and Education.* OPRE Report No. 2015-93, Washington DC: Office of Planning, Research and Evaluation, Administration for Children and Families, U.S. Department of Health and Human Services.

Nowell, L. S., Norris, J. M., White, D. E., & Moules, N. J. (2017). Thematic analysis: Striving to meet the trustworthiness criteria. *International Journal of Qualitative Methods, 16,* 1–13.

Phillips, B. M., & Morse, E. E. (2011). Family child care learning environments: Caregiver knowledge and practices related to early literacy and mathematics. *Early Childhood Education Journal, 39*(3), 213–222.

Porter, T., Paulsell, D., Del Grosso, P., Avellar, S., Hass, R., & Vuong, L. (2010). *A review of the literature on home-based child care: Implications for future directions.* Princeton, NJ: Mathematica Policy Research.

Roopnarine & Johnson (2013). *Approaches to Early Childhood Education* (6th ed.). Boston: Pearson.

Tamis-LeMonda, C., Shannon, J., Cabrera, N., & Lamb, M. (2004). Fathers and mothers at play with their 2- and 3-year-olds: Contributions to language and cognitive development. *Child Development, 75,* 1806-1820

Tarrant, K., & Huerta, L. A. (2015). Substantive or symbolic stars: Quality rating and improvement systems through a new institutional lens. *Early Childhood Research Quarterly, 30,* 327–338.

Tonyan, H. A., Nuttall, J., Torres, J., & Bridgewater, J. (2017). Engaging with quality improvement initiatives: A descriptive study of learning in the complex and dynamic context of everyday life for family child care providers. *Early Education and Development, 28*(6), 684–704.

Van Hoorn, J. L., Monighan-Nourot, P., Scales, B., & Alward, K. R. (2014). *Play at the center of the curriculum.* New York: Pearson.

Vermeer, H. J., & van IJzendoorn, M. H. (2006). Children's elevated cortisol levels at daycare: A review and meta-analysis. *Early Childhood Research Quarterly, 21*(3), 390–401.

Vu, J., Han, M., & Buell, M. (2012). Preserving play in early childhood classrooms: Suggestions for early childhood teacher education and policy. *Play and Culture Studies. 12,* 207–221.

Williams, M., & Rask, H. (2003). Literacy through play: How families with able children support their literacy development. *Early Child Development and Care, 173*(5), 527–533.

Wood, E. (2014). The play-pedagogy interface in contemporary debates. In Booker, Blaise, Edwards (Ed.) *The SAGE Handbook of Play and Learning In Early Childhood.* (pp. 254–261). London, UK: Sage.

Wood, E. & Hedges, H. (2016). Curriculum in early childhood education: Critical questions about content, coherence, and control. *The Curriculum Journal, 27*(3), 387–405.

Section II

PLAY AND CURRICULUM IN STEM

Chapter Four

Facilitating Mathematical Thinking in Preschool Play

Findings of the CECE Math-Play Studies

Sudha Swaminathan and Jeffrey Trawick-Smith

"How many dollars for this tomato?" a four-year-old asks, holding a wooden vegetable up to a peer, who is pretending to be a cashier in a make-believe grocery store. "Oh," says his peer, studying the pretend tomato. "That's about 48 dollars, I think."

"Forty-eight dollars!" says the child who is buying the tomato in an incredulous tone. "No, not that much." He looks at the small number of make-believe dollar bills he has in his hand. "Okay," says the cashier. "Then let's say five dollars, because the tomato's littler than the other vegetables. See? (Points to other make-believe vegetables.) So, it's five dollars and cents."

The shopper counts out five bills, most of the play money that he is holding. "That's five," he says. "But I don't have too much money left." The cashier places the toy bills into a wooden cash register drawer and says, "Thanks, and have a nice day."

As shown in this vignette, young children's play is often a rich context for mathematical thinking and conversation. In naturalistic play, children have been observed solving different kinds of math problems—counting dots on dice, comparing the lengths of blocks with which they are building, sorting shapes in a math game, negotiating the cost in play money of vegetables in a make-believe grocery store, keeping score in a beanbag game, and experimenting with the amount of water needed to fill up a container at the water-play table (Baroody, 2004; Edo, Planas & Badillo, 2009; Ginsberg, 2006; Trawick-Smith, 1992). Despite such anecdotal reports showing how children think mathematically as they play, only a small number of empirical studies have examined the relationship between play and math learning.

The symbolic quality of preschool children's sociodramatic play—make-believe role playing—has been associated with math abilities in third-grade (Hanline, Milton, & Phelps, 2009). Playing board games and making puzzles have been found to predict knowledge in several math domains—an understanding of number and spatial knowledge (Ramani & Siegler, 2008; Ramani, Siegler, & Hitti, 2012). An association has been found between block and Lego play in early childhood and math performance later in school (Wolfgang, Standard, & Jones, 2001, 2003).

Much of this research on play and mathematics has been conducted in isolated laboratory settings—sometimes with only one choice of play material provided to children and often without peers to play with. Additional research is needed on the association between naturalistic free play in classrooms and math learning. Too, little research has examined the impact of many types of play in preschool classrooms that have not been studied—waterplay, art, or even play in a classroom book center. Do all activities available to children during classroom free play time provide the same opportunities for mathematical thinking?

An interrelated question raised in the literature is whether teachers of young children can, or should, take steps to facilitate children's math learning as they play (Clements, Sarama, Swaminathan, Weber, & Trawick-Smith, 2018). Play, by definition, is self-chosen and intrinsically motivated (Rubin, Fein, & Vanderberg, 1983). So, wouldn't it be best for teachers to hold back and allow purely independent play to work its magic? Or does some unobtrusive teacher involvement in play strengthen its contributions to math learning? A growing body of research suggests that *guided play*—free play in which teachers ask questions, give hints, or pose problems—is more likely to contribute to academic outcomes in classrooms than autonomous free play alone (Weisberg, Hirsh-Pasek, Golinkoff, Kittredge, & Klahr, 2016). In one study, such guided play was found to enhance an area of mathematics learning—geometry (Fisher, Hirsh-Pasek, Newcombe, & Golinkoff, 2013).

Findings on the effects of guided play and learning lead to additional questions. Can teachers guide young children in mathematical thinking in play without interfering or overdirecting their chosen activities? If so, what kinds of interactions with children will best support both math learning as well as meaningful, autonomous play? At the Center for Early Childhood Education (CECE)—a research center at a small, public, liberal arts university—we pursued these questions in a series of six investigations on play and mathematics. Each of these studies was reviewed by the Institutional Review Board of our university and found to adhere to ethical principles for research on children and teachers. In this chapter we highlight our findings and suggest their implications for classroom practice.

STUDY 1: WHICH ASPECTS OF BLOCK
PLAY CONTRIBUTE TO MATH LEARNING?

"Hey, we used to have three long blocks," a four-year-old declares, looking directly at a peer's block structure, in which she has incorporated all of the longest blocks available in the block area. She continues building, oblivious to his intense expression, which seems to suggest he might snatch one of her long blocks for his own use. But after a pause, he says, "I know. This can be a long block." He places two shorter blocks together so that they comprise the longer length that he needs.

As illustrated in this vignette, several previous investigations have indicated a relationship between block play and math knowledge (Wolfgang, Standard, & Jones, 2001, 2003). So, we chose to conduct an initial study on the specific elements of this type of play in preschool that predict positive math outcomes (Trawick-Smith et al., 2017). We built upon previous work by identifying features of naturalistic block play—peers, teachers, play materials, and the type of block play, itself—that impact math learning.

Method

Participants. We video-recorded 41 three- and four-year-olds as they engaged in naturalistic block play in four preschool classrooms in a high-quality, nationally accredited child development center over the course of a year. Children were of diverse cultural and socioeconomic backgrounds and included an equal number of boys and girls. Recordings were made with cameras mounted in the classroom and controlled from a remote site, so children were not aware they were being observed. During recording periods, any children who entered the block area in their classrooms during free play time were captured on video, yielding over 2,500 minutes of block play for analysis.

Measures. We administered a pre- and posttest to all participants, using *Tools for Early Assessment in Mathematics—TEAM* (Clements, Sarama, Wolfe, & Spitler, 2013). This instrument is used regularly in preschool research and measures knowledge of number, geometry, measurement, and patterns. TEAM has been found to be a reliable and valid measure of early math knowledge (Clements et al., 2015; von Eye & Mun, 2005).

Video captured for each participant was analyzed, using the following measures: 1.) *number of structures built during the year,* 2.) *total time spent in blocks,* 3.) *mean block structure complexity* (Hanline et al., 2010), 4.) *mean score on social participation in block play* (Coplan & Rubin, 1998), 5.) *frequency of teacher interactions in blocks,* 6.) *percentage of building without miniature toys.* Interrater agreement was high for all measures; *kappas* ranged from .84 to 1.00.

Results

Conducting hierarchical multiple regression analyses, we found that these block play variables, all together, explained an additional 13 percent of variance in posttest TEAM scores over and above the influence of pretest scores, age, SES, and gender, R^2 change = .13., F (6, 29) = 11.59, $p < .001$. Three individual block play variables were found to contribute significant variance to these posttest scores: block structure complexity, ß = .27, $p < .01$, social participation in block play, ß = .25, $p < .05$, and percentage of building without miniature toys, ß = .25, $p < .01$.

Discussion

That block play variables explained 13 percent of math learning during a year of preschool provides strong evidence to support including blocks in preschool classrooms. Findings suggest that it is the complexity of structures, not their frequency, that has the strongest impact on math growth. The degree of collaboration with peers in block building is also highly related to math ability. One reason for this may be the scaffolding that peers provide one another when building. This finding might also reflect how math conversations and negotiations in play with peers promote learning. An interesting finding—and one that challenges common classroom practice—is that building *without* miniature toys—vehicles, people, and animals—leads to greater math knowledge. It may be that such toys—while beneficial in other areas of development—distract children from complex block building and the mathematical thinking that goes with it. This finding is consistent with earlier research indicating that realistic replicas, compared to nonrealistic materials such as blocks, can restrict children's choices of play themes and inhibit their open-ended play activities (Sear, 2016; Trawick-Smith, 1990; Trawick-Smith, Wolff, Koschel, & Vallarelli, 2014).

STUDY 2: HOW DO PRESCHOOL TEACHERS ENGAGE CHILDREN IN MATHEMATICAL THINKING IN PLAY?

A teacher is playing a farm board game with four-year-olds. She rolls a large die and asks, "What did I roll?" One of the children shouts, "A four, so you land on the pig." The teacher responds, "Well, let's see," and counts four spaces, moving her game piece to a space beyond the picture of the pig. "No!" the child says, pointing to the pig. "You go here." The teacher challenges him gently. "But I rolled four, so I'm here." The child thinks a moment then says, "But let's say you rolled three, okay?"

This vignette illustrates our focus in study 2, in which we looked at how teachers guide children's mathematical problem solving in play. Our objective was to determine if and how experienced, highly educated preschool teachers naturally engage in play with children to promote mathematical thinking.

Method

Participants. The four head teachers in four classrooms in the same child development center as in Study 1, were the adult participants in this investigation. All were female and held either bachelor's or master's degrees in early childhood education and had 10 years of classroom teaching experience. The 44 three- and four-year-olds enrolled in these classrooms—an equal number of boys and girls who were of diverse socioeconomic and cultural backgrounds—were included in the study.

Recording and analysis. Each teacher was recorded interacting with children in weekly, one-hour free play periods over a two-month period, yielding 32 hours of teacher-child interactions for analysis. As in Study 1, recordings were made from mounted cameras that were manipulated from a remote site, so teachers and children were not aware that they were being observed. Segments of teacher-child interactions that contained math content were isolated for analysis; sixty-three video clips of such interactions were obtained across the four teachers. These clips were transcribed. Following a method recommended by Lincoln and Guba (1985), two researchers, in continuous collaboration with one another, categorized, named, and defined units of math-play interactions, guided by the math domains and processes outlined by the National Council of Teachers of Mathematics standards (NCTM, 2000). The researchers also coded teacher scaffolding using an observation system that measured how well teacher math interactions matched children's play needs (Trawick-Smith & Dziurgot, 2010a & 2010b).

Results

Our data indicated that teachers naturally addressed math content and processes during play interactions with preschoolers. Our analysis delivered a framework of 7 items that fully captured these math-play interactions: *good-fit versus poor-fit interactions*—whether an interaction supported or interrupted children's play; three *math domains*—specific math areas addressed in an interaction—number, geometry, and measurement; and three *math processes*—problem-solving, reasoning, and math communication.

Discussion

Results of this study provided a window into the nature of teacher-child math-play interactions. Teachers interacted in various ways to support young children's thinking across specific math domains and thinking processes emphasized by NCTM. One important finding was that in some math-play interactions the math content or process evinced by the child was not matched by the math content or process evinced by the teacher. For example, a child might be working on solving a problem—determining how many and what sized shapes would fit on her collage—and the teacher might instead ask her to count the shapes. A child might be in deep concentration while counting the number of cups he is filling at the waterplay table, but a teacher might ask him which cup was largest. A child might be setting the table for a make-believe party, without thinking mathematically at all, but a teacher might ask her to name the shapes of the plates. These were considered *poor-fit interactions*.

In contrast, we observed many good-fit interactions (such as the illustration above) in which a teacher matched the kind of support they gave to what children were currently playing and thinking about. Because we observed both poor- and good-fit interactions, we determined that it would be worthwhile to study this pattern of interaction more closely in our next investigation.

STUDY 3: WHICH TYPES OF TEACHER-CHILD PLAY INTERACTIONS CONTRIBUTE TO MATH LEARNING?

Two five-year-olds are playing a classic card game, Memory, in the math center of their preschool classroom. When the game is over, one child announces, "I won, see? I have more cards." He holds up the pile of cards he has won. A teacher says, "So tell me how you figured out that you won the most cards." The child pauses. "Well," he says, "just look at my cards. My pile is thicker than hers." This causes his peer to challenge his thinking. "Wait a minute," she says. "That's not right." The teacher asks, "Do you have a different way to figure out who won?" The protesting child creates a line on the floor with her cards, then lines up her peer's cards next to hers. "Oh," she says. "So what did you figure out?" the teacher asks. "Well, he did win," she concedes, "because his line is longer."

This vignette is an illustration of how teachers can prompt mathematical problem-solving in play (Trawick-Smith, 1992). Through prompting and questions, this teacher guides the child away from relying solely on appearances to solve a problem toward a more reasoned solution (Piaget, 1952). Previous research suggests that such interactions can enhance academic abilities, generally, and math learning, specifically (Edo, Planas & Badillo, 2009; Fisher, Hirsh-Pasek, Newcombe, & Golinkoff, 2013). However, this prior work has not identified the specific types of interactions that are most effective. In Study 3 we examined the relative impact on math learning of each of the categories of teacher-child play interactions that were identified and defined in Study 2 (Trawick-Smith, Swaminathan, & Liu, 2016).

Method

Participants. Participants were 47 three- and four-year-olds enrolled in the same four classrooms in the child development center where Studies 1 and 2 took place. As in previous studies, an equal number of boys and girls, and those of diverse cultural and socioeconomic backgrounds were included. Adult participants were the four, highly educated and experienced head teachers as in our previous studies, along with 12 teacher associates and assistants who held associates or bachelor's degrees.

Measures, recording, and analysis. Children's mathematical knowledge was assessed at the beginning and at the end of the study, using the Test of Early Mathematics Ability—TEMA (Ginsberg & Baroody, 2003). Widely used in preschool research, TEMA is a reliable and valid measure of number-related skills and knowledge. Each child was recorded in five, 20-minute free play periods in the classroom over eight months. Video was edited to isolate all clips containing math interactions between a child and an adult. These clips were coded by two independent researchers, using the framework from Study 2. Agreement for coding all categories was high between raters; *kappas* ranged from .87 to .96.

Results

To determine the relative contributions of teacher-child interactions to mathematics ability, a hierarchical multiple regression analysis was conducted with TEMA posttest scores as the dependent variable and pretest TEMA scores, demographic variables, and frequency of categories of math interactions as independent variables. Math-play interaction variables were found to contribute 23 percent additional variance to posttest TEMA scores, beyond what was explained by pretest scores and demographic variables, R^2 change = .23, $F(9, 37) = 35.48$, $p < .001$. Three individual teacher-child math interactions contributed significantly to the variance in posttest performance—good-fit interactions, $\beta = .22$, $p < .01$, interactions related to number, $\beta = .23$, $p < .01$, and math communication interactions, $\beta = .19$, $p < .01$.

Discussion

These results confirm that teachers' math-play interactions are effective for enhancing math learning. Our findings suggest that teachers should engage in three particular interactions in play that accounted for increases in math ability—interactions to support number, good fit play interactions, and math communication. Number interactions are common in preschool classrooms (Swaminathan & Trawick-Smith, 2018). As teachers engage in these, the present study suggests, they should also strive for good-fit math interactions—those which support children's play and thinking—while avoiding those that disrupt their activities. Our findings also indicate that teachers use math communication interactions in play—that is, converse about math ideas using math-rich language. These findings are consistent with those of other studies in which such *math talk* in non-play settings was found to predict math learning (Boonen, Kolkman, & Kroesbergen, 2011; Klibanoff, Levine, Huttenlocher, Vasilyeva, & Hedges, 2006).

STUDY 4: DO INCREASES IN TEACHER MATH TALK DURING PLAY LEAD TO GREATER MATH LEARNING?

A teacher joins a group of four-year-old children who are pretending to make dinner in the dramatic play area of their classroom. "Honey," one of the children says to the teacher in a very serious adult tone, "you need to set the table." The teacher says, "Okay. How many plates do we need?" When the child looks at him with a puzzled expression, the teacher says to himself, as if thinking out loud, "Well, let's see . . . how many people will be eating? I'm going to count." He counts, pointing to each child as he does. "So, we have three people eating. No wait. I'm going to eat dinner too, so that's one, two, three, four. So, we need four plates." Another one of the children enthusiastically says, "I'll do it," and, just as the teacher has done, counts the plates aloud. "See? Four," the child announces pointing to the plates on the table.

The teacher in this vignette is modeling mathematical thinking by talking to himself and counting out loud. In Study 3, we found that such teacher verbalizations predict growth in math learning. In our next investigation, we sought to determine if a professional development program to increase teacher math talk during free play would promote math learning (Trawick-Smith, Oski, DePaolis, Krause, & Zebrowski, 2016). Our previous (and subsequent) investigations were conducted in a child development center that served a diverse population and was staffed by highly experienced and educated teachers, many with master's degrees. In the present investigation, we wanted to assess the impact of a math talk professional development strategy on professionals who had lower levels of education and who taught in more typical community-based programs.

Method

Participants. Participants were 13 teachers and assistants and the 66 preschool children they cared for in four classrooms in a large, community-based child development center in a low-income urban neighborhood. Teachers held associate degrees; assistants held high school diplomas or GEDs. Thirty-five boys and 31 girls of low SES Latino and African American backgrounds were included in the sample.

Training, measures, and coding. An eight-hour training program for center staff was implemented over a five-month period to increase and diversify math talk during free play. Strategies were presented for engaging children in unobtrusive ways in math talk across areas of play and all domains. Each child was assessed at the beginning and end of the study, using five "snapshot" math assessments that were developed in previous research (Levine, Ratliff, Huttenlocher, & Cannon, 2012; Vanderheyden et al., 2011). These assessments were conducted within the classroom, utilizing available play materials. They yielded one score in number, two in geometry, one in spatial knowledge, and one in measurement of length. Reliability was established in previous research, *kappas* = .77 to .99. One morning a week during free play, math talk was coded, over a 16-week period. As in our previous studies, number, geometry, and measurement talk were noted. In addition, spatial knowledge talk was coded, based on emerging research on this domain (Ferrara, Hirsh-Pasek, Newcombe, Golinkoff, & Lam, 2011).

Results

A significant increase in teachers' math talk during play was observed over the course of the study, $X^2 = 296.25$, $p < .001$. One source of this increase was a growth in teachers' use of geometry and measurement talk. We conducted a series of multiple regression analyses, with pretest assessment scores, age, gender, and the frequencies of the four math talk domains entered as independent variables and posttest scores on each of the math assessments as dependent variables. Each type of math talk was found to predict significant growth in one or more specific posttest assessments. Number talk and measurement talk by teachers during children's play predicted significant gains in the number assessment, ß = .34, $p < .05$ and ß = .31, $p < .01$, respectively. Measurement, geometry, and spatial knowledge talk contributed significantly to gains in the geometry assessment, ß = .51, $p < .001$, ß = .34, $p < .05$, and ß = .35, $p < .05$, respectively. Spatial talk in play predicted growth in the spatial knowledge assessment, ß = .42, $p < .05$. Measurement talk and spatial talk predicted growth in measurement assessment scores, ß = .21, $p < .05$ and ß = .77, $p < .01$, respectively.

Discussion

Our findings suggest that community-based child care providers, with minimal levels of education, can, through professional development, increase and diversify their math talk during children's play. Consistent with findings of Study 3, this increase in math talk was found to contribute to learning in various math areas. The study also suggests that the type of talk teachers use in play will determine which math domains it enhances. An implication is that teachers should engage children in conversations across varied math domains, not just counting. Based on our data, measurement talk—discussions about length, quantity, and size—will have the broadest impact across domains of math learning.

STUDY 5: WHICH MATH TOPICS DO TEACHERS TALK ABOUT, HOW DO THEY TALK ABOUT THEM, AND WHY?

A three-year-old is building a tower with blocks. "Look!" the child says to a nearby teacher. "See how tall? Take a picture!" The teacher responds, "It is tall. And I like how you put this block right on the top. It's called a cylinder." The child looks confused. "No, it's a circle," she protests. The teacher explains gently, "See it's a block, a shape that's thick, an object you can hold. See? So it's called a cylinder." The child says, impatiently, "Cylinder, okay. But take a picture."

This vignette shows that teacher math talk can vary greatly, not just by domain (in this case geometry), but also in how it is phrased (here as a declarative statement), and by its intended purpose (here to directly inform a child of a math concept). In this next investigation we sought to identify, in naturally occurring math talk, not only which domains teachers and children discuss, but also the syntactic structure of teacher utterances, and their intended purposes. Our goal was to develop a math talk coding system that would differentiate among these varies types of utterances and could be used in subsequent research.

Method

Participants. Participants were four preschool teachers, who held bachelor's or master's degrees, and four associates with bachelor's degrees (three female and one male), who were working in classrooms in the same high quality, nationally accredited child development center where Studies 1, 2, and 3 were conducted. Child participants—an equal number of boys and girls—represented the same diverse socioeconomic and cultural distributions as previous studies.

Recording and analysis. Participants were recorded interacting with children in weekly, one-hour free play periods in each classroom for two months. As in previous studies, cameras were manipulated from a remote site, so teachers were not aware of when they were being individually recorded. Video was edited so that segments of teacher-child interactions that included math talk were isolated for analysis. Over 100 clips of math talk were captured across the eight adult participants. These clips were transcribed. Working from both the video clips and transcripts, two coders, in continuous collaboration with one another, categorized each teacher math talk utterance that was recorded, following Lincoln and Guba's (1985) "looks like, feels like" method. This process resulted in a categorization of distinct math talk units that were named and defined.

Results

Math talk utterances could be categorized in three different ways. First, they could be sorted by the math domains that were being discussed—number, geometry, measurement, and patterning. These categories could be further divided into 17 sub-categories under these domains. Math talk utterances could also be categorized according to three syntactic structures—*declarative statements*, *open-ended questions*, and *closed questions*. Finally, utterances could be sorted according to their discourse purpose—that is, the assumed intent of a statement within a conversation. Seven such discourse purposes were delineated—*informing* a child about a mathematics concept, *giving instructions* on how to solve a math problem, *narrating* a child's math activities or thinking, *modeling* mathematical thinking, *clarifying* a child's mathematical reasoning, *posing a closed mathematical problem* with a correct answer, and *posing an open-ended problem* with multiple solutions. Altogether, a total of 27 sub-categories of math talk during play were identified and defined. These are presented in Table 4.1.

Table 4.1. Teacher Math Talk Categories Related to Domains, Syntactic Structures, and Discourse Purposes, Identified in Study 5

Math Domains in Teachers' Math Talk

Number	Geography	Measurement	Patterning
Counting Objects	Spatial Knowledge	Measuring Objects	Identifying Patterns
Abstract Counting	Shape Identification	Comparing Measures	Creating Patterns
Number Symbols	Shape Composition	Ordering by Size/Amount	Continuing Patterns
Cardinality	Attributes of Shapes		
Ordinality	Transformation		
Addition/Subtraction			

Syntactic Structures Used in Teachers' Math Talk

Declarative Statements	Open-Ended Questions	Closed Questions

Discourse Purposes for Teachers' Math Talk

Informing	Giving Instructions	Narrating	Modeling	Clarifying Reasoning	Posing Closed Problem	Posing Open Problem

DISCUSSION

Our findings indicate that the natural classroom math talk of teachers as they interact with preschool children in play is exceedingly complex. In a single interchange, a teacher must first observe play and consider the possible math domains that they might discuss with children. When children build tall block towers, a teacher might discuss measurement (e.g., "Which of these is the tallest?"), and during a board game, the conversation might be about number (e.g., "How many more spaces do you have to move to get to the end?"). In many cases, a teacher might decide to converse with children about non-mathematical topics.

In addition, teachers must decide how to phrase their math talk utterances. Research suggests that open-ended questions prompt deeper reflection, greater reasoning, and more extensive conversation in young children that other types of queries (Säre, Tulviste, & Luik, 2019). For this reason, some teachers might strive to frame their questions in more open-ended ways during children's play ("How did you figure that out?") rather than asking only those that have a single answer ("How many spaces did you move?"). In the present study, there was great variation across the teachers, with some readily asking such questions and others doing so very infrequently.

Teachers must also consider the purposes for their math talk, based on what children are currently doing in their play. Do they directly instruct children who are having difficulty solving a problem ("Why don't you count the dots on the dice to see how far you move?"), model or narrate mathematical thinking ("Let's count the dots. One, two, three . . ."), or pose a more open-ended problem ("You rolled the dice, so now what will you do?") We concluded that research was now needed to explore the unique impact of each of these dimensions of math talk on children's learning.

STUDY 6: WHICH DOMAINS, STRUCTURES, AND PURPOSES OF MATH TALK PREDICT LEARNING?

Two five-year-olds have invented a game at the waterplay table. They pour water into different shaped containers, then carefully line them up on counter. "Tell me what you're doing," a teacher says. "See, we're putting them in order like we did that one time," one child explains, referring to an ordering activity that the teacher had created in the science center several weeks ago.

"So, they're in order by how much water is in each of them?" the teacher asks to clarify their thinking. "Yeah, see?" the other child says pointing to the row of containers. "These are the most and these aren't very much." The

teacher nods, pauses, then asks, "So how did you figure out which ones are the most or least." One of the children says confidently, "Oh, easy as pie." She bends down so her face is inches from the containers and holds her hand at the water level of each in turn. "This one's higher water, then this one . . ." She continues until she has commented on the water level of each container.

In this vignette a teacher is using open-ended and closed questions and a discourse purpose—seeking to clarify children's mathematical thinking—to talk about the measurement domain. Is this interchange useful in supporting children's math learning? In Study 6, we utilized our math talk framework, constructed in Study 5, to examine the impact of the 27 specific types of math talk, including domains discussed, syntactic structures used, and intended purposes (Swaminathan & Trawick-Smith, 2018).

Method

Participants. Participants were 40 three- and four-year-olds—an equal number of boys and girls—of diverse cultural and SES backgrounds, and who were enrolled in the same four preschool classrooms and with the same sixteen teachers and assistants as in Studies 1, 2, 3, and 5.

Measures and Recording. Children's math knowledge was assessed at the beginning and end of a school year, using the Tools for Early Assessment in Mathematics, TEAM (Clements et al., 2013), which has been used in previous research, including Study 1. The instrument evaluates early knowledge of number, geometry, measurement, and patterning. Reliability and validity of this measure are reported under Study 1. Each child participant was videorecorded in five separate 30-minute observation periods during free play in the classroom over eight months. From resulting video, subclips were created for any instance in which an adult moved to within five feet of the child being recorded. Each syntactically complete teacher utterance that included math content was transcribed and coded by two independent researchers for its math domain, its syntactic structure, and its discourse purpose. Interrater agreement was high, mean *kappa* = .91.

Results

A series of hierarchical regression analyses were conducted with posttest TEAM scores as the dependent variable and all math talk categories—domains, syntactic structures, and purposes—and demographic factors as independent variables. Overall math talk frequency, across all domains, was found to explain 33 percent of variance of posttest scores, over and above the influence of pretest performance and demographic variables, R^2 change =

.33., *F* change (17,18) = 204.27, *p* < .001. A number of individual categories and subcategories of math-talk were found to contribute significant variance to TEAM posttest scores. These math talk variables, beta weights, significance, and examples of each are presented in Table 4.2.

As shown in the table, the four sub-categories of math talk related to the domains of number and geometry were found to contribute significant variance to TEAM posttest scores: Math talk related to abstract counting, ß = .32, *p* < .001, cardinality, ß = .11, *p* = .05, ordinality, ß = .12, *p* < .01, number symbols, ß = .10, *p* < .01, and attributes of shapes, ß = .16, *p* < .01. As shown in the table, one syntactic structure variable, open-ended questions, explained significant variance in posttest scores, ß = .50, *p* < .001. Two math talk discourse purposes contributed significant posttest TEAM score variance— modeling mathematical thinking, ß = .19, *p* < .05, and posing open-ended math problems, ß = .50, *p* < .001.

Discussion

Results of this study indicate, once again, that math talk in play by preschool teachers explains a substantial percentage of math learning over the course of a year. Findings suggest that teachers should converse with children in play about five sub-domains of math talk, in particular: abstract counting,

Table 4.2. Math Talk Categories That Contribute Significant Variance to Posttest TEAM Scores in Study 6, Their Beta Weights, Significance, and Examples

Math Talk Categories	Beta	Sig.	Example
Abstract Counting	.32	.001	"How many tickets do you need for your whole family?"
Cardinality	.11	.004	"How many animals are in the farm all together?"
Ordinality	.12	.001	"Jamal was first; who's going to roll second?"
Number Symbols	.10	.041	"Here's the doctor's phone number. See? It's 355–3244."
Attributes of Shapes	.16	.012	"You're right, it (a triangle) does has three corners. But not the circle, see?"
Open-Ended Questions	.50	.001	"How can you figure out which has the most?"
Modeling Mathematical Thinking	.19	.040	"I'm going to feed the monkey two more bananas, so now he has one, two, three, four."
Posing Open-Ended Problems to Solve	.48	.000	"Can you put out enough cups so all of you (mothers) can have coffee?"

cardinality, ordinality, number symbols, and attributes of shapes. Examples of such math talk, presented in Table 2, illustrate that these categories promote deeper levels of thinking and conversation about math concepts than do simple counting of objects or naming shapes, which we did not find to predict math learning. Our findings are consistent with previous research indicating that young children benefit from experiences requiring higher-level mathematical thinking than those traditionally provided in preschool (Engel, Claessens, & Finch, 2013).

Based on our results, teachers should also often frame their math talk in play as open-ended questions. Similarly, they should engage children in conversations that pose open-ended problems for them to solve. These findings underscore the value of constructive conversations rather than one-right-answer discussions as children play. Since modeling of mathematical thinking in play predicted math learning in this investigation, teachers might more often "think out loud," as they interact in play. In so doing, they demonstrate problem solving and reasoning that have an impact on math abilities.

GENERAL DISCUSSION

Findings of our CECE math-play studies have important implications for classroom practice. Across studies, we found evidence that play in classrooms often includes mathematical thinking and conversations. This finding is consistent with previous anecdotal descriptions of how children are regularly confronted with and solve math-related problems in natural play settings (Ginsberg, 2006; Hanline, Milton, & Phelps, 2009; Park, Chae, & Boyd, 2008). Further, our studies indicate that this mathematical thinking and conversation in play contributes to children's math learning in preschool. So, our research establishes that play in early childhood classrooms can promote, not only the many social and emotional outcomes that are often reported in the literature (Veiga, Neto, & Rieffe, 2016), but also an important area of academic learning. In our Study 1, for example, building complex structures with peers during block play was found to explain 13 percent of children's math growth over the course of a year of preschool. In this investigation, it was block play alone, not any special adult intervention, that predicted these gains—a finding that is consistent with several other block play investigations (Hanline, Milton, & Phelps, 2010; Jirout & Newcombe, 2015; Wolfgang, Standard, & Jones, 2001, 2003). Our study adds, then, to the growing body of research supporting the inclusion of blocks, along with other forms of play, in early childhood classrooms (Parker & Thomsen, 2019; Whitebread, Basilio, Kuvalja, & Verma, 2012)

In our studies, we also determined that preschool teachers can and do as-sume an important role in guiding mathematical thinking in play. In Study 2, we found that teachers often naturally interact with children in all kinds of play and in a variety of ways to promote math learning. Many of these inter-actions were found to align with math learning standards recommended for preschool children (NCTM, 2000). However, only some of these interactions supported play as well as math learning, we discovered. Some were identified as "poor fit" interactions—those that actually interfered with what children were playing and thinking. Such obtrusive adult interventions have been ob-served in other studies as well, and have been found to limit children's play activities. (Trawick-Smith & Dzuirgot, 2010a, 2010b). These findings raise questions about the benefits versus risks of teacher math-play interactions for both math learning and play development.

In Study 3, we examined the impact of various math related play interac-tions, including those that were considered a good- or poor-fit with children's current play activities. Our findings showed that specific teacher math inter-actions in play can enhance learning. Interactions related to number and those that included language—that is, math talk—were found to be most predictive of math learning. These findings extend the work of other researchers who have reported that adult math talk in non-play settings in preschool and kin-dergarten supports children's understanding of number (Boonen, Kolkman, & Kroesbergen 2011; Klibanoff, Levine, Huttenlocher, Vasilyeva, & Hedges, 2006). An implication for classroom practice is that teachers should strive to use rich math language, where appropriate, as they interact with children in play, particularly related to number. An additional finding of Study 3, with significant implications for teaching, was that only those teacher interactions that were coded as a good-fit with children's play activities were strongly as-sociated with math learning. Those that interrupted what children were play-ing had no relationship to math outcomes. This finding highlights the impor-tance of sensitive and supportive teacher interactions in play and reinforces a concern raised in the literature that adult interference in play can diminish its benefits (Trawick-Smith, 2012; Tsai, 2015).

Can teachers be taught to use good-fit math talk in play within typical, community-based preschool classrooms? This was the question addressed in Study 4. Through professional development, teachers with associate's degrees in urban preschools serving children of low socioeconomic status were inspired to increase the frequency and variety of their conversations about math in play. These increases in math talk resulted in significant gains in various domains of math learning. This is an important finding for professionals working with children living in poverty, who have been found to enter elementary school with lower levels of math knowledge than their middle-class peers (Lee, Autry, Fox, & Williams, 2008; Lee & Moon, 2007). Math talk in play appears to be an effective strategy for helping to close this math achievement gap. Too, our findings suggest that a limited professional development program—only eight hours over five weeks—can improve math-play interactions among professionals with varying backgrounds—even those with limited education and training. We conclude that urban school districts might consider a low-cost intervention—one that requires no special curriculum or materials—to promote good-fit math talk play interactions among all preschool teachers, childcare providers and assistants, and even parents within the community.

Our investigations confirm that math talk with young children in play is extremely complex. This is consistent findings of previous studies that adult math talk goes far beyond simple counting (Levine, Suriyakham, Rowe, Huttenlocher, & Gunderson, 2010; Gunderson & Levine, 2011). Teachers in our Studies 5 and 6, for example, were found to utter 27 different categories of math talk, including 17 different sub-domains, three distinct syntactic structures, and six specific purposes during play. Each category was found to have a distinct impact on children's learning. Our study 6 revealed that teacher math talk in play had a stronger association with math learning if it was related deeper math concepts—not just counting or naming shapes. Conversing about abstract counting (with no objects are present), cardinality, ordinality, number symbols, and attributes of shapes—topics that are not always addressed in a preschool curriculum—contributed most to math growth. This finding supports the position that young children should be more fully challenged in their mathematical thinking (Engel, Claessens, & Finch, 2013).

Too often, some researchers argue, children spend too much classroom time on things they already know. For example, in some of our observations, teachers regularly asked children to simply name shapes, which they were readily able to do. But discussions about features of shapes—their angles, curves, sides, area, size or position in space—which were more strongly related to math learning—were less frequent. Our findings on the effects of syntactic structures and discourse purposes of math talk in play further support the idea that children should be challenged more fully in their thinking. Open-ended questions and utterance that posed open-ended problems were strongly associated with learning. Questions and posed problems with only a single right answer did not predict math growth. We conclude that a play setting, with its multiple and unpredictable problems to solve, may be the ideal context for stretching children mathematical thinking and problem solving.

In summary, our studies support the importance of play as well as of teacher play interactions in promoting math learning, with one caveat. Observations in all of our studies suggest that teachers should use caution to avoid what Sutton-Smith (1990) calls "didactic play bumblings" (p. 5). Teachers must respect and support children's play, itself, even as they strive to support mathematical thinking. Only when math talk contributes to what children are currently playing and thinking will it have an important impact on learning.

ACKNOWLEDGMENT

This research has been funded by two generous grants for the Spencer Foundation

REFERENCES

Baroody, A. J. (2004). The developmental bases for early childhood number and operations standards. In D. H. Clements, J. Sarama, & A. DiBiase. (2004). *Engaging young children in mathematics: Standards for early childhood mathematics education* (pp. 173–220). New York: Psychology Press.

Boonen A. J., Kolkman M. E., & Kroesbergen E. H. (2011). The relation between teachers' math talk and the acquisition of number sense within kindergarten classrooms. *Journal of School Psychology, 49*, 281–299.

Clements, D. H., Sarama, J., Swaminathan, S., Weber, D., & Trawick-Smith, J. (2018). Teaching and learning geometry: Early foundations. *Quadrante: Revista de Investigação em Educação Matemática, 2*, 7–31.

Clements, D. H., Sarama, J., Wolfe, C. B., & Spitler, M. E. (2013). Longitudinal evaluation of a scale-up model for teaching mathematics with trajectories and technologies: Persistence of effects in the third year. *American Educational Research Journal, 50*(4), 812–850.

Clements, D. H., Sarama, J., Layzer, C., Unlu, F., Wolfe, C. B., Spitler, M. E., & Weiss, D. (2015). *Effects of Triad on mathematics achievement: Long-term impacts.* Washington, DC: Society for Research on Educational Effectiveness.

Coplan, R. J., & Rubin, K. H. (1998). Exploring and assessing nonsocial play in the preschool: The development and validation of the Preschool Play Behavior Scale. *Social Development, 7*(1), 72–91.

Edo, M., Planas, N., & Badillo, E. (2009). Mathematical learning in a context of play. *European Early Childhood Education Research Journal, 17*(3), 325–341.

Engel, M., Claessens, A., & Finch, M. A. (2013). Teaching students what they already know? The (mis) alignment between mathematics instructional content and student knowledge in kindergarten. *Educational Evaluation and Policy Analysis, 35*(2), 157–178.

Ferrara, K., Hirsh-Pasek, K., Newcombe, N. S., Golinkoff, R. M., & Lam, W. S. (2011). Block talk: Spatial language during block play. *Mind, Brain, and Education, 5*(3), 143–151.

Fisher, K. R., Hirsh-Pasek, K., Newcombe, N., & Golinkoff, R. M. (2013). Taking shape: Supporting preschoolers' acquisition of geometric knowledge through guided play. *Child development, 84*(6), 1872–1878.

Ginsberg, H. (2006). Mathematical play and playful mathematics: A guide for early education. In D. Singer, R. M. Golinkoff, & K. Hirsh-Pasek (Eds.) *Play-learning: How play motivates and enhances children's cognitive and social-emotional growth* (pp. 145–165).

Ginsberg, H. & Baroody, A. (2003). *Test of early mathematics ability (3*rd *edition).* Austin, TX: Pro-Ed.

Gunderson, E. A., & Levine, S. C. (2011). Some types of parent number talk count more than others: relations between parents' input and children's cardinal-number knowledge. *Developmental science, 14*(5), 1021–1032.

Hanline, M. F., Milton, S., & Phelps, P. (2009). A longitudinal study exploring the relationship of representational levels of three aspects of preschool sociodramatic play and early academic skills. *International Journal of Early Childhood Education, 2,* 55–75.

Hanline, M. F., Milton, S., & Phelps, P. C. (2010). The relationship between preschool block play and reading and maths abilities in early elementary school: A longitudinal study of children with and without disabilities. *Early Child Development and Care, 180*(8), 1005–1017.

Jirout, J. J., & Newcombe, N. S. (2015). Building blocks for developing spatial skills: Evidence from a large, representative US sample. *Psychological science, 26*(3), 302–310.

Klibanoff, R. S., Levine, S. C., Huttenlocher, J., Vasilyeva, M., & Hedges, L. V. (2006). Preschool children's mathematical knowledge: The effect of teacher "math talk." *Developmental Psychology, 42,* 59–69.

Lee, J., Autry, M. M., Fox, J., & Williams, C. (2008). Investigating children's mathematics readiness. *Journal of Research in Childhood Education, 22,* 316–328.

Lee, J., & Moon. S. (2007). *Gender and racial/ethnic difference in early mathematics achievement.* Paper presented at the meeting of the American Educational Research Association, Chicago, IL.

Levine, S. C., Ratliff, K. R., Huttenlocher, J., & Cannon, J. (2012). Early puzzle play: a predictor of preschoolers' spatial transformation skill. *Developmental psychology, 48*(2), 530.

Levine, S. C., Suriyakham, L. W., Rowe, M. L., Huttenlocher, J., & Gunderson, E. A. (2010). What counts in the development of young children's number knowledge? *Developmental psychology, 46*(5), 1309.

Lincoln, Y. S., & Guba, E. G. (1985). *Naturalistic inquiry.* Newbury Park, CA: Sage.

NCTM. (2000). *Principles and standards for school mathematics.* Reston, VA: National Council of Teachers of Mathematics.

Park, B., Chae, J. L., & Boyd, B. F. (2008). Young children's block play and mathematical learning. *Journal of Research in Childhood Education, 23*(2), 157–162.

Parker, R., & Thomsen, B. S. (2019). *Learning through play at school: A study of playful integrated pedagogies that foster children's holistic skills development in the primary school classroom.* Billund, Denmark: The Lego Foundation.

Piaget, J. (1952). *The origins of intelligence in children.* New York, NY:International Universities Press.

Ramani, G. B., & Siegler, R. S. (2008). Promoting broad and stable improvements in low-income children's numerical knowledge through playing number board games. *Child development, 79*(2), 375–394.

Ramani, G. B., Siegler, R. S., & Hitti, A. (2012). Taking it to the classroom: Number board games as a small group learning activity. *Journal of educational psychology, 104*(3), 661.

Rubin, K. H., Fein, G. G., & Vandenberg, B. (1983). Play. *Handbook of child psychology, 4,* 693–774.

Säre, E., Tulviste, T., & Luik, P. (2019). The function of questions in developing a preschooler's verbal reasoning skills during philosophical group discussions. *Early Child Development and Care, 189*(4), 555–568.

Sear, M. (2016). Why loose parts? Their relationship with sustainable practice, children's agency, creative thinking and learning outcomes. *Educating Young Children: Learning and Teaching in the Early Childhood Years, 22*(2), 16.

Sutton-Smith, B. (1990). Playfully yours. *The Association for the Study of Play Newsletter, 16,* 2–5.

Swaminathan, S., & Trawick-Smith, J. (2018, April) *Preschool teachers' math talk: Effective math domains, syntax, and purpose.* Paper presented at the annual meeting of the American Educational Research Association, New York.

Trawick-Smith, J. (1990). Effects of realistic vs. non-realistic play materials on young children's symbolic transformation of objects. *Journal of Research in Childhood Education, 5,* 27–36.

Trawick-Smith, J. (1992). *Interactions in the classroom: Facilitating play in the early years.* Columbus, OH: Merrill.

Trawick-Smith, J. (2012). Teacher-child play interactions to achieve learning outcomes in preschool: Risks and opportunities. In R. Pianta, S. Barnett, L. Justice, & S. Sheridan (Eds.), *Handbook of Early Childhood Education.* New York: Guilford.

Trawick-Smith, J., Dzuirgot, T. (2010a). "Good-fit" teacher-child play interactions and subsequent autonomous play in preschool. *Early Childhood Research Quarterly, 26,* 110–123.

Trawick-Smith, J., & Dzuirgot, T. (2010b). Untangling teacher-child play interactions: Do teacher education and experience influence "good-fit" responses to children's play? *Journal of Early Childhood Teacher Education, 31,* 1–24.

Trawick-Smith, J., Oski, H., DePaolis, K., Krause, K., & Zebrowski, A. (2016). Naptime data meetings to increase the math talk of early care and education providers. *Journal of Early Childhood Teacher Education, 37,* 157–174.

Trawick-Smith, J., Swaminathan, S., & Liu, X. (2016). The relationship of teacher-child play interactions to mathematics learning in preschool. *Early Child Development and Care 186,* 716–733.

Trawick-Smith, J., Swaminathan, S., Baton, B., Danieluk, C., Marsh, S., & Szarwacki, M. (2017). Block play and mathematics learning in preschool: The effects of building complexity, peer and teacher interactions in the block area, and replica play materials. *Journal of Early Childhood Research, 15*(4), 433–448.

Trawick-Smith, J., Wolff, J., Koschel, M., & Vallarelli, J. (2014). Which toys promote high-quality play? Reflections on the five-year anniversary of the TIMPANI toy study. *Young Children, 69*, 40.

Tsai, C. Y. (2015). Am I interfering? Preschool teacher participation in children play. *Universal Journal of Educational Research, 3*(12), 1028–1033.

Vanderheyden, A. M., Broussard, C., Fabre, M., Stanley, J., Legendre, J., & Creppell, J. (2011). Measurement of kindergartners' understanding of early mathematical concepts. School Psychology Review, 40 296–306.

Veiga, G., Neto, C., & Rieffe, C. (2016). Preschoolers' Free Play—Connections with Emotional and Social Functioning. *International Journal of Emotional Education, 8*(1), 48–62.

von Eye, A., & Von Eye, M. (2005). Can one use Cohen's kappa to examine disagreement? *Methodology, 1*(4), 129–142.

Weisberg, D. S., Hirsh-Pasek, K., Golinkoff, R. M., Kittredge, A. K., & Klahr, D. (2016). Guided play: Principles and practices. *Current Directions in Psychological Science, 25*(3), 177–182.

Whitebread, D., Basilio, M., Kuvalja, M., & Verma, M. (2012). *The importance of play*. Brussels, Belgium: Toy Industries of Europe.

Wolfgang, C. H., Standard, L., & Jones, I. (2001) Block play performance among preschoolers as a predictor of later school achievement in mathematics. *Journal of Research in Childhood Education, 15*, 173–180.

Wolfgang, C., Stannard, L., & Jones, I. (2003). Advanced constructional play with LEGOs among preschoolers as a predictor of later school achievement in mathematics. *Early Child Development and Care, 173*, 467–475.

Chapter Five

Exploring the Role of Free Play in Elementary Science

Brian A. Stone, Lora Lorentsen,
and Meghan Schmidt

When a child chooses to engage in play, an entire realm of possibilities opens. As a child begins to playfully imagine, construct, socialize, discover, wonder, inquire, experiment, and meaningfully interact with the environment, a high level of cognitive, emotional, and social growth can occur (International Play Association, 2014b). Some may attempt to capture the essence of play, but with a goal or objective in mind. However, when the play becomes a task, and ownership no longer belongs to the child, the power of play diminishes. The goal is the play itself, not for an adult or other to achieve an objective through it. When a child has the opportunity to play, a profoundly powerful ownership experience emerges. This experience is unique to each individual, as the child develops for his or her own purposes a world one can understand, manipulate, and construct without barriers. It is in this world, the play world, where a child can begin to discover and develop meaningful and relevant conceptual understandings with significant personal connections. It is important to note that this can often happen through play or in play settings, even without being set up by an adult/teacher to achieve some curriculum-motivated outcome. This descriptive field study was designed to explore the role and opportunities for freely chosen play in 3rd and 4th grade science classrooms, specifically within the context of static electricity content, and with regard for concept learning.

REVIEW OF LITERATURE

Previous studies have provided evidence for the many benefits of play, even within specific contexts. For example, play aids in conceptual development in science (Bruner, 1983; 1985). Johnson, Christie, and Wardle (2005) suggest that play is a necessary process for concept development in many areas including problem solving, divergent thinking, and higher-order thinking processes. Others suggest that play shifts behaviors to a higher-conceptual level "using the powerful natural engine of free play" (Gmitrova & Gmitrov, 2003, p. 245).

Despite substantial evidence showing the varied benefits of play, the school context shows that play is severely undervalued, with little to no time given for play activities, especially free play, and the play of older children. Lewis (2017) states, "the creeping erosion of play is occurring across several landscapes" (p. 11). The IPA (2014b) suggests that schools have an overemphasis on theoretical and academic studies, and that there is a societal indifference to play. Gray (2013) contends that there has been a rise in adult control over children, which has led to several decades of declining play opportunities for children. Others suggest "play is being shunted aside in favor of more direct forms of instruction" and that "teachers increasingly regard play as a waste of instructional time with no clear benefits for high-priority cognitive outcomes" (Christie & Roskos, 2006, p. 57). Therefore, the design of this study is situated in the disconnect between the known benefits of free play, and the virtual lack of such play in schools other than during recess periods.

Benefits

According to the IPA (2014b), play is an essential component of childhood with multiple benefits including social, emotional, and cognitive development. Play leads to stronger autonomy, sharing, and equality, as children learn through play to direct themselves and their world, share through social interaction, and respect/attend to everyone's needs (Gray, 2013). Lewis (2017) suggests that play has epistemological and ontological significance in our species, and that play is universally observed and recognizable across cultures, though it may vary widely. Unfortunately, play is eroding, especially in school contexts, as there are "fewer spaces and places" for play in the classroom and there seems to be a growing indifference to play in society (Lewis, 2017, p. 11; IPA, 2014b).

Play helps children develop physically, emotionally, socially, cognitively, creatively, and helps children develop effective communication skills (The Genius of Play, n.d.). Play enhances brain structure and executive functioning, and in the presence of adversity, play has a critical role in regulating the body's stress response (Yogman, Garner, Hutchinson, Hirsh-Pasek, & Golinkoff, 2018). Furthermore, play has an important role in developing problem-solving skills, collaboration, creativity, and helping individuals learn to take risks, experiment and test boundaries (Yogman, et al., 2018).

Play in Learning Contexts

According to Talu (2018), the necessities for play are given when children feel free and have free time to engage in play. Furthermore, the materials should neither dominate the play, nor dictate the pattern of play. In education settings, children should have opportunities to play, and should be left to play on their own (Ariel, 2002). Most importantly, the adult should not control the child's activity, which is more important than having designed materials (Talu, 2018).

Lewis (2017) stresses the "importance of play in the holistic development of children," but that increasingly, play is "highly structured, orchestrated by teachers," and "has some learning goal or outcome attached to the play," which is "constantly under surveillance" (p. 16). This is known as the curricularization of play. Vandenberg (2004) sums up this approach, stating that the "danger of the play curriculum is that the focus on adult intentions renders the activity no longer playful" (p. 58).

Play and Science Concept Development

According to Laszlo (2004), science has elements of play, and in fact, "there is some cognitive value to the playful element in science" (p. 400). Ashbrook (2010) takes it further by stating that play and science inquiry are essential components of childhood, and that "imaginative play, unscripted yet guided by children's own rules, allows students to use their imagination and develop self-regulation, symbolic thinking, memory, language, and social skills, as well as construct their knowledge and understanding of the world" (p. 26). Furthermore, play reflects learning through scientific inquiry and helps children make sense of the world and engage as scientists (Ashbrook, 2010). In studying children in "water play," Gross (2012) found that children developed deep understandings of varied science concepts simply through water play activities. These activities were slightly more teacher-directed, but still allowed for substantial free play opportunities. Talib, Norishah, and Zulkafly (2013) suggest that children who explore science concepts creatively, and through play, will develop a sustained interest to understand the scientific concept. In a study on free play, researchers found that "robust learning" takes place through free play and "young children's self-directed learning supports the higher-order generalizations, laying the foundations for building larger conceptual structures and intuitive theories" (Sim & Xu, 2017, p. 642).

Traditional Science Contexts

Using Siegfried Engelmann's original designs for Direct Instruction, many teachers have developed more traditional approaches to science education that explicitly teach carefully sequenced and chunked information in more scripted ways (Carnine, Silbert, Kame'enui, & Tarver, 2010). Direct Instruction features teacher-directed, scripted experiences that are usually high-paced, and cue students for responses (Athabasca University, 2017).

Science curriculum has been reduced to textbook readings, superficial memorization, and low-level workbook tasks (National Science Teachers Association, 2000). Curriculum-centered pedagogy is "most effectively and efficiently transmitted through methods that impose curricular order and is characterized by pedagogical methods that presume teacher as authority, learning through repetition, and learning as a quantifiable outcome" (Pinnegar & Erickson, 2010, p. 849–850). However, Zion and Mendelovici (2012) recommend educators move away from this "instructionism," and that teachers use a child-centered approach to teaching science. The National Research Council (2012) suggests science education move away from the focus on discreet skills, and that educators focus on depth of understanding. Also, the NRC framework strongly suggests the need for connecting material to student interest and experience (NRC, 2012).

THEORETICAL FRAMEWORK

The theoretical framework for this study draws from constructivism, in which individuals build knowledge through meaningful, relevant activities. When engaged in play, children develop conceptual understanding through activity, interacting with their environment, and constructing knowledge through exploration (Kirova & Bhargava, 2002). Play is an essential component of constructivism. Piaget (1952) believed play was a critical component necessary for cognitive growth. As children develop their play worlds, and engage in play activity, ample opportunities exist for discovery learning, scientific inquiry, and concept development. According to Bruner (1961), discovery learning is constructivist in nature as children interact with the world by exploration and manipulation of objects, and as children consider questions and perform experiments. Discovery learning would encourage active engagement, intrinsic motivation, autonomy and independence, creativity, and problem-solving skills (Learning Theories, 2017). Some define the benefits of play similarly to discovery, as play develops problem solving, collaboration, creativity (Yogman, et al., 2018), and is independently owned through the autonomous actions of the individual (Lewis, 2017; IPA, 2014a). A parallel exists between constructivism, discovery learning, inquiry and play.

Furthermore, wonder and curiosity are developed, influenced, or enacted through play activity. The Importance of Play (2019) suggests that play is a key trigger for curiosity, which stimulates development and authentic learning. Perry (2001) contends that curiosity leads to exploration, discovery, pleasure, and eventually mastery.

Finally, a play environment is child-centered. Coughlin, Hansen, Heller, Kaufman, Stolberg, and Walsh (2000) define child-centeredness as the intrinsic involvement of children in their own learning, while the teacher responds to the interests of learners, respects the personal strengths and needs of each learner, and maintains the natural curiosity of the individual. Play is the heart of child-centeredness as children explore, take risks, inquire, test boundaries, and develop understandings through pleasurable, necessary activity.

METHODS

Research Question

The main research question for the study was as follows: How does free play in science impact students' concept development of static electricity content in 3rd and 4th grade classrooms?

Procedures

This qualitative, descriptive field study took place in six classrooms at two separate public schools in the southwestern United States, with over 130 participating students in grades three and four. The students represented an ethnic composition of Caucasian (71.1 percent), Hispanic (16.8 percent), Native American (7.7 percent), and Other (4.4 percent), and both schools were solidly middle class. Gender was split at 51 percent female and 49 percent male across the observed classrooms.

Each of the classrooms was randomly assigned to one of two groups including a play group, and a traditional instruction (reading science content) group. Participating students were not randomly assigned to groups, but stayed with their class. In total, there were three play groups and three traditional groups. Prior knowledge of static electricity content was assessed using a three-question survey, which was given to fifty-four randomly sampled students (26 play/28 traditional) prior to the content reading and play opportunities.

Within the span of two weeks, the investigators visited all six classrooms and set aside a 35–50 minute block of time for each class to either give direct instruction (in the form of reading in the content area of static electricity – See Appendix A) to the traditional groups, or provide direct instruction plus free play with static electricity-related materials, including balloons, plastic combs, wool cloths, and salt. The science content of static electricity was imposed on each of the groups, but the play groups were given free time to play with the materials however the students saw fit, or even just to play (they did not need to play with given materials). Each of the play groups were given 7–10 minutes of undirected, free playtime, in which there were no given objectives, no desired outcomes, and no teacher guidance. Students were observed during this time. The observational protocol involved all three researchers intensely watching participants during play events. Furthermore, the researchers specifically looked for types of play, related play activities (in terms of science content), verbal or observable connections, scientific process, inquiry, and social play. During observations, researchers wrote low and high inference notes as they related to the main research question. After the teaching event in the traditional group, or the play event in the play group, students were randomly selected in each class to participate in an authentic assessment to gauge concept development. These students were interviewed in a one-on-one setting with one of the researchers for a period of three to five minutes. In total, the three researchers took ten to fifteen minutes per class after the teaching or play events to administer the authentic assessment to the randomly sampled students.

Participating students were sampled prior to the study using student permission slips, and assigning numbers to the students. Because the Prior Knowledge Survey and Authentic Assessment (See Table 5.1.) were time intensive, fifty-four students were selected to receive the assessment. Prior to the science content reading in both groups, students who were selected, were given time to write their answers to the Prior Knowledge Survey. Then, after the reading for the traditional group, and the free play of the play group, those same students who recorded their answers on the Prior Knowledge Survey were given a qualitative, Authentic Assessment in a one-on-one setting with the researchers. Unlike the survey, the researchers asked the questions for the Authentic Assessment and recorded student responses. All randomly sampled participants in both the play and traditional groups were given materials (balloons, combs, wool cloths, and salt) to use to demonstrate their knowledge on the Authentic Assessment.

RESULTS AND DISCUSSION

During the observations of classrooms during traditional instruction (content area reading) and play, an immediate point became evident to the researchers. Despite the lack of any guided instruction, scripted procedures, objectives, or expected outcomes, the play groups had higher engagement and expressed deeper interest in the content than the traditional groups. This data was

Table 5.1. Prior Knowledge Survey and Authentic Assessment

Prior Knowledge Interview (Before Lesson or Play)

1. Have you learned about static electricity before?
   a. If you have, did you learn about it in school or at home
   b. What do you remember about static electricity?

Authentic Assessment Protocol

Materials: Plastic combs, wool cloth, pepper, balloons (inflated)

Conceptual Understanding: Atoms make up everything and can gain or lose electrons, which cause the atoms to be positively or negatively charged. Like charges will repel each other and opposite charges will attract.

Social Transmission (Vocabulary): Protons, Neutrons, Electrons, Ions, Attraction (attract), Repulsion (repel), Insulator, Conductor

Prompts for Students:

1. Using these materials (balloons, combs, wool cloths, salt), can you demonstrate static electricity concepts?
   a. Can you describe what you are doing?
   b. What are the relationships between the objects?
2. Do you remember the terms used in class to describe static electricity?
   a. What are they?
   b. How do they connect with the materials on the table?

noted in the high-inference field notes taken during the observations. The two groups had different climates. The traditional groups were motionless, sitting at desks, and though each student had a copy of the reading, and was instructed to follow along, many students were overtly not reading along with the researcher. Students' expressions were solemn, and participation, even when prompted by the script, was minimal. Students had no social interaction during this time.

Conversely, when the play groups were given the opportunity to play freely, almost all students immediately stood up, and moved around, using the balloons, wool, combs, and salt in various ways. Social play became commonplace, as students worked together, inquired, and even performed small-scale, testable experiments based solely in curiosity and mutual interest. Students' expressions showed excitement, and most were smiling and laughing. Play is a pleasurable experience.

Observational Evidence of Concept Development

The data from the observations was coded into two main types: unassociated play (the play did not connect with the concepts of static electricity in any perceivable way), and associated play (the play connected with concepts of static electricity).

Unassociated Play

Not all students played in a manner that connected with static electricity concepts, which the researchers called unassociated play. This was not only considered acceptable, but encouraged. According to Parten's (1933) types of play, students engaged in some solitary play (students playing by themselves with the balloon or salt), onlooker play (some students did not engage right away in play, but instead watched others), parallel play (students copied what others were doing without interacting), and associative play (activities were not synced, but students interacted with each other). Students extensively engaged in social play, and there were multiple organized activities, even with assigned roles, which constituted cooperative play. Many students passed the balloons back and forth in a game of catch, or bounced the balloons with the goal of not letting them touch the floor. Some combed their hair with the combs, and some drew patterns in the salt pile on their table. Some just repeatedly pushed on their balloon or squashed it against their table.

Using the cognitive levels of play (Piaget, 1962; Smilansky, 1968; Stone, 1993), students also exhibited constructive play, dramatic play, games with rules, and a lot of functional play. Some students tried to stack balloons, and others shaped the salt piles on the table, representing constructive play. For dramatic play, one student said "we need to shine the balloons" and made a show to his classmates of making the balloons shiny by rubbing with the wool cloths. Another student imagined that there was something inside the balloon and repeatedly put his ear to the balloon to hear it (there was nothing inside). Others joined in by listening to their balloons. For games with rules, as mentioned previously, students played games of catch and "don't let the balloon hit the floor." These games had established rules (although they were not always explicitly stated) with active players. Functional play, or repetitive movements with (or without) objects, was frequently observed as students bounced or squashed their balloons.

Not all players used the materials. Rarely, students decided to use their time for social interaction, or to play in other ways. An area for future research would be to explore why some students did not play with the materials, and why most students decided to play with the materials.

During one play event in one of the classrooms, the teacher, despite knowing the parameters of the study, intervened in the play of students. Some were playing catch with the balloons, and the teacher yelled across the room for the students to stop playing catch. She told them they needed to do their activities as instructed by the researchers, which is noteworthy because the researchers did not provide any instruction for what to do, other than to just play. This type of interference shows the lack of value in play and the high control of teachers in classroom contexts even when another adult is ostensibly in charge doing a special play enrichment activity with the children.

Associated Play

The majority of students decided to play in a way that connected with the static electricity materials in some way, at least for a portion of their play time. Simple frequency counts were used to note when children in the play groups were outwardly demonstrating a connection to the science content in some way. Some children played the entire time while connecting to the science content. Others began to play in the science content area and then shifted to unassociated play, or conversely, played in an unassociated way, but then shifted to content area play. Some students shifted back and forth, particularly with social influences. For example, a student might be bouncing a balloon repetitively (unassociated), and then see others using the wool cloths to rub their balloons and stick them to the wall. The solo player would join a group or engage in parallel play for a while (associated), then shift back to an unassociated activity. This type of free-flowing shifting landscape of play was common. The below quotes represent common phrases (direct quotes) of students while engaged in associated play. It is important to note that multiple children across the three play groups said similar phrases to those listed in here.

Common Phrases (Direct Quotes) of Students During Associated Free Play
"Rub the salt while it's on the balloon, see if that makes a difference."
"I need another cloth, this one isn't working."
"Look, it's picking up the salt, too."
"We discovered if you rub the balloon on your hair, it picks up the salt."
"Make the comb pick up the salt."
"The balloon sticks to the wall and to the underside of the table."
"It sticks to me."
"It attracts like a magnet."
"It's like a magnet with the salt."
"It sticks to hair."
"It's like a vacuum."
"It works with combs."

Within the associated play activities, other behaviors were noted and used for coding, including *evidence of concept development, problem-solving, critical thinking, comparing/contrasting, discovery, and inquiry.* Using students' verbal expressions and responses and the observational evidence of behavior, students engaged in the associated play activities demonstrated a high level of concept development.

Concept development occurred authentically through play and related inquiries. The script that all students read (Appendix A) mentioned rubbing a balloon with a wool cloth produces static cling, but did not mention rubbing balloons together, or sticking balloons to walls or tables. The script mentioned nothing of combs or salt. However, when free to play with the materials, students chose to explore these avenues. As evidenced from the quotes, students connected the material to magnets often (concept of static cling), and some apparently had the idea of a vacuum (the balloon picking up salt after being rubbed with a wool cloth). The magnet connection is actually conceptually similar, and although the vacuum connection is not conceptually related, the students were thinking divergently and creatively through their observations. These actions/behaviors suggested expanded concept development (beyond the content in the script). Furthermore, when students used the combs by rubbing them with wool cloths (not mentioned in the script) and picking up salt, students were demonstrating transfer and application of conceptual understanding. Others transferred and applied understanding through rubbing the balloons on their hair and testing whether they would pick up salt.

Students were not observed using terms like protons, neutrons, electrons, static cling, ions, or repulsion in their play, but many did use the term attraction. Most students who engaged in associated play were able to demonstrate static cling in a variety of ways through their social and object free play.

Problem solving was observed in some cases in the associated play. For example, one child rubbed his balloon with the wool cloth, and it would not stick to the salt or anything else, so he mentioned his wool cloth was not working and asked the researchers to replace it. He repeated his procedure and finally was able to pick up the salt. Another group of students mentioned they wanted to rub the salt while it was on the balloon after static cling had already taken place to see if it would come off of the balloon.

Students frequently compared and contrasted the balloons and the combs, often making connections between the similarities in how they both picked up salt. They also frequently used their hair and rubbed their balloons on their head. This type of behavior was picked up by others and mimicked often. Students were creative with their balloons, seeing if they would stick to themselves or other objects. Some tried to transfer the salt to other objects after it stuck to the balloon. Some tried to stick multiple balloons to the walls or ceiling (stacked balloons). Students were analyzing and applying their understandings. They were creative, and made judgments based on their knowledge. For example, a student said, "no that won't work" in response to a peer's suggestion to try and stick a comb to the balloon. These types of critiques were common.

The most commonly coded activities were inquiry and discovery. Students outwardly expressed scientific process starters such as, "I wonder what happens if. . . ." Many small experiments were conducted, and some students were verbalizing and testing hypotheses often. The students were the owners and stakeholders in their inquiry processes, and their science-related intentions and actions were interconnected with their play. Comments like, "we discovered if you rub the balloon on your hair, it picks up the salt," or "the balloon sticks to me" were also frequently heard.

Prior Knowledge Survey

In an attempt to understand if prior knowledge had an influence on concept development or the exhibition of content knowledge, the researchers had administered the Prior Knowledge Survey (Table 5.1.). The results showed that a slight majority had received some prior instruction in static electricity, mostly at school. Frequencies can be observed in Table 5.2. The vast majority had no reported understandings or limited understandings like "it shocks you," or "it sticks to stuff." Only two students out of those sampled had a deeper knowledge base. One student stated, "I remember opposites attract,

Table 5.2. Frequencies Recorded in Prior Knowledge Survey

Total (All Groups)	
Prior Instruction	32/54 (59%)
Recalled Information (Terms or Concepts)	19/54 (35%)
No Reported Understandings	35/54 (65%)
Depth of Understanding	2/54 (4%)
Limited Understandings	17/54 (31%)
Play Groups (Total = 26 Students)	
Prior Instruction	14/26 (54%)
Recalled Information (Terms or Concepts)	5/26 (19%)
No Reported Understandings	21/26 (81%)
Depth of Understanding	1/26 (4%)
Limited Understandings	4/26 (15%)
Traditional Groups (Total = 28 Students)	
Prior Instruction	18/28 (64%)
Recalled Information (Terms or Concepts)	14/28 (50%)
No Reported Understandings	14/28 (50%)
Depth of Understanding	1/28 (4%)
Limited Understandings	13/28 (46%)

friction, and you can get shocked. Everything is made of atoms, and atoms have protons, neutrons, and electrons in them, and electricity can be very dangerous." This student with a deeper knowledge base was in the traditional group. The other student (in the play group) stated, "Static is made by two things rubbing together constantly, and when you touch something metal, you get a shock."

Based on the prior knowledge survey, the researchers concluded that most students had very little understanding of static electricity concepts or terms. It is important to note that despite some level of prior knowledge, the quality of free play was not noticeably influenced. The current data suggested prior knowledge was not a significant factor in students' concept development.

Authentic Assessment

The Authentic Assessments (Table 5.1) were administered by the researchers after the teaching and play events to both traditional and play groups. Students were given the play materials (balloons, combs, wool cloths, and salt) and the researchers recorded their verbal responses and outward behaviors. Again, a total of fifty-four students were authentically assessed. These were the same students who took the Prior Knowledge Survey before the teaching and play events. The following codes emerged from the authentic assessment data: *No Recollection*, *Action without Understanding*, *Vocabulary Recall*, and *Conceptual Understanding*.

The researchers were able to use sub-questions (Table 5.1) to prompt students for verbal responses if necessary. Each response or action on the part of the student was coded according to the categories listed previously. *No Recollection* was used when students couldn't answer the questions, or recall concepts/terms. *Action without Understanding* was used when students picked up the materials in response to the questions, but could not demonstrate static electricity concepts, and could not verbalize any concept. *Vocabulary Recall* was used when students were able to use any of the terms used in the reading including Atoms, Static Cling, Protons, Neutrons, Electrons, Charge, Ions, Attraction, Repulsion, Insulator, or Conductor. Finally, Conceptual Understanding was used to mark students' demonstrated actions (e.g., a student rubbed the wool cloth on the balloon), and their verbalization of what was happening (e.g., "the balloon takes electrons from the cloth, and it sticks to the wall").

Play Groups

Of the twenty-six students assessed, a strong majority demonstrated *Conceptual Understanding* in some way (Table 5.3). Students used a variety of ways to demonstrate their understandings through actions including: rubbing the balloons and wool cloths, rubbing the balloons on their hair, picking up salt from the table, and using the combs in a similar way to the balloons (i.e., rubbing with a cloth and picking up salt). Verbal responses corresponded with students' actions including statements like, "When I rubbed the wool on the comb, it picked up the salt," "the cloth has electrons taken off," or "the wool has a positive charge and the balloon has a negative charge." These types of responses were common among the nineteen with *Conceptual Understanding*.

Some took action by picking up the materials, but could not demonstrate any conceptual understanding, nor could they verbalize any understanding (*Action without Understanding*). Typically, students would pick up the materials when asked the first question, and then say, "I don't know." One child coded in this scenario wiped the balloon with the wool cloth, but said, "I'm wiping away dirty stuff."

In response to question two, a majority was able to demonstrate *Vocabulary Recall* including eleven students who recalled multiple terms. Eleven students showed *No Recollection* of vocabulary terms.

Traditional Groups

Twenty-eight students in the traditional group were authentically assessed, and overall, sixteen demonstrated *Conceptual Understanding* in some way (Table 5.3.). Similarly to the play groups, students used many ways to demonstrate their understandings through actions including: rubbing the balloons and wool cloths, rubbing the balloons on their hair, picking up salt from the table, and using the combs in a similar way to the balloons (i.e., rubbing with a cloth and picking up salt). Verbal responses corresponded with students' actions including statements like, "I am making electricity," "the comb gives

Table 5.3.   Frequencies Recorded in Authentic Assessments

Play Groups (Total = 26 Students)	
Demonstrated Conceptual Understanding	19/26 (73%)
Action without Conceptual Understanding	7/26 (26%)
Vocabulary Recall	15/26 (58%)
No Recollection	11/26 (42%)
Traditional Groups (Total = 28 Students)	
Demonstrated Conceptual Understanding	16/28 (57%)
Action without Conceptual Understanding	12/28 (43%)
Vocabulary Recall	19/28 (68%)
No Recollection	9/28 (32%)

off electrons," or "the cloth gives electrons to the balloon." These types of responses were common among the sixteen with *Conceptual Understanding.*

Twelve students took action by picking up the materials, but could not demonstrate any conceptual understanding, nor could they verbalize any understanding (*Action without Understanding*). Typically, students would pick up the materials when asked the first question, and then say, "I don't know."

In response to question two, nineteen students were able to demonstrate *Vocabulary Recall* including fifteen students who recalled multiple terms. Nine students showed *No Recollection* of vocabulary terms.

Play and Authentic Assessments

The prior knowledge survey was used to determine if participating students already had a substantial knowledge base from which to draw when playing and/or during authentic assessments. However, most students had limited understandings or no understanding of static electricity concepts. Therefore, the play could be considered mostly original with little to no influence from prior knowledge. For example, if a child had been instructed in the past to rub balloons with wool cloths and pick up salt from a table, then that child may have demonstrated those actions during free play, and those actions could have been attributed to concept development as a result of their play. The authentic assessments presented an opportunity for students to apply what they had learned or discovered during free play, and the results showed that students were better able to apply conceptual understandings using the materials provided. Free play does not necessarily exist in isolation, but can be informed by the curriculum, or prior experiences (at home, or socially). Furthermore, the benefits of play can be used to guide further instructional experiences. Teachers can even use play experiences to aid in concept development and scientific process use. Authentic assessments can be used to help teachers develop play activities or opportunities for free play.

CONCLUSIONS

According to the observational data, students in the play groups (when they chose to play in a content-associated way) demonstrated conceptual understandings through their actions and verbalizations, and also engaged in high-level scientific process skills, using critical thinking, problem-solving, inquiring, discovering, and comparing through their play. The students in the traditional groups were deprived of the opportunities to engage in these behaviors. The Authentic Assessment, given to both play and traditional groups showed overall similarities, but the play groups demonstrated a slightly higher conceptual base of knowledge, and many were able to confidently use the materials to demonstrate static electricity concepts. Interestingly, the students in the traditional groups demonstrated a slightly higher recall of terms, but were less confident in demonstrating conceptual understanding. The research question for the study is what the role of free play is in science concept learning. Students in the play groups had a slightly higher conceptual knowledge base than did their traditional counterparts. They were able to undertake freely chosen play activities that led to higher-level scientific process skills and a high level of engagement. Teachers at the grade levels used here can try to structure play-like activities to develop conceptual understanding and guide students to content ends. It is recommended based on the present exploratory study, however that teachers should value spontaneous child-initiated play and allow students to freely play, even within subject-area content like science. This is true even when teachers may be tempted to step in and guide the play.

RECOMMENDATIONS

As discussed earlier in this chapter, play lacks value in many educational settings, and when teachers do make use of play, they tend to curricularize the play through scripted play-like activities with a content objective in mind. However, free play is highly beneficial for students, and when given the opportunities to play in an unhindered way in the content area, students can develop conceptual knowledge and engage in high-level scientific process skills. However, it is important to note that teachers can build on play activities, attach content like terminology to concepts developed during free play, and guide further instruction based on these experiences. Authentic assessments can be used to determine the extent and depth of concept development and scientific process skills, and can be used to aid the teacher in constructing curriculum. Therefore, it is recommended by the researchers that teachers and schools develop policies to protect and expand free play opportunities, even free play opportunities within content areas like science. Furthermore, it is recommended that teachers value and provide opportunities for free play experiences in science content areas.

LIMITATIONS AND FURTHER RESEARCH

Being a qualitative study, this research is situation specific, and does not generalize but may nevertheless provide insights into the benefits of free play activities in science. Further research is needed in the assessment of students' prior understandings, long-term benefits and retention of concept development through free play, and teacher perceptions of play as they relate to classroom content. In practice, many teachers may use the traditional approaches described in this paper for a variety of reasons, but in theory, a Five-E (Engage, Explore, Explain, Elaborate, Evaluate) Learning Cycle approach could combine discovery learning, play, and guided content as the teacher leads students through the material. In future studies, researchers could explore how different approaches compare to free play in science content areas.

This study has provided evidence for the benefits of free play in science, and how children can develop conceptual understandings. In summary, this study demonstrates that children can exhibit higher-level scientific process skills, creativity, problem solving, and deeper concept development through the mode of play as compared to a more traditional approach.

REFERENCES

Ariel, S. (2002). *Children's imaginative play: A visit to wonderland.* Westport, CT: Praeger Publishers.

Ashbrook, P. (2010). The early years: Inquiry at play. *Science and Children*, 48(1), 26–27.

Athabasca University. (2017). Siegfried Engelmann and direct instruction. Retrieved from https://psych.athabascau.ca/open/engelmann/

Bruner, J. (1961). The act of discovery. *Harvard Educational Review*, 31, 21–32.

Bruner, J. (1983). Play, thought, and language. *Peabody Journal of Education, 60*(3) 60–69.

Bruner, J. (1985). *Models of the learner. Educational Researcher*, 14(6), 5–8.

Carnine, D. W., Silbert, J., Kame'enui, E. J., & Tarver, S. G. (2010). *Direct instruction reading.* Boston, MA: Pearson.

Christie, J., & Roskos, K. (2006). Standards, science, and the role of play in early literacy education. In D. Singer, R. Golinkoff, & K. Hirsh-Pasek (Eds.), *Play-learning how play motivates and enhances children's cognitive and social-emotional growth* (57–73). New York, NY: Oxford University Press.

Coughlin, P. A., Hansen, K. A., Heller, D., Kaufman, R. E., Stolberg, J. R., & Walsh, K. B. (2000). *Creating child-centered classrooms: 3-5 year olds. Step by step: A program for children and families.* Washington, DC: Children's Resources International, Inc.

Gmitrova, V., & Gmitrov, J. (2003). The impact of teacher-directed and child-directed pretend play on cognitive competence in kindergarten children. *Early Childhood Education*, 30(4), 241–246.

Gray, P. (2013). *Free to learn: Why unleashing the instinct to play will make our children happier, more self-reliant, and better students for life.* New York, NY: Basic Books.

Gross, C. M. (2012). Science concepts young children learn through water play. *Dimensions of Early Childhood*, 40(2), 3–12.

International Play Association (2014a). The child's right to play. Retrieved from http://ipaworld.org/childs-right-to-play/the-childs-right-to-play/

International Play Association (2014b). Declaration on the importance of play. Retrieved from http://ipaworld.org/wp-content/uploads/2015/05/IPA_Declaration-FINAL.pdf

Johnson, J. E., Christie, J., & Wardle, F. (2005). *Play, development and early education*. Boston, MA: Pearson.

Kirova, A., & Bhargava, A. (2002). Learning to guide preschool children's mathematics understanding: A teacher's professional growth. *Early Childhood Research & Practice*, 4(1), 1–20.

Laszlo, P. (2004). Macroscope: Science as play. *American Scientist*, 92(5), 398–400.

Learning Theories (2017). Discovery learning (Bruner). Retrieved from https://www.learning-theories.com/discovery-learning-bruner.html

Lewis, P. J. (2017). The erosion of play. *International Journal of Play*, 6(1), 10–23.

National Research Council. (2012). *A framework for K-12 science education: Practices, crosscutting concepts, and core ideas*. Washington, DC: The National Academies Press.

National Science Teachers Association. (2000). *NSTA pathways to the science standards*. Arlington, VA: NSTA Press.

Parten, M. B. (1933). *An analysis of social participation, leadership, and other factors in preschool play groups*. Princeton, NJ: Princeton.

Perry, B. D. (2001). Curiosity: The fuel of development. *Early Childhood Today*, 15(6), 22–23.

Piaget, J. (1952). *The origins of intelligence in children*. New York, NY: International Universities Press.

Piaget, J. (1962). *Play, dreams, and imitation in childhood*. New York, NY: Norton.

Pinnegar, S., & Erickson, L. (2010). Teacher-centered curriculum. In C. Kridel (Ed.), *Encyclopedia of curriculum studies*. Thousand Oaks, CA: Sage Publications.

Sim, Z. L., & Xu, F. (2017) Learning higher-order generalizations through free play: Evidence from 2- and 3-year-old children. *Developmental Psychology*, 53(4), 642–651.

Smilansky, S. (1968). *The effects of sociodramtic play on disadvantaged preschool children*. New York, NY: Wiley.

Stone, S. J. (1993). *Playing: A kid's curriculum*. Culver City, CA: GoodYear Books.

Talib, O., Norishah, T. P., & Zulkafly, N. A. (2013). Understanding the wonder of science through creative play. *Procedia Social and Behavioral Sciences*, 141, 1378–1385.

Talu, N. (2018). Symbolic creativity in play activity: A critique on playthings from daily life objects to toys. *International Journal of Play*, 7(1), 81–96.

The Genius of Play (2016). *6 benefits of play*. Retrieved from https://www.thegeniusofplay.org.

The Importance of Play (2019). *Play boosts children's curiosity*. Retrieved from http://www.importanceofplay.eu/news/article/play-boosts-children-s-curiosity.

Vandenberg, B. (2004). Real and not real: A vital developmental dichotomy. In E. Zigler, D. Singer, & S. Bishop-Josef (Eds.), *Children's play: The roots of reading* (pp. 49–58). Washington, DC: Zero to Three Press.

Yogman, M., Garner, A., Hutchinson, J., Hirsh-Pasek, K., & Golinkoff, R. M. (2018). The power of play: A pediatric role in enhancing development in young children. *Pediatrics*, 142(3), 1–16.

Zion, M., & Mendelovici, R. (2012). Moving from structured to open inquiry: Challenges and limits. *Science Education International*, 23, 383–399.

APPENDIX. DIRECT INSTRUCTION SCRIPT
STATIC ELECTRICITY

1. Objective: Students will be able to identify and define the following terms relating to static electricity: Atoms, Protons, Neutrons, Electrons, Ions, Attraction, Repulsion, Insulator, and Conductor.

    Additionally, students will understand the concept of static electricity: an imbalance of electrical charges caused by the movement of electrons in materials

    Give randomly selected students Prior Knowledge Interview.

2. (The teacher will read the following passage on static electricity while students follow along with their own copy): Atoms are very small. In fact, they are so small we cannot see them. They make up all matter (all materials that we can see and touch). Atoms are made up of even smaller pieces called Protons, Neutrons, and Electrons. Protons and Neutrons make up the nucleus, or center of an atom. Electrons orbit or spin around the nucleus. Look at the diagram (picture of an atom provided to students):

    *   Take a moment and look at where the Protons, Neutrons, and Electrons are in the atom.
    *   Count each type. How many Protons are there?
    *   How many Neutrons?
    *   How many Electrons?
    *   Does this picture remind you of anything?

(Pause and let them answer –do not confirm any answers or answer any questions)

Have you ever been shocked when you touched a door handle or another person? (Pause and let them answer –do not explain any content). Maybe you went down a slide and got shocked at the end. Why does that happen? (Pause and let them answer –do not confirm any answers or answer any questions). Well, two of the particles in an atom have electric charges. Protons have a positive charge, and Electrons have a negative charge. Neutrons have no charge. Now, look at the diagram again. When two materials rub against each other (called friction), the electrons can move from one material to another. Count the number of Protons and Electrons in the picture. There are 4 Protons and 4 Electrons. Remember, the Protons have one positive charge, and the Electrons have one negative charge. This means there are 4 positive charges and 4 negative charges. The atom is stable (the number of positive charges and negative charges are equal). Now, what if one of the electrons in the picture moved to another material? There would still be 4 positive charges, but only 3 negative charges, so the atom would have a positive charge. What about the material that gained an electron? It might have 4 positive Protons, but 5 negative electrons. This means it would have a negative charge. When electrons move from one material to another, the charges are imbalanced (not equal). When an atom has a positive or negative charge, it is called an ion. Like charges will repel each other (push away from each other, also known as repulsion). Unlike charges will attract each other (come together, also known as attraction). When you rub a balloon with a wool cloth, electrons are moving from the wool to the surface of the balloon. This makes the balloon more negative and the wool more positive. The two will stick to each other. We sometimes call this static cling. Please see the diagram (a picture of balloons and wool cloths with charges will be presented to students):

- What do you notice about the balloon and wool cloth before rubbing them together?
- What do you notice about the balloon and wool cloth after rubbing them together?
- Why are there plus and minus signs on the picture?

(Pause and let them answer –do not confirm any answers or answer any questions)

When a material's electrons move freely, the material is called a conductor. In other materials, the electrons are held tightly and do not move easily. These materials are called insulators. Good conductors are usually metals while insulators are glass, rubber, and wood.

3. Play Groups are handed materials (one to two balloons per table, one to two combs per table, wool cloths, and salt) and told they have 7–10 minutes of free time to play and/or use the materials in any way they see fit.
4. Authentic Assessment for Participants (Non-Participants will draw another picture).

Chapter Six

Thinking Outside the Woods

Teacher Stories of Urban Nature and Inviting the Wild into the City Classroom

Heather J. Pinedo-Burns

We climb the steps to the park and look out to see no one. On this rainy day we have the park to ourselves, a rarity in New York. My toddler daughter walks ahead and stops at the first puddle. Autumn leaves float on the surface, an invitation to look further. She bends down to inspect and study, leaning forward with her hands on her knees, spying acorns lying at the bottom of the pool of water. She pauses at the storm drain to dip her fingers into the water streaming into it. She turns her head to smile at me, joyful in the light force of the flow. This is our morning, walking slowly, stopping often, as busy commuters cross the park on their way to the subway. In my hands, I hold the leaves and acorns she gathers to carry home. She'll ask for them after we return home.

The importance of and value in nature play has long been observed and recognized within early childhood education (Carson, 1965/1998; Cadwell, 1997; Wilson, 1995). Nature offers children the opportunity to learn through inquiry and experience (Louv, 2008). Early childhood education programs situated in urban areas are challenged to provide children with rich experiences exploring nature as both access to natural spaces and natural materials may be limited. The idea of opening the classroom doors and letting children play in the woods behind the school, unfettered with the concerns and restrictions of adults, is an impossibility that urban educators have faced at least since industrialization (Hirsch, 1974; Pratt, 1948/2014; Rivkin & Schein, 2014). Despite the obstacles urban educators face in providing their students with nature-based experiences, early childhood educators must not burden themselves and children with the weight of romanticized memories of outdoor play of yesteryear (Louv, 2008; Fraiberg, Adelson, and Shapiro, 1987). We need to rethink what nature play is and why we believe nature play is important. Rather than live in the nostalgia of what used to be and is no longer possible, we must consider what is possible (Miller, 2010). Nature play in its most basic form happens when children are afforded the opportunity to physically play outside using natural materials (Moore, 2014). It can extend to the wider concept of nature play, one that embraces children's playfulness with nature and the outdoors; it can include inquiries into environmental concepts such as conservation, and entail the use of natural materials (Louv, 2008; Rivkin & Schein, 2014).

I am the director of a small university-based lab preschool located in a large metropolitan city, and we embrace the challenge of urban nature play each day because of our firm beliefs that nature play matters for all children. In our work with children, teachers, and families, we advocate for nature as an integral component of our early childhood curriculum, as a way of living life (Macdonald, 1971). We encourage our community to engage in nature play because we believe it is important; it gives children first-hand experience with nature, something that should be valued and preserved (Wilson, 1995). We do it as a community because children inquire about natural materials; this leads to explorations into sciences, and children can learn about geology, gravity, change, states of matter, and more (Inan,Trundle, & Kantor, 2010; Wilson, 1997). We do it because nature play supports the development of the whole child: sparking and stretching the mind, tactile sensory exploration, social-emotional development, and gross motor activity (Davis, 1998; Wilson 1997). We also do it because it fosters children's sense of wonder (Carson, 1998/1965; Wilson 1997).

Perhaps most importantly we believe in nature play because it sets the stage for early scientific inquiry and aesthetic appreciation (Inan, et al, 2010; Wilson, 1997), perhaps even giving to each individual a sense that there is something greater than oneself and a connectedness to life and wonder (Louv, 2008; Wells, & Lekies, 2006). Davis, 1998). Moreover, you do not need to be in the woods to make this possible, as Louv (2008) states, "cities are and ought to be places where nature occurs" (p.26). We posit that there are certain actions educators can take to support our students' early positive experiences with nature. While the first-hand experience of being in nature is preferable, we ask, what is made possible when educators carry nature into the classroom inviting the children to play with nature?

METHODS

This research is rooted in my lived experiences: a childhood in the country with vast amounts of time outdoors; as a mother raising my daughters in a city environment as an urban naturalists; and as a teacher and director of a small lab preschool on the campus of a large university in New York City that embraces the overarching themes of nature, conservation, and the importance of citizen science.

Methodologically, I rely on narrative inquiry (Chase, 2005). Narrative inquiry is a way of collecting and analyzing data, as well as representing outcomes and results (Chase, 2005; Richardson, 1997, 2000). Particularly, I use Richardson's (2000) "writing as method." Writing as method is one form of narrative inquiry. In writing as method, the researcher uses brief notes of stories of lived experiences that provoke ongoing questions about pedagogical and theoretical issues (Pinedo-Burns, 2015). These stories, which work much like field notes, are a central facet of the inquiry process as the stories are embedded in all aspects of the inquiry (Sullivan & McCrary, 2002).

Relying on autobiography, a form of narrative inquiry, as an approach to research, Sullivan (2000) asks a few questions that frame my inquiry: "What is the nature of the researcher's attention? How do we learn to attend with keen eyes and fine sensibilities? How do we teach others to do it?" (p. 211–212). Thus, as an observer of children and a teacher at play in natural surroundings, and as an educational leader and professional development facilitator, these questions for me not only gesture to research, but also to engagement with nature. Chase (2005) writes, "Narrative is a way of understanding one's own and others' actions, of organizing events and objects into a meaningful whole, and of connecting and seeing the consequences of actions and events over time" (p. 656). Written narratives thereby serve as not only working data but also as representations of the data (Pinedo-Burns, 2015). Further, Sullivan (2000) suggests that narratives are reflective of an "autobiography of attention" (p. 222) and thus:

> It may seize a moment in order to stare at it and see more fully, more deeply, but aesthetic vision does not assume that what one sees in the moment is what one will always see. It perceives the potential for transformation within any apparent fixity—a block of wood, a piece of clay, a display of words, the configuration of a classroom, or the behavior of an individual child. (p. 221)

Compatible with standard ethnographic approaches (Chase, 2005; Richardson, 1997, 2000), I relied upon different forms of the "field notes" (Richardson, 2000, p. 156) including narrative and photographic data, observational notes, e-mail communications, and teacher-researcher journal entries collected over ten years at one university-based lab preschool, as well as personal narratives and artifacts collected over a lifetime. In particular, the school narratives I previously composed for family communications served as sparks for my inquiry serving as "writing stories" (Richardson, 2000, p. 943). These writing stories served as points of data that shaped my inquiry. The writing stories also allowed me to depict moments of engagement with nature as I advocate for cultivating natural experiences as a child responsive educational practice. Much like other illustrations of research—charts, graphs, and tables—in this chapter I include selections of the writing-stories to share aspects of my methodological process as well as to illustrate my argument. Thereby I simultaneously present my narrative data as I engage in the process of analysis, which is reflective of the integration of process woven into the writing as method (Richardson, 1997, 2000).

Using the methods of narrative inquiry, I specifically seek to explore the following questions: How can urban educators provide their students vital experiences with nature, even when nature may appear to be absent? How can educators support children's knowledge, understanding and love of nature within classroom contexts? In doing so, how can we challenge our collective romantic notions, memories, and conceptions of outdoor play?

Educational Context

The setting is a university-based lab preschool where I have worked at since 2003. Located in New York City the school serves 16 toddlers aged 20 months-40 months in a non-separation, family-engagement weekly program and 34–38 children ages 3–5 in a half day full year program. The enrollment is reflective of the ethnic, racial, and religious diversity of the city with 65 percent children of color. Typically, 50 percent of the student population speaks more than one language. The teachers are all graduate students enrolled in programs within the university. The students hail from across the borough of Manhattan. The program utilizes one main classroom, a smaller sensory studio space, and a shared gross motor room. Access for outdoor play is limited to a shared internal brick courtyard within the university, the campus lawns located at least four city blocks away, as well as the local public parks.

A key component of early childhood education at any center is family education. At our school we work to foster home-school connections through stories, most often communicated through letters. Our communications with families reflect the multi-layered nature of life in a university-based early childhood classroom. We not only need to share the update on the events of the classroom, but also a window into our pedagogical rationale for doing so. To foster inclusivity, we use the language "loved ones" to represent the many familial individuals in the children's lives, avoiding the less inclusive terms such as parents.

The philosophy of the preschool focuses on embracing children's sense of wonder through our child-responsive approach. As in many other child-responsive early childhood programs, much work at the preschool originates from the interests, questions, curiosities, connections, wonderings, and experiences of the children. We believe in engaging in community inquiries that are shaped by the wonderings of the children and supported through the intentional actions of the teachers. Balanced with this and inspired by Maxine Greene's (1973) conceptions of the roles of teachers, we also believe in the importance of inviting the passions of the teachers into the curriculum. We hope that with each exploration we endeavor to wonder as a community of children and teachers and that we will draw each adventure to a close with new thoughts, questions, and ponderings which loop in a cycle of inquiry.

APPROACHES TO NATURE PLAY IN URBAN CLASSROOMS

What is nature play in the urban classroom? What is possible for urban educators and students if we look beyond romantic notions of nature play, such as illustrated by children running through meadows of wild flowers and deep in the thicket as dusk approaches? In response to these specific questions, I argue that there are certain actions educators may take to support nature explorations in the urban classroom. Educators can adopt a nature mindset: a sense of comfort with nature, a willingness for getting dirty in the classroom. Second, educators can actively create opportunities for nature study, exploration, and experience through specific provocations in the classroom. Finally, educators must be willing to think "outside the woods" so to speak, when conceptualizing and incorporating nature play in the urban classroom.

In considering how to educate children and their loved ones in developing nature mindsets, I composed the following family correspondence:

Each session we offer the children different hand lenses, also called magnifying glasses to explore. We find hand lenses are a fun way to encourage children to study nature up close and notice the details. And they are fun! When going on nature hikes, I'll often keep one in my to-go bag and offer it to my daughter as we begin our trail. Many families maintain a special nature observation area in their home to house the artifacts their children discover. Keeping a hand lens near this area can encourage your child to really study and explore natural treasures.

For the next session, we'll offer the children an opportunity to explore the chorus of spring— birds! The early-morning chirping sounds of the spring time birds can now be heard throughout New York. When you hear birds, we encourage you to pause with your child and listen. All of the birds have different calls and songs. From the peck peck peck sound of a woodpecker busy at work, to the distinctive coo of a city pigeon, to the sweet chirp of excited robins after a springtime rain shower, we often hear birds but may not see them. Birding often asks us to first listen and then look. To help us look in the classroom we'll also have special homemade binoculars!

Although nature is often thought of as a thing—trees, wild animals, dirt, rocks, or rain, I suggest that the experience of being in nature and playing with(in) nature is an educative process. Experiencing, studying, playing, and being in nature, like academic rigor, grit, or potential (Dweck, 2008) is a mindset. A mindset is a way of thinking, believing, and/or acting that most defines an individual's way of being. To encourage our children to experience nature holistically through play, especially our children in urban areas, we must embrace a nature mindset. A nature mindset is a way of thinking, a way working, a way of teaching, a way of inquiring . . . it is a way of living in which nature is part of life. Nature is not something you go to, you visit, you study or explore. Nature is a part of you (Greene, 1973). A nature mindset means you go beyond seeing nature while visiting a park, or strolling on a river walk; a nature mindset means nature is a way of being, woven into the daily facets of life, even urban life. It is the sturdy dandelion forcing its way through the crack in the sidewalk; it is the interplay of skyscraper shadows; the afternoon sunshine on the trees of the city; it is the hawk who resides on the fire escape of the prewar building; it is the actions of the child who pauses on a walk to grasp the schist, the sparkly rocks found in Manhattan's uptown parks. A nature mindset enables nature to be both the natural item and the experience of it, or the propensity to play with it or have it play with you.

Sullivan (2000) said, "My mother, the scientist, taught me to see. She taught me attention to the complexities of surface detail and also attention to what lies beneath those surfaces. She taught me the rhythms of tide and regeneration, and the syllables of the natural world rubbing against each other" (p. 221). As with any mindset, a nature mindset can be cultivated, supported, and enriched through hands-on play experiences beginning in early childhood. Educators need to take the actions to help each of students see the nature that surrounds us all (Louv, 2008).

This often entails educators being comfortable with bringing a little dirt into the classroom. This is to be expected from nature activities such as collecting rocks on walks in the neighborhood to bring back to have the children wash, finding a piece of rotting wood and sharing it with the children to observe, composting our waste as a community, having a worm bin to support our efforts, adding soil to the sensory table and letting children just dig in! As a parent this means not only pausing with my daughter to marvel at a puddle and peer below the surface but also that I need to actively model my engagement with the natural world, wondering beside her. This is the legacy of wonder sparked by engagement with nature as Sullivan (2000) suggests, and this is an example of a nature mindset.

To actively foster a nature mindset is a journey that can begin in early childhood with active collaboration from all stakeholders, especially families, or loved ones as we say at the preschool. I recall a letter I shared with our preschool loved ones during an inquiry into the Humpback Whale, about exploring nature and conservation with the children.

Although there is beauty to the children's inquires and play into the life cycle and migration of the Humpback Whale, there are also the harsh realities of the natural world. The children learn of the challenges the different species face—changes in environment, loss of habitat, pollution, over-hunting, decreased access to food, and more, balanced with the recognition and celebration of the efforts and successes of conservation groups. There is hope. At this very early age, the children learn that every life matters and the work of every individual on this earth matters. These are important lessons we hope will guide the children as they move onward and upward in their individual life journeys becoming mindful, empathetic, contributing members of a more just society.

The nature mindset enables us as a community to embrace the interdisciplinary invitations that weave nature into the world of early childhood, similar to how early literacy and early numeracy opportunities abound in the early childhood classroom (Wilson, 1995). Seeing the possibilities for nature in any classroom, especially the urban classroom, opens worlds of possible inquiry and experience for the children. The theme of conservation is central within many of our inquiries. Still, even with these integrated opportunities to explore nature, conservation, and the environment, there is no replacement for time spent outside playing or interacting with natural materials (Louv, 2008; Rivkin & Schein, 2014). Nevertheless, we as educators provide planned possibilities for the children to play with nature and natural materials at school, encouraging the children's inquiries into conservation, the environment and nature play.

Amazing innovations are occurring in nature education. As an example forest schools are emerging everywhere, even in New York City! (Moore, 2014). There are pocket parks, tree planting initiatives that children and schools can support. As urban educators there are times we need to think "outside the woods" to provide our students with ample and rich opportunities for engagement and play with nature.

At our school, each time we choose to go on a nature walk, we must dress all 18–19 children in their layers, line up in the classroom, walk to the elevator to wait to go down from the third floor to the ground floor, then, walk through two buildings before we are outside. Then, it is another 4–5 blocks at least before we arrive at a park! Many obstacles impede nature experiences for urban educators, mittens and gloves, being only two of the most benign! We must not assume that if we do not take the children outside to play in the park every day that nature play is not possible.

We must think outside the woods; we must carry the woods indoors. At our preschool we do this in a variety of ways, by using natural materials including woven baskets, twigs, seeds, pinecones, rocks as loose parts for invitations to play (Daly, & Beloglovsky, 2014). Our children have affection for nature guides, park maps, and other outdoor hiking materials that serve as resources to naturalists, and imaginative play props for our children. Nature is something we explore, read about, play with, sing about, and with carry with us always.

All this means, in a sense, that we work to create a forest of inquiry in classroom, minds, and hearts. To elaborate, one winter I composed this letter to our loved ones to describe how we do this through play and community inquiry.

During our first session, the children immersed themselves in both sensory play and nature play! We truly enjoyed watching you follow your children's lead as they engaged with our natural materials, white snow playdough, and our pretend snow. The hand lenses were a hit as children explored how they could see the world a bit differently with their use! The children were busy with their play they were actively exploring the classroom and its materials with their senses, looking, touching, listening, and grasping the various natural materials. As the children initiated their imaginative play, they were involved in important approaches to learning in early childhood including: stacking, filling & dumping, sorting, classifying, tossing, and pulling (and more!). With each of these approaches to learning the children were developing their sense of self while exercising their fine motor, social, and mathematic, scientific, and linguistic skills.

The natural materials, with the exception of the small twigs, the pussy willows, and wooden tree discs were all collected around the greater tri-state area over time. For example, I collected many of the pine cones including the small black spruce pine cones at my mother's farm in upstate New York. Our executive director and her husband, also collected many of the fresh greens, including the blue spruce, the white pine boughs, and the evergreens we used in the classroom from their home.

In discussing the nature of attention in research Sullivan (2000) suggests that autobiography is "of attention—learning it, teaching it, discovering its role in research. It's a story that began when I was very young." And so, I too share a story of an invitation to wonder sparked by memory:

Growing up in the country, in the winter days my brother and I would spend hours on the skating pond. The skating pond was a walk from our home, up to the barn and across the fields. We often would go out with our Dad, he liked to skate and had since he too was a child. One day he decided to take me and my brother Jim past the barn, beyond the ice-skating pond, up the knoll, to the woods. The trees were bare but still created a dense canopy of branches overhead. There we skated, beneath the cover of winter branches amidst the trees.

We only skated here once but my brother and I carry that one experience with us deeply. Did my Dad know he was creating a moment of awe and wonder for me and my brother? More to the point of this chapter, how might we as educators create these planned possibilities for wonder and awe in nature for our students? Sullivan asserts that this is vital, sharing: "...years later I remember with a vividness and intensity that compel me to poetry. On some level, in some hidden and inarticulate way, I must have been attending and recording extremely well. I was learning, internalizing, without any direct instruction" (p. 222).

Perhaps that is why last fall I found myself writing this in a letter to our families about how scientific inquiries, specifically studies of migration shape young children's experiences with nature:

The migration studies also offer us an opportunity to explore a scientific inquiry at the beginning of the year to shape our approach to our community inquiries for the school year. Within a scientific inquiry we seek to provide the children vital and viable experiences working as scientists—studying their subject, formulating questions, doing research, observing, creating theories or hypotheses, and of course, thinking of more questions! There is a balance of play within all of this—the teachers pull materials to support our invitations to play that encourage the children's sense of wonder, and exploration of the collective knowledge. Of course, we also read as a community! Shared books serve as an important touchstone for our inquiries, as reading together we often learn more about our questions, but in the process of doing so, develop even more questions!

There is something magical to explore the life cycle and migration of any of these amazing animals knowing that scientists at this very moment are also studying them filled with wonder and curiosity, driving their own inquiries. We often as a class will read about the work of researchers or view video clips of their work. It is our hope the children will carry the importance of having life-long passions, as well as themes of conservation and ecology with them beyond their time at school, recognizing the influence, impact, and responsibilities of humans within this beautiful world.

Once again, I return to Sullivan to ponder the invitations for explorations in nature we may provide our students: "How important were the tactile impressions of sun on my skin, mud beneath my feet, the water's salt at my lip, the rockings of my Mother's wooden boat? How did they matter, those lappings and squishing, the bubblings. . . ." (p. 222). While our students may not travel by boat on the open waters in the hopes of spying a humpback whale, we can gather around the green rug, lights dimmed to project the images of marine biologists on a mission to track the migratory journey of these gentle giants. To the children, we are there, we can feel the tickle of water lapping at the sides of the boats, our hearts racing as the whale breaches, dancing before our eyes, we can smell the ocean surf all from the four walls our Manhattan classroom.

This metaphorical journey we co-construct with our children conveys a sense of the foundational experiences that we hope will shape the students' lives' perspectives. Yet there are not necessarily tangible outcomes that can be specifically tested or proven. Further, Sullivan (2000) explores the educational implications more directly, "What are the implications of this for education in a society that demands artificial attention and immediate testable results?" (p. 222) Can we test the children's sense of kinship with these gentle giants? Moreover, should we?

CONCLUSION

I write on a winter day. My daughter, a city kid, is napping after a busy morning at Grandma's farm. She woke up extra early, ready to embrace the day. We filled our morning with nature, first feeding the birds, and then going on a nature hike. As we walked up to my mother's barn and around the pine trees, with my daughter seated in a red sled, the country quiet highlighted the crunching sounds of my boots. A piece of lichen, pine needles, and other natural flotsam and jetsam accompany my daughter in the sled as found treasures. On the way back to the house, we spy the maple trees in my mother's yard, and I hold my daughter high so she can study the early buds forming on the branches. I take photographs, and share a tweet with our families, asking, "What are you noticing this February break?"

My life as a teacher and my life otherwise are inextricably woven; I am teacher, as I am a mother, as I am a naturalist. I do not separate these worlds (Greene, 1973). Rather, my life experiences both in and outside the classroom work to shape my conceptions of learning, nature, play, and early childhood education. I believe we, as educators, are working to shape the world by teaching; thereby I teach as I live and as I believe (Macdonald, 1971). Nature play and experiences with natural materials are important to me as a mother, as a teacher, within my foundational memories of childhood. I recognize these positive experiences influence my conceptions of the possible within early childhood education. For me, nature is all around us, even in urban of environments.

To embrace nature play in the classroom teachers must first embrace nature and nature play outside the classroom. I recognize that there are also levels of comfort with nature for all individuals, not just urban educators, as there are levels of comfort with the messiness of early childhood for all educators. There are educators who find the benefits of the sensory play at the sand table to be more important than the reality of always having the grittiness of sand everywhere in the classroom. And there are educators who choose to leave the cover of sand table always closed. Teaching asks of us to move beyond our own personal challenges for the benefit of the children we teach, support, and care for each day. It asks of us to accept, if not embrace, the grit of early childhood play: dirt, leaves, twigs, seeds, worms, and bugs, and all.

Experiences with and in nature afford children chances to form potential foundational memories that may shape how they chose to live with and within the world. I recall a snippet published in *Utne* magazine, entitled, "Music to Our Ears: Utne Staffers Chime in on Their Favorite Sounds" (2005) that made me think of the senses and nature play, and pushed me to consider the potential of sensorial memories. The list includes:

horses chewing carrots
sisters in the kitchen . . .
the sigh/gurgle/grumble of a dog getting comfortable on the couch . . .
beans or rice being poured into a pan
snow under my boots
the heavy "thud" a dictionary makes when you close it
a head of lettuce being ripped open
snow falling on my jacket (n.p.)

With nearly each sound listed, I could hear the noise in my mind. What is the sound the snow falling on jackets? If you've walked with children in the snow, you'll know it is often accompanied by giggles and smiles and a looks of wonder as heads turn up towards the sky and down to study the snowflakes gathering on mittens before they melt. Classrooms should ring with sounds of nature and children engaged in nature play—the clunk of rocks pounding together, the shifting of sand being pushed aside by tiny hands, the plink, plunk, plink of acorns and pinecones dropping into a basket, the drumming bump of tree blocks momentarily transformed into musical instruments, or the brittleness of dried leaves.

Sullivan, & McCrary (2002) address the heart of the potential of natural experiences in early childhood and the potential legacies such experiences with the natural world may afford: "by teaching me attention to detail and nuance, by bringing me into personal, emotional engagement with the natural world; by modeling a delight in the varieties of ways that one can name the world" (p. 365). And that is one of our hopes as early childhood educators, that our students' foundational educational experiences position the children to confidently and joyfully not only embrace the world, but also make it their own.

Extensive early playful experiences with nature are planting seeds for growth, inquiry, and potentially life-long passions of conservation and environmentalism. The perceived challenges urban early childhood educators must face—from the time devoted to properly attiring children for nature walk, the lack of access to parks and nature trails, can be shifted to offer other possible avenues of exploration. To do this we, as urban educators, need to move beyond fixed, romantic conceptions of nature play and embrace the possible with(in) the classroom and beyond.

REFERENCES

Cadwell, L. B. (1997). Bringing Reggio Emilia home: An innovative approach to early childhood education. New York, NY: Teachers College Press.

Carson, R. (1998). The sense of wonder. New York, NY: Harper Collins. (Original published 1965).

Chase, S.E. (2005). Narrative Inquiry: Multiple lenses, approaches, voices. In N. K. Denzin & Y. S. Lincoln (Eds.), Handbook of qualitative research (3nd ed., pp. 651–679). Thousand Oaks, CA: Sage Publications, Inc.

Daly, L., & Beloglovsky, M. (2014). Loose parts: Inspiring play in young children. St. Paul, MN: Redleaf Press.

Davis, J. (1998). Young children, environmental education, and the future. Early childhood education journal, 26(2), 117–123.

Dweck, C. S. (2008). Mindset: The new psychology of success. New York, NY: Random House, Inc.

Fraiberg, S., Adelson, E., & Shapiro, V. (1987). "Ghosts in nursery: A psychoanalytic approach to the problems of impaired infant-mother relationships." In L. Fraiberg (Ed.), Selected writings of Selma Fraiberg. Columbus, OH: Ohio State University Press.

Greene, M. (1973). Teacher as stranger. Belmont, CA: Wadsworth Publishing Company, Inc.

Hirsch, E. S. (1974). The block book. National Association for the Education of Young Children.

Inan, H. Z., Trundle, K. C., & Kantor, R. (2010). Understanding natural sciences education in a Reggio Emilia-inspired preschool. Journal of research in science teaching, 47(10), 1186–1208.

Louv, R. (2008). Last child in the woods: Saving our children from nature-deficit disorder. Chapel Hill, NC: Algonquin Books.

Macdonald, J.B. (1971). The state of the art: Curriculum theory. The journal of educational research. 64(5), 195–200.

Miller, J. (2010). Nostalgia for the future: Imagining histories of JCT and the Bergamo conferences. Journal of curriculum theorizing, 26, p. 7–23.

Moore, R. (2014). Nature Play & Learning Places. Creating and managing places where children engage with nature. Raleigh, NC: Natural Learning Initiative and Reston, VA: National Wildlife Federation.

Music to our ears: Utne staffers chime in on their favorite sounds. (2005, July-August). Utne reader. Retrieved July 16, 2007, from http://www.utne.com/issues/2005_130/promo/11704-1.html

Pinedo-Burns, H. (2015). Puffins, butterflies, and clouds in the preschool: The importance of wonder. In J. Iorio & W. Parnell, Eds., Rethinking readiness in early childhood education: Implications for policy and practice. New York, NY : Palgrave Macmillan, 165–178.

Pratt, C. (2014). *I learn from children: An adventure in progressive education*. New York, NY: Grove Press. Original 1948.

Richardson, L. (1997). *Fields of play: Constructing an academic life*. New Brunswick, NJ: Rutgers University Press.

Richardson, L. (2000). Writing: A Method of Inquiry. In N. K. Denzin & Y. S. Lincoln (Eds.), Handbook of qualitative research (2nd ed., pp. 923–948). London: Sage.

Rivkin, M. & Schein, D. (2014). The great outdoors: Advocating for natural spaces for young children. Washington, DC: NAEYC.

Sullivan, A.M. (2000). Notes from a marine biologist's daughter: On the art and science of attention. *Harvard educational review.* 70(2), 211–227.

Sullivan, A., & McCrary, A. B. (2002). Mudflat: the aesthetics of a marine biologist's engagement with her work. Curriculum inquiry, 32(3), 357–365.

Wells, N. M., & Lekies, K. S. (2006). Nature and the life course: Pathways from childhood nature experiences to adult environmentalism. Children youth and environments, 16(1), 1–24.

Wilson, R. A. (1995). Nature and young children: A natural connection. Young children, 50(6), 4–11.

Wilson, R. A. (1997). The wonders of nature: Honoring children's ways of knowing. Early childhood news, 9(2).

Section III

PLAY, TEACHERS
AND HIGHER EDUCATION

Chapter Seven

Play in Higher Education

Emergent Understandings of Play Pedagogy for Adult Learners in Early Childhood Teacher Education Programs

Marleah Blom and Miranda D'Amico

When childhood ends and adulthood begins, human beings do not stop learning nor do they lose the capacity to play. Documented opportunities for adult learners to learn about and through play are limited particularly within the context of formal university and college post-secondary settings. "Play is ubiquitous and normal in childhood, but play in adulthood is less well understood, even more so when it comes to being playful in higher education" (Nørgard, Toft-Nielsen, & Whitton, 2017, p. 274). College, university and early childhood classrooms can all be potential spaces where play can come to life and foster student learning. By synthesizing content, skills and creative processes for learners of all ages, both higher education and early childhood settings are 'play's conceptual fermenting grounds' (Ranz-Smith, 2007).

Early childhood teacher education (ECTE) programs, which are geared to prepare educators to create spaces and experiences for children's learning and development, are fertile grounds for adult learners to explore and experience play in higher education settings. When educating upcoming leaders and advocates, these programs help shape the discourse about play, develop adult learners' skills and understandings as well as promote students' awareness about play and learning throughout the lifespan. With ongoing concerns and conversations about the decline and evolution of children's free play (Gray, 2011; Lewis, 2017) as well as play's longstanding history within early childhood education, attention needs to be placed on strengthening these educational programs so early childhood educators can support play practices and policies in early childhood settings (Vu, Han, & Buell, 2012). In order to help strengthen programs, a better understanding of play and curriculum with adult learners is required, both in terms of play content and play-based teaching practices. Currently there is a paucity of information about play in terms of what is being taught as well as how play is facilitated by instructors for adult learning in post-secondary ECTE programs. In Canada, the majority of recognized ECTE programs are housed in colleges (Jacobs & Adrien, 2012), including publicly funded pre-university and technical colleges referred to as Collèges d'Enseignement Généraux et Professionnels (CÉGEPs) in Québec.

This chapter includes details about a qualitative research study, which investigated 19 instructors' beliefs about play and learning and related teaching practices when educating pre-service educators in 13 college and university ECTE settings in six different provinces and territories across Canada. Post-secondary instructors' self-reported teaching practices as well as influential factors at institutional, classroom and societal levels are outlined. Findings are discussed using Wood's (2014) notions of 'play *as* educational practice' and 'play *in* educational practice' within the play–pedagogy interface, which refers to how play is positioned in relation to and as a form of pedagogy. Various considerations, including suggested adaptations to modes used within Wood's analysis and recommendations for professional development efforts for teacher educators in ECTE programs are provided.

PLAY IN HIGHER EDUCATION

Formal higher education settings have an influential role in shaping the future and instructors are key players. Instructors' pedagogical decisions affect not only the development of students' knowledge, skills and competencies, but also their teaching practices may influence ways students experience and view education. It is not known how many college and university instructors create spaces and opportunities for adult learners to experience play and embrace the notion that learning can be fun.

There have been increasing pressures on instructors to create learning spaces and innovative practices to engage, motivate and prepare diverse student bodies for the complex twenty-first century global marketplace and a lifetime of learning (Entwistle, 2011; Kinzie, 2011). With the shift toward a "learning paradigm" at the latter part of twentieth century (Barr & Tagg, 1995), higher education settings have been adopting constructivist approaches to teaching and learning. An emphasis on learners and the learning process rather than imparting education has contributed to efforts that aim to support adult learners in "lifelong learning" as compared to "lifelong education" (Hasan, 2012).

Instructors are encouraged to integrate instructional methods that promote active learner engagement, active construction of knowledge, applied skills and deep approaches to learning (Marton & Säljö, 1976). Active, collaborative, and experiential learning practices are considered high impact practices as they have been found to foster increased rates of student retention and engagement (Association of American Colleges & Universities, n.d.). Hands-on learning and 'learning by doing' are recommended to help students develop skills, adapt to change as well as help instill a mindset of lifelong learning (Universities Canada, 2018).

Positive effects of play on adult learning have been reported (Goldmintz & Schaefer, 2007; Harris & Davey, 2008; Meyer, 2010), and although higher education settings are described as becoming 'increasingly performative risk-aversive environments' (Nørgard et al., 2017), it is claimed that there has been an increase of playful approaches to teaching and learning in higher education over the past decade (Whitton, 2018). Due to what it affords, play may be a good fit in terms of recommended teaching practices and the goals of higher education.

In play, individuals are actively engaged in experiences and learn by doing. Using the 'magic circle' as a metaphor, Whitton (2018) and Nørgard et al. (2017), describe how playfulness and playful approaches foster educational liminal spaces, where failure, risk, exploration, experimentation, participation, ideation and intrinsic motivation becomes possible. Play allows students to take risks, learn from mistakes and learn to be adaptable to change by trying on new or alternative thoughts and behaviors. Play encourages possible encounters with content, ideas, behaviours and others within the nonliteral, safe space it creates. The suspension of disbelief, or 'as if' reality, created through play is beneficial as it allows for possibilities and innovation. Within a playspace, new problems, change, innovation, relational and transformational learning are fostered (Meyer, 2010) and a ludic or play space is one that promotes deep learning with a self-organizing community with its own set of traditions (Kolb & Kolb, 2010). In a model of *Play and Problem Based Learning*, play has also been described as a mediator for knowledge creation, which helps students become more creative (Thorsted, Bing, & Kristensen, 2015). Engagement, through play, may also be enjoyable, which can foster a desire for lifelong learning.

While digital games and gamification are increasingly becoming popular in post-secondary settings (Norgard et al., 2017), there is evidence that traditional games, board games, role plays, and simulations are nevertheless used in post-secondary settings (Whitton, 2018). Other examples of play and playfulness used by instructors for teaching and learning in higher education outside of ECTE programs have been reported (Aying, 2012; Blom & Henle, 2013; James, 2013; James & Brookfield, 2014; James & Nerantzi, 2019; Nørgard et al., 2017; Thorsted et al., 2015). Contextual information about what helps or hinders the implementation of play and playful approaches within the context of higher education helps inform what is happening along with the why and how with adult learners.

Ideally play and playful approaches to teaching can be used in higher education and promote innovative teaching practices that fit within the 'learning'
paradigm. Play-based pedagogy may help address the needs of students who
are in post-secondary classrooms. As Scott (2015) writes, play-pedagogies
support learners in acquiring new competencies and skills to tackle twenty-
first century challenges while providing opportunities for learners to become
comfortable initiating, producing and sharing their creations. These pedagogies are stated to include such things as participation as well as collaborative, personalized and project-based learning. Play, due to its active, applied,
experiential and creative nature, may fit within such approaches to learner-
centered teaching, particularly for learners who will be working with young
children.

It is not enough for preservice educators to know what play is. Preservice
educators also need knowledge as to how to put play into practice, particularly as educators have voiced how they believe in the value of play in early
childhood settings but do not necessarily know how to put play into practice
(Lobman, 2005). Educators need to accept the importance of play (Graue,
2010; Hewes, 2006; Moyles, 2010) be comfortable with uncertainty, and
be adept at being a flexible planner (Nell & Drew, 2013; Wood & Attfield,
2005). Not only has it been recommended that teacher education promotes
competence in observation and identification of children's play needs as
well as making decisions about when and how to intervene during children's
play (Trawick-Smith, 2012), preservice educators may also be provided opportunities to develop awareness as to the role of play in their own lives as
adults (Nicholson, Shimpi, & Rabin, 2014). These aptitudes may potentially
be achieved through teacher education. To best support adult learners in post-
secondary ECTE programs, instructors' pedagogical decisions may benefit
from the inclusion of both play content and play-pedagogy.

PLAY IN ECTE PROGRAMS

Geared to prepare adult learners learn knowledge and skills related to child
development, play and early childhood curriculum, ECTE programs in post-

secondary environments are an ideal context for adult learners to closely engage with play content and learning experiences. ECTE programs must include content, strategies and policies to support positive changes that help preservice educators' development of play-based curriculum (Vu et al., 2012).

In their examination of various aspects of ECTE Certificate and Diploma programs across Canada, Jacobs and Adrien (2012) found that content of programs may be the result of 'best practice' information as interpreted by college instructors. Through an analysis of course lists and course content gathered from websites of a sample of colleges that offer Diploma and Certificates in Early Childhood Education and Care (ECEC) programs across Canada, the authors found that in attempts to deliver the message about the importance of play, some programs provided play specific courses whereas other programs embedded play material in other courses. These results are similar to Vu et al.'s (2012) review of 20 NAEYC accredited teacher education programs for early childhood where they found that specific courses or content related to play theory and practice were not a requirement to receive certification by the association.

With concerns about the future of children's free play, which the authors define as child-initiated play whereby an adult is not guiding the play or constructing it with learning objectives in mind (Yogman, Garner, Hutchinson, Hirsh-Pasek, & Golinkoff, 2018), the authors call to include playful learning for healthy child development. It is thus essential to examine what pre-service educators are learning about play as well as ways play is positioned in relation to and as a form of pedagogy when instructors facilitate students' learning. Practices in early childhood teacher programs can help early childhood educators understand, value and support play in children's lives and play in children's educational experiences in early childhood classrooms (Kemple, Oh, & Porter, 2015).

Evidence of play in ECTE has been reported in terms of instructors engaging preservice educators in play-based action research (Patte, 2012), eliciting student participation in improvisation (Lobman, 2005), modelling play and using playful teaching modules (Hyvoven, 2011), and using play-based pedagogy to teach play in teacher education (Harris, 2007). Others have reported on their own practices within the play specific courses that they teach (Bredikyte & Hakkarainen, 2011; Johnson, 2014; Kemple et al., 2015; Lord & McFarland, 2010). Additional examples have been provided by Nell and Drew (2013), who address the importance of hands-on, open-ended play and recommend having educators actively engage in intentional play themselves to better understand play for children. Nicholson, Shimpi and Rabin (2014) suggest meaningful play experiences can help develop early childhood professionals' understanding and passion to advocate for children's right to play. Most examples within the literature are single cases from the United States, Europe and Australia. A detailed snapshot as to what is happening within various courses and institutions in terms of helping early childhood educators develop play knowledge and skills within the landscape of Canadian ECTE has been missing from the literature.

'PLAY *IN* EDUCATION' OR 'PLAY *AS* EDUCATION'

Play is a topic of ongoing study and research in various disciplines and has a longstanding place in the field of education due to its complex relationship with learning. Across examples of play in higher education, including practices used within the context of ECTE programs, there is great variability in terms of how the term 'play' is used in practice. Play, for example, is described as an activity, method, approach, and space. Whitton (2018) has gone further to describe ways practices that are considered 'playful learning within the magic circle' may be classified into tools, techniques and tactics. Tools, including artefacts and technology such as toys and puzzles, can be used to develop playfulness, whereas techniques (e.g., role playing, quests) are described as approaches that naturally possess elements of play. Tactics, on the other hand, are strategies that add playfulness. Examples include surprise, humor and storytelling. This classification system helps conceptualize potential relations between play and pedagogy in terms of using play in higher education settings. A distinction is not made in terms of play being used in education or play being used as a form of education. Whitton addresses how there is more work to be done in terms of establishing a coherent definition, providing evidence for pedagogic rationale for the use of play in higher education as well as establishing an overarching framework.

Scholars have readily focused their efforts on children's play and potential ways it may be incorporated in childhood settings for educational purposes. For the purposes of this chapter, research findings will be discussed in terms of the play-pedagogy interface, which includes the notions of play *as* education and play *in* education (Wood, 2014). The interface acknowledges pedagogical implications that arise from contrasting interpretations of what play is and what it does for learning as well ideological underpinnings, which influence how play is constructed within practice and justify its inclusion as play *as* or *in* education. Play *as* education positions play as a universal source and driver of learning and development, play *in* education implies using play as intentionally planned and facilitated for educational purposes.

Wood discusses her analysis of the play-pedagogy interface based on different modes of educational play in early childhood settings. While spontaneous and natural play can be educational due to what the player may learn through play, "the difference between educational play and non-educational play reflects purposes and proposed outcomes from a play activity" (Saracho, 2012, p. 75). The term educational play thus represents play, including child-initiated play, that is perceived to have intentional educational value, educational play thus also implies some level of control by the adult or teacher, who may be present, supervising, monitoring, and intervening during play or terminating the play (Johnson, 2016). This differs from natural, recreational or real play (King, 1986), where play is voluntary, there are no intended educational purposes, goals are created by the players, and children are free from adult interference. When planning for educational play, teachers are faced with the challenge to allow for spontaneity and student initiative yet plan so that the activity is educational (Saracho, 2012). Free, child-initiated play may also be considered educational, yet it is undervalued if both children and adults' goals are not taken into consideration when planning for play (Wood, 2014).

In her analysis of the play-pedagogy interface, Wood (2014) conceptualizes three main modes of play, which include child-initiated play (Mode A), adult-guided play (Mode B), and technicist version of educational play (Mode C). All three modes are considered educational play however, there is some overlap between them. Within each mode, the play-pedagogy relationship is considered in terms of (a) goals for the pedagogy, (b) practitioner's assumptions about learning, play and the child, (c) the purpose of play and the interaction between play and pedagogy, as well as (d) outcomes of the interaction for the child and the practitioner (Wood, 2014). Play *as* education may include both recreational, real, types of play as well as some instances of child-initiated educational play (Mode A) as it is closest to the ideological tradition of free play whereby play's qualities are valuable for children's learning (Wood, 2014). Modes B and C (the adult-guided and technicist versions) of educational play are more aligned with the notion of play *in* education.

Other continuums have been created to illustrate varied perspectives on how play can be integrated into teaching practices within early childhood educational settings (Miller & Almon, 2009; Pyle & Danniels, 2016; Trawick-Smith, 2012). These continuums essentially place free, unstructured play, or child-initiated play on one side, didactic, structured play or play to meet specific curriculum needs and learning outcomes on the opposite end, with adult-guided play somewhere in the middle. All continuums suggest a relationship between children and adults within the educational process in early childhood settings. Based on findings from the research study, potential adaptations and suggestions for future research on the play-pedagogy interface within higher educational settings will also be addressed.

A QUALITATIVE ENQUIRY

Methodology

A qualitative, exploratory and descriptive design was used to investigate faculty's reported beliefs on play and learning and related teaching practices used with preservice educators within the context of accredited Canadian post-secondary Early Childhood Education (Diploma or Certificate) Teacher Education programs. Faculty's reported teaching practices within post-secondary ECTE programs, which reflected their personal conceptions of play and learning were examined. In addition, this study investigated contextual factors that support or hinder implementation of faculty's beliefs about play and learning and faculty's insights on professional development initiatives centering on play as well as learning were also explored.

Multiple methods and data forms were used to embrace complexity and multiple ways of knowing, creating and representing data. The research design was inspired by interpretative phenomenological analysis (IPA), narrative inquiry and arts-based research, which were incorporated at various parts of the research process. The research study, which focused on exploring each faculty member's personal meanings of play and related teaching practices, was not framed by one definition or theory, nor did it take into account recreational versus educational types of play.

Participants

Nineteen female faculty members representing 13 post-secondary institutions in 6 different Canadian provinces and territories volunteered to participate and completed the study. Participants were female between 26 and 61 years at the time of data collection, with a mean age of 47.4 years. Sixteen participants (84 percent) were between the ages of 40 and 59 years. The highest level of education held by participating faculty included a Diploma (5 percent), a Bachelor's degree (11 percent), a Master's degree (73 percent), or a Master's/Ph.D. combined degree that was currently in progress (11 percent). All participants reported having education within areas of Early Childhood Education or Child and Youth Studies. Two participants reported having a Master's degrees in areas related to adult learning.

Participating faculty all held a teaching position with six participants also indicating having a coordinator role within their respective institution. Participants reported a varied list of courses they had taught or were currently teaching with 26 percent reporting teaching courses where play was explicitly noted in the title.

Research Process

Data, including images, narratives and transcripts of semi-structured interviews, were collected throughout a four-stage process. Throughout all stages of the research, a journal was used to help the researcher be explicit about her own beliefs and assumptions as well as to note observations and memos throughout the process.

During stage one, numerous individual institutional ethics requirements were adhered to before participants were recruited for the study. Faculty members were first asked to submit via e-mail written answers to demographic questions and questions about their beliefs on how children and adults learn. Questions sent to participants prior to interviews and interview protocols for stages two and three are listed in the Appendix.

Once the requested information was collected, interview dates were scheduled with each faculty member, who was asked to send two images depicting how they see (a) play and learning for children in ECEC and (b) play and learning for adults in ECTE. Images could include photographs, cartoons, paintings, and text. They could be created by faculty members or found elsewhere. The decision was left to participants so they could choose what best depicted their beliefs about play and learning. The only requirement was that images needed to be in a format that could be sent via e-mail to the researcher prior to the first interview. More details about the use of images to elicit faculty members' beliefs can be found in Blom and D'Amico (2016).

During stage two, a one-hour photo-elicitation inspired interview was conducted with each faculty member using faculty's self-chosen images to elicit their self-reported beliefs about play and learning in ECEC and ECTE. As indicated in the interview protocol within the Appendix, "*Tell me about the picture. . . .*" was used as the opening question for both images. Due to geographical constraints, interviews were conducted either in person, or via telephone or Skype. Participants were provided the option. During this stage, 19 interviews about participants' beliefs were completed. Two interviews were done face-to-face, one via Skype and all others were completed over the telephone. At the end of the interview, a date for a follow up interview was scheduled with each faculty member. Each participant was asked to reflect on their stated beliefs and create a written narrative about how they put their beliefs into practice when teaching in post-secondary ECTE environments. This document was to be submitted to the researcher via e-mail prior to the second interview. All interviews were audio-recorded, transcribed, and reviewed prior to stage three.

Stage three included one-hour semi-structured interviews with each participant, which centered on (a) play related teaching practices, (b) factors that help or hinder their practices, and (c) information about faculty professional development initiatives. Nineteen individual interviews were completed during this stage. One was done face-to-face, two via Skype and all others were completed over the telephone. All interviews were audio-recorded, transcribed, and reviewed prior to stage four.

Based on all data gathered, the last stage of the process (stage four) involved reviewing data collected from each faculty member during stages one, two and three, which included demographic information, images, narratives and interview transcripts from both interviews. A written summary of the researcher's understanding was sent to each faculty member, respectively. Participants were asked to verify the document and were invited to make any changes deemed necessary. All nineteen participants completed all stages involved in the study.

Data Analysis

A three-step approach to data analysis was used in this study. The steps include (a) becoming familiar with data and devising a coding framework, (b) summarizing and verifying individual cases, and (c) conducting a thematic analysis across cases. Each step fed into the next and the individual's accounts are at the center of the analysis process. The process was an inductive and iterative one. Each stage informed the next and built the foundations of understanding. Throughout the process, the researcher was also able to clarify participants' meanings that were being created with participants themselves.

Data for each individual faculty member were reviewed between each stage of data collection. During step one, becoming familiar with data through ongoing review, transcription and reflection aided in the development of emergent codes that became a part of the coding framework that was used within the next two steps of the analysis. The coding framework was developed keeping in mind a priori codes (King & Horrocks, 2010) as well as redefined codes that emerged through stages of data collection. Aligned with approaches used within IPA, triangulating data and verifying summaries with each participant during step two, respected individual faculty members' subjective meanings. All 19 verified cases then provided the basis for a thematic analysis across the group (Attride-Stirling, 2001). This third step helped to unveil and report broader themes for the group of Canadian faculty participating in the study.

DISCOVERIES: TEACHING PRACTICES AND INFLUENTIAL FACTORS

Faculty Members' Self-Reported Teaching Practices

Overall, while participants were not specifically asked to voice examples of play-pedagogy and learning outcomes, all participants reported using play for the purpose of learning within their professional teaching practices. This, in addition to faculty members perceiving their role as very important in creating relationships with students, creating and facilitating activities as well as modelling playful behaviors, suggests that practices are aligned with educational play in ECTE programs. There were no examples of practices that included or encouraged students engaging in recreational play (Johnson, 2016), real play (King, 1986) or free play on their own nor were there examples of illicit (King) or disruptive forms of play.

Play was reported to promote student engagement, understanding and retention of course material. Play was perceived beneficial to ECTE students, namely as play helps teach child-centeredness, develop specific skills, become comfortable with play, advocate for play, as well as understand the benefits of play in their own lives. One faculty member, for example, voiced that "if you are going to be an early childhood educator who values children's play you have to play." When and how play is used was highly dependent on the individual faculty member. For example, play was reported by five faculty members who taught play content within courses specific to play. Participants also voiced how they implement play in other courses. Some participants incorporated play in all courses, regardless of content and subject matter, used at different times throughout the course. One faculty member reported using play every 15 minutes during each class and another reported implementing play every 30 minutes. Other participants described using play more at later points during the course or only after material was presented.

There was tremendous variability in specific play-related teaching practices that faculty members reportedly use in university and college classrooms. Many examples of in-class, outside the classroom, assignments and working directly with children within the context of the course were provided. Examples are outlined in Table 7.1.

After a detailed analysis of all reported examples, key features of instructors' practices emerged. Instructors' practices included active engagement on behalf of the student, social interaction between students or between students

Table 7.1. Examples of Play Related Teaching Methods Reportedly Used by Faculty

In the classroom	Outside the classroom	Assignments	Children
Physical energizers	Go outdoors to collect materials, bring them back to discuss	Create play spaces, activities or kits	Photos and videatives
Facilitate and observe play scenarios	Go on nature walks	Create choreography	Field experiences
Engage with play stations or invitation centers	Visit a child care center when no children are present	Create videos	Visits by children to the ECTE classroom
Role play and simulations	Field experiences in child care centers or schools in the community	Create online profiles	
Mock interviews		Reflect on own childhood play experiences	
Debates		Engage in experience and write about it (not just about theory)	
Games (e.g., Jeopardy)		Choices within assignments	
Ball toss		Providing suckers while students write exams	
Constructive or sensory activities			
Puzzles			
Construct own play definitions			
Visualizations			
Use of the arts (clay, paint, draw play, write poems, engage in art making)			
Inductive problem solving			
Group activities			
Explore websites			
Playing with ideas			
Discussions			
Engaging with content in playful ways			

and children, and some type of real-life application. One faculty member expressed how her practices involve "keeping it real for students" and "keeping the students as active as possible in class."

Although most participants expressed implementing play by facilitating activities and assigning assessments that they, themselves, considered play, one faculty member described play as an approach to teaching. Play was not deemed a specific activity per se. Instead, various methods and strategies were reportedly used, regardless of the course, to help foster a mindset or play state in students. An example was the use of 'energizers' in all of her classes. Every 15 or 20 minutes she has students do something. "Even if it's just if I put on music and they're dancing around the room and when the music stops they're chatting with a partner about what we just covered." This was voiced "to takes you out of that mind space of 'I'm sitting here having to learn something' to 'oh my goodness, I'm actually having a good time' . . . it just puts you in a space I think where you're then more open to learning." It was reported that it is important to not become focused on setting up play environments solely to meet learning outcomes as it takes away the essence of play itself. She stated that "play is about a mode or mental state." Creating environments and experiences within courses so students are "in that state of joy where anything is possible and that's such an important learning space. Where not worrying about what others are thinking. Present moment."

Not only were play-based practices used alongside other teaching methods, instructors' practices were reportedly used to help connect theory and practice and were aligned with course outcomes and goals. Safe environments were deemed necessary to implement play-related activities. Faculty members expressed the importance of taking the time to create conditions for students to be comfortable with play.

Although positive feedback was reportedly received about play as a teaching method in their courses, participants reported that students were sometimes hesitant to participate due to various reasons, including appearing silly in front of teachers and peers, being embarrassed, being scared to do something that is not accepted, caring about others' opinions, not being used to having choice, and not being familiar with play-based practices in educational contexts. Direct feedback from students was not collected within this study.

Participants provided examples of what they considered play in their teaching yet overall, play related practices were not specifically discussed as being similar or different to experiential or active learning methods. Only one participant referred to play and active learning. She stated how active learning may be a form of play but it is not called play. Another participant addressed the importance of terms to gain support for play in educational settings. She suggested that play might be called 'active engagement' due to society's views that play is only for children. Prompted by a specific question to help understand their practices, different views on the terms play, playful, playful practice and playfulness emerged. Distinctions are listed in Table 7.2.

Influential Factors

Faculty members were directly asked what factors are perceived to support and hinder implementation of their play-based practices in ECTE. Questions are listed within the protocol for Interview 2 within the Appendix. Insights in terms of institutional, classroom, societal and faculty related factors emerged. A list of these factors and examples are outlined in Table 7.3.

Overall, having freedom in course design, small class sizes, funding and reasonable schedules were voiced to help foster play-pedagogy in ECTE program. For example, one faculty member voiced "I'm drained if I have to do two three hours classes in a day. I'm really drained and I have done them back to back." It was suggested that programs create schedules that allow more time and freedom for students to engage fully in meaningful play-based experiences during classes. Support from colleagues, department head or administrators was also deemed beneficial. It was shared that senior administration needs to understand and support the benefits of doing things in a way that differs from students "sitting in desks listening to teachers deliver theory."

Courses described as being more theoretical were perceived by various participants to require more content be 'delivered.' One faculty member, however, expressed "it is more important in those courses that are heavy in theory and sort of academic learning that you try to bring some fun into it, some play." Play was also described by many faculty members to be more readily applied with some topic areas, including curriculum and creativity. "So, the subject itself kind of dictates what you can do with it," voiced one instructor. Others described incorporating play in all their courses, regardless of the topic. For example, a couple of participants discussed how they have brought play into teaching about serious topics such as childhood diseases, and child abuse.

In addition to classroom and faculty related factors, perceptions of others within the institution and society, including lack of respect for those working in ECTE and early childhood settings were reported to influence faculty members' teaching practices. Faculty members expressed how their work and teaching practices may be undervalued. One particular incident was discussed as an instructor talked about her students engaged in play within her class. "As they were dancing and the music was blaring, somebody opened the back door of my classroom and just screamed, 'This is an academic institu-

Table 7.2. Distinctions Made by Participants between Play, Playful and Playfulness

Play	Playful	Playful practice	Playfulness
Sequenced; doing something (physical); act of playing	light, carefree, relaxed; cognitive, emotional or personal expression; being playful, which can occur in situations that do not warrant or that are not set up for play		
spontaneous		planned activities or involves educator being engaged in the play; can include element of play but is not fully play; creates structure, develops safety and trust to better spontaneously jump into play	
what person is doing			how person is acting; term used to justify play for adults

Table 7.3. Contextual Factors That Support or Hinder Play Related Practices

Factor			Examples (Support)	Examples (Hinderance)
Institutional	Departmental policies and requirements	Course design	flexibility when creating courses	having to include on-line or group components, using standardized textbooks, late submission policies
		Class sizes	small class sizes	
		Class schedules	longer classes	teaching many classes in one day or teaching classes back to back, scheduling classes early morning and at night
		Length of program		2-year programs
	Social network and support		support from colleagues, similar philosophical approaches, support from department heads and senior administration	
	Course related factors	Content, level, year	teaching topics related to curriculum, play or creativity	teaching theory or theory-heavy courses
		Delivery method		on-line courses or on-line components of courses
		Practicum sites		having good model educators in practicum settings with similar approaches to play and learning
	Job related factors		teaching educators to work with children	lack of time, heavy workload, marking exams and assignments,
	Funding		having adequate funding for materials and children' visits to ECTE classrooms	

Classroom				
	Students	Reactions to activities	interest and high levels of participation	fear of judgment and doing the wrong thing; unfamiliarity with others and certain teaching methods; uncomfortable with choices and control
		Diversity		variety of ages, education levels, experience working with children, cultures, needs, interests and learning preferences
	Logistics	Classroom	large classrooms, windows	
		Furniture	moveable furniture, preferably round or 'puddle tables'	
		Materials	access to a variety of open ended and loose materials	having to cart around materials around or no accessible space for storing materials and resources
		Additional space considerations	space to post and store students' work, access to outdoor or gym spaces, child center close or central to classrooms	

(continued)

Table 7.3. *(Continued)*

Factor		Examples (Support)	Examples (Hinderance)
Societal	Views about play		play not being valued for society, play viewed solely for children, views that time and resources are not needed to study play
	Views from ECEC settings		feeling undervalued and unintelligent
	Views on education		focus on knowledge and overachievement, post-secondary studies are 'serious'
Faculty-related	Beliefs		
	Education and training	staying current, engaging in ongoing professional development	
	Experience	continued work with children	

tion!' and closed the door." Societal views that play is natural and does not need to be taught, that play is only for children and that higher education is 'serious,' were also deemed to influence faculty members' teaching practices. "And especially in the context of university, people want to, or they're told 'university is serious. You're coming and you're studying. So when you throw play at them they're like, 'what?' Like this is not within my realm of university.'".

DISCUSSION

This study elicited many examples of play in college and university class-rooms, which reflected the multitude of ways that play can be implemented to foster student learning within educational settings. Within the play-pedagogy interface (Wood, 2014), a detailed analysis of reported practices across all 19 cases suggests that all were examples of 'play *in* education.' Within faculty's self-reported practices, all play experiences were structured and controlled and designed and facilitated by the faculty members to meet specific objectives. All instructors described using play in their pedagogy. Play was used as a tool or approach within a broader teaching orientation to achieve a particular purpose.

The idea that play is perceived as a driver of learning in and of itself, did not emerge. Rather, it was apparent that the focus was to intentionally implement practices coined as 'play' for educational purposes. There was an apparent alignment between play with learning goals created by someone other than the learner. At the end of the study, one faculty member stated her desire to use play as a tool for learning, questioning whether her current practices align with her intentions. "I guess what I've realized throughout this process is that I think I use play as a tool for learning but actually do not . . . yet!"

The closest examples of play *as* education are considered opportunities where students engage in interactive activities, engage with open ended materials or to 'have fun.' When engaged in experiences perceived to be play by the instructor, there is a perceived challenge to help students understand that learning can happen when one experiences qualities of play, such as fun.

I think also another constraint a little bit is the idea that learning can be fun and when they are having fun they are learning. That's a leap. You have to make that leap to get it and that's what the debrief is all about. The debrief is all about, okay, what happened? What happened and what did you learn?

There is a sense that instructors who cultivate experiences for students to 'play' believe that play is a driver for learning for adult learners. In cases where conditions are set up for students to engage in "play," instructors ensure that connections between play and learning are made explicit. These types of experiences are used for set purposes, such as applying new ideas or knowledge, practicing course content or theory, or the experiences are designed and facilitated with specific learning objectives in mind. There are educational intentions that guide the activities. There is no apparent choice or control on the side of the student, particularly in terms of creating and pursuing learning goals that emerge from the experience and are based on students' own interests. These practices are thus considered educational yet the way in which they are implemented suggest they too fit within the notion of play *in* education.

Another close example of play *as* education that was discussed, was the approach used to help students get into a "play state." Facilitating "energizers" and creating play environments were not reportedly done to meet learning outcomes and play was not perceived as an activity. Rather, the instructor described an overall approach to value the essence of play itself. This approach is still considered "play *in* education" as scheduled activities were intentionally facilitated within the classroom. The instructor determines when to facilitate these short activities, decides when the activity begins and ends as well as instructions for what the experience will entail. There is still an implicit goal: to help students be open to learning.

Participants in the study acknowledged that play is not only something that students should understand, but it should also be experienced. As stated by a faculty member during the study, "if you are going to be an early childhood educator who values children's play" and someone who understands play as a vehicle for teaching and learning with children "you have to play." Instructors' self-reported teaching practices were identified as "play," yet they were not described in ways that hone into play's ability to disrupt, defile, disturb rules, routines and social conventions (Wood, 2014). "Play *in* education" may help students learn about content, develop skills and achieve predetermined learning outcomes, yet "play *as* education" can allow learners to drive their own learning as well as control and initiate activities, which can in turn develop interdependence, ownership and autonomy. In this light, instead of viewing play only as part of a direct process explicated through learning goals, play has the potential to open-up the unexpected and give birth to new knowledge (Thorsted et al., 2015).

Opportunities for students to take control, fully engage and immerse themselves in play, and create new ideas, knowledge, and goals through their experiences, were not apparent in teaching practices as they were described by faculty members within the study. Play for students' own sake, where goals emerge from the process itself, was not discussed. Free, unstructured play experiences in ECTE, whereby adult learners had spontaneous engagement that was intrinsically valuable to the learner, was not present. This does not imply that all forms of play are appropriate within ECTE programs. Rather, if ECTE programs are meant to help students develop knowledge and personal conviction to advocate support for the value of play in early childhood settings (Kemple et al., 2015), students may benefit from experiencing various play pedagogies, including both play *as* and *in* education. It may even be possible for play *as* education to be nested in play *in* education. Instructors may provide a loose structure within which students have freedom to engage a process-oriented experience in which they can make decisions, discover, create their own goals, take ownership and follow their own interests. This may include both educational and recreational play, depending on the design.

Goals, beliefs, interactions and outcomes are considered within each mode used for Wood's (2014) analysis of the play-pedagogy interface. Examining play-pedagogies in ECTE programs is complex in that it involves an examination of these factors, including assumptions about play, learning, learners and pedagogy for both children and adults. It involves thinking about what play-pedagogies with adults are effective for preservice educators to understand so that they can then implement effective play-pedagogies for children. It was acknowledged by participants that play looks different for students in ECTE programs than it does for children in educational settings. The analysis of faculty's practices also reveals a potential disconnect between what faculty members reportedly put into practice and their beliefs about types of play (free, child-initiated) they hope early childhood educators foster in early childhood settings. This echoes how "there is a discontinuity between the nonlinear ways that young children learn and the linear educational institutions where teachers and caregivers are trained" (Fromberg, 1999, p.33). Future conversations may need to take into account alignments between play-pedagogies in both contexts.

Wood's (2014) model, and other continuums that illustrate forms of play-pedagogy (Miller & Almon, 2009; Pyle & Danniels, 2017; Trawick-Smith, 2012) are created based on early childhood and kindergarten settings. To examine the play-pedagogy interface in higher education, terms must be adjusted to include adult learners or preservice educators and instructors instead of basing continuums on 'child-initiated' and 'adult-guided' categories (Wood, 2014). Additional modes may also be added to include learning outcomes and curriculum goals at both course and program levels.

Developmentally, children and adults are at different stages, which impacts how they play and how they learn. These differences need to be addressed in a model for it to be suitable for higher educational settings. As participants in the study voiced, adult learners bring knowledge, experience and familiarity with educational settings to the post-secondary context. They may also bring expectations in terms of what education involves, fear of judgement from peers, awareness of evaluative components and competitiveness to succeed. Factors such as these may impact how much adult learners are willing to initiate, choose and control their learning and create their own learning goals without consideration of the instructors and programs goals. These factors also impact ways in which adult learners may be hesitant to engage in play related activities or their levels of intrinsic motivation to do so.

All reported practices in the study are perceived to fall between the adult-guided (Mode B) or technicist version (Mode C) within Wood's (2014) educational play continuum. A more complex model is needed to not only name adults as learners but to (a) better represent the students' role in learning, (b) represent the instructors' role and responsibilities in teaching, and (c) reflect the relationship between students and instructors and curriculum within the context of post-secondary ECTE programs. Mode A in Wood's model, child-initiated play, positions play in which children drive their own learning by initiating play activities. Within formal post-secondary settings, adult learners may not necessarily initiate activities or assignments yet there may be opportunities to engage in qualities of play, such as making choices, following interests and formulating goals at different times. The relationship and interactions between instructors and students differ with this context and the role of an instructor differs from that of an early childhood educator. Modes must be developed to represent the context, relationships, and responsibilities of instructors and learners as well as ECTE programs. Modes can then be used to analyze different elements of different courses in terms of play-pedagogy, such as assignments, in-class activities, out of class activities, and delivery methods. By contextualizing the framework and examining each element, we can gain a better understanding the play-pedagogy interface in ECTE programs.

As indicated by participants, there are various influential mediating factors operating at various levels to consider when attempting to practice play-pedagogy in higher education. For example, is play *as* education realistic within a context that depends on assessment and evaluation? What are the needs, interests and expectations of adult learners in ECTE programs? Participants voiced how creating welcoming and safe learning environments was deemed very important when implementing play in practice within ECTE programs. This is supported by research, including Whitton (2018) who addresses how others have reported that 'safe' playful spaces provide low stakes, which increases students' enjoyment of learning as well as supports such things as learning from failure, management of risk-taking, creativity and innovation. Additional research is called for on contextual factors, conditions needed for play-pedagogy, and their impact on play-pedagogy; such research is especially needed when developing modes of play in post-secondary ECTE settings.

The play-pedagogy interface includes pedagogical implications resulting from various perspectives of what play is and what it does for learning. The term 'play' itself, when used to identify instructors' teaching practices, needs to be better defined. Some participants also came to the realization that they distinguish between terms such as 'play' and 'playful.' Others voiced how they implement elements of play in their teaching as compared to true forms of play. Further investigations on how instructors perceive their practices in terms of recreational play or educational play as well as what they perceive as key elements of each type are needed. It may also be beneficial to engage in further investigations to distinguish between play, and playful practices as well as play and active or experiential learning methods.

Teaching practices may potentially be classified into more specific types. Whereas Wood uses three modes along a continuum within her analysis, Pyle and Danniels (2017) address the variation of types within their continuum of pedagogies for play-based learning in kindergarten settings. While they provide a similar continuum that includes child directed, collaborative and teacher directed play, they indicate where each of the following types of play fit within the continuum: free play, inquiry play, collaborative play, playful learning and teaching through games. Existing categories to identify tools, techniques and tactics (Whitton, 2018), may be used in further research or new modes of play used within pedagogy may be named to better showcase what is being done in ECTE programs.

LIMITATIONS, IMPLICATIONS, AND RECOMMENDATIONS

The study described in this chapter was conducted to contribute information on how college and university instructors in 13 different ECTE programs within six different provinces and territories across Canada incorporate play within their teaching practices. The study included a small sample (19 faculty members) and relied on self-reported information. Faculty members' practices were unique to their own respective experiences and were not observed or discussed within the context of each course, group of students and respective institution. More research is needed to gain a broader and deeper understanding of what is happening in terms of play and learning with adult learners within post-secondary ECTE program within and outside of Canada.

Continuing conversations about play and curriculum for adult learners, especially with programs designed to help in fostering spaces and opportunities for children's play, are essential. Critical conversations that center on play, including content and programs outcomes are needed at the program level. What knowledge, skills, or competencies do programs aim to foster? Do program level outcomes include developing an awareness about the importance of play in the lives of early childhood educators (Nicholson et al., 2014)? Are programs open to play opportunities that provide freedom for students to perform who they are and who they are becoming (Lobman & Perone, 2018)?

Conversations thus need to focus on instructors teaching within ECTE program. ECTE has been viewed to operate within a larger early childhood professional development system, in which faculty, pedagogy and content are all seen as key players in higher education (Hyson, Horm & Winton, 2012). What instructors do and how they do it may impact student learning and yet what teacher educators do is by and large unexamined within educational research (Kemple et al., 2015). Continued research and ongoing conversations with instructors in ECTE programs will help showcase instructors' practices, encourage teacher research and can improve practices for quality teaching and learning experiences with preservice educators. It is also important to learn more about play as an educative process to benefit preservice educators and the young children they will be working and playing with in the future.

Perceptions of how preservice educators are engaging in play-pedagogy, what they are taking away from it (and if such practices are even considered 'play') may differ between instructors and students themselves. It is imperative that ongoing investigations include the students' voices. These insights will contribute to understanding what the place of play is in pedagogies in ECTE programs, as well as their effectiveness. Findings indicated that faculty members unanimously agreed that support within the ECTE programs and institutions helped with the implementation of play-based practices in university and college classrooms. ECTE programs need to find ways to acknowledge and encourage play for adult learners in post-secondary classrooms. Conducive spaces, moveable furniture, and access to materials can support innovative and play-based practices. Visionary leadership that creates a culture for innovative instructional practice in higher education along with recognition for instructors who plan, develop and lead educational innovation are needed (Lock, Kim, Koh & Wilox, 2018).

By the time they arrive in ECTE post-secondary settings, students have learned how to be students (Lobman & Perone, 2018), have expectations about formal education settings and bring culturally framed notions of play. Students' ideas of what is or is not play and beliefs about the role of play in educational contexts may be very different. Efforts are needed to help instructors create inclusive environments and meet the needs of various students while navigating beliefs and understandings about play within and across

ECTE settings. To foster quality learning experiences, instructors need pedagogical competencies. Yet many universities around the globe do not require or provide such pedagogical training (Kaynardağ, 2019). Instructors, with the help of professional development initiatives, may develop pedagogical knowledge and competencies needed to design, facilitate and justify active, collaborative and experiential methods that allow students to take ownership and control of their own learning in college or university contexts.

When asked about recommendations for professional development, all faculty members in the study voiced that professional development on play and learning would be beneficial for instructors. Experiential and research-based professional development initiatives, tailored to the needs and interest areas of attendees, were recommended. Even though initiatives that center on play in higher education may not necessarily be embraced or funded, professional development on play was deemed beneficial for faculty across institutions, including faculty in programs other than ECTE. By listening to those who teach in ECTE settings, we may learn more as to what is happening and what can be done in terms of play *in* and *as* higher education.

Opportunities for instructors to reflect on their own notions of play as well as practices they implement in higher education may be beneficial. Entwistle (2018) suggests that the individual instructor is the only one who can decide specific implications that have an impact on one's teaching. Individual program and institutional requirements may also influence what can or cannot be done within instructors' courses. Encouraging more open dialogue with faculty about their practices and providing more opportunities to engage in teacher inquiry or action research may thus help generate insight about what ECTE instructors are doing as well as what issues they may be grappling with themselves. Teacher inquiry may not only help instructors' own teaching practices, it may help model reflective practices to students (Kemple et al., 2015). Case studies on instructors' practices and student feedback, which provide a rich detailed look at conditions for play *in* and *as* education are recommended, including the interplay between modes of play that are contextualized based on ECTE programs in higher education settings.

Teaching is multifaceted and involves various factors including the context in which it takes place (Entwistle, 2018). When considering the ways in which play is incorporated *in* and *as* education in ECTE contexts, influential factors like those elicited in this study need to be taken into consideration. It must also be acknowledged that factors do not operate in isolation (Lock et al., 2018), when describing how instructors are expected to incorporate innovative pedagogical practices in higher education, argue that conflicting views at micro- (classroom or practicum), macro- (program) and meso- (institution) levels must be navigated in a way to support such innovations.

Further research is needed on factors that may support or impede instructors' play-based teaching practices in ECTE programs to be able to improve policies and practices.

It was revealed that an overemphasis on achievement in education was one of many factors that faculty members perceived to hinder play in post-secondary ECTE classrooms. This is in accordance with Nørgard, et al. (2017) who argue that there will always be a conflict between intrinsic motivation to learn and goal-oriented behaviors and extrinsic rewards in higher education. Implementing 'play *as* education' in higher education settings, where quantifiable assessments and outcomes are a priority can be a challenging feat. ECTE programs need to create desired programs and policies, including course content and scheduling, which fit within higher educational systems, yet do not perpetuate messages that play is only meant as a tool for learning. Play can also be a way of learning in educational settings.

CONCLUSION

With increasingly more examples of play-based teaching and learning in higher education as well as support for learner-centered, active, collaborative, experiential and innovative practices, now is an opportune time to advocate for play and adult learning. This is especially pertinent for early childhood teacher education programs, where play content and play pedagogy can provoke discussions and understandings about children's play as well as potentially provide opportunities for adult learners to experience the value of play.

Examples from a qualitative study, which explored instructors' teaching practices in post-secondary ECTE programs, provided the foundation to examine how play is incorporated in the education of pre-service educators in Canada as well as influential factors. Practices were deemed to fit within Wood's (2014) notion of 'play *in* education' as compared to play *as* education. This chapter only begins to address some of the nuances involved within the play-pedagogy interface in hopes to provide insights for further conversations. Based on the findings, suggestions and considerations for adapting modes used within Wood's analysis, were outlined.

One main implication centers on ECTE programs doing what they can to ensure students' learning experiences in formal education settings, develop understandings about what play is, as well as ways to implement sound play-pedagogies with young children in educational contexts. Due to the key role ECTE instructors have in preparing pre-service educators to work with young children, instructors must be provided support and be given a voice within discourses on play and learning in higher education. Ongoing inquiries on play and learning can provide more insights and support for play *in* and *as* education, regardless of one's age.

REFERENCES

Association of American Colleges & Universities (n.d.). High-impact practices. Retrieved from: https://www.aacu.org/leap/hips

Attride-Stirling, J. (2001). Thematic networks: An analytic tool for qualitative research. *Qualitative Research, 1*(3), 385–405.

Ayling, P. (2012). Learning through playing in higher education: Promoting play as a skill for social work students. *Social Work Education, 31*(2), 764–777.

Barr, R. B. & Tagg, J. (1995). From teaching to learning: A new paradigm for undergraduate education. *Change, 27,* (6), 12–26.

Blom, M., & D'Amico, M. (2016). Using images to capture faculty's beliefs about play and learning in early childhood education and care settings. *Journal of Studies in Education, 6*(4), 93–109. http://dx.doi.org/10.5296/jse.v6i4.10151.

Blom, M., & Henle, S. (2013, March). Play as a pathway for teaching and learning in higher education. Paper presented at The Association for the Study of Play and American Association for the Child's Right to Play (IPA/USA) joint conference, Newark, DE.

Bredikyte, M. & Hakkarainen, P. (2011). Play intervention and play development. In C. Lobman, B. O'Neill Eds.), *Play and performance* (pp. 59–83). Lanham: University Press of America.

Entwistle, N. (2018). *Student learning and academic understanding: A research perspective with implications for teaching.* London, UK: Academic Press.

Entwistle, E. (2011). Taking stock: An overview of key research findings . In Christensen Hughes, J. & Mighty, J. (Eds.). *Taking stock: Research on teaching and learning in higher education,* (pp. 15–60). Kingston, ON: Queen's University, School of Policy Studies.

Fromberg. D. P. (1999). A review of research on play. In C. Seefeldt (Ed.), *The early childhood curriculum: Current findings in theory and practice* (pp. 27–53). New York: Teachers College Press.

Goldmintz, Y., & Schaefer, G. E. (2007). Why play matters to adults. *Psychology and Education, 44*(1), 12–25.

Graue, E. (2010). Reimagining kindergarten. *The Education Digest, 17,* 28–34.

Gray, P. (2011). The decline of play and the rise of psychopathology in children and adolescents. *American Journal of Play, 3*(4), 443–463.

Harris, P. (2007). Developing an integrated play-based pedagogy in preservice teacher education: A self-study. *Studying Teacher Education, 3(2),* 135–154.

Harris, P., & Daley, J. (2008). Exploring the contribution of play to social capital in institutional adult learning settings. *Australian Journal of Adult Learning, 48*(1), 50–70.

Hasan, A. (2012). Lifelong learning in OECD and developing countries: An interpretation and assessment. In: D. Aspin, J. Chapman, K. Evans & R. Bagnall (Eds.)

Second international handbook of lifelong learning, (pp. 471–48). New York: Springer.

Hewes, J. (2006). *Let the children play: Nature's answer to early learning.* Montreal: Early Childhood Learning Knowledge Center, Canadian Council on Learning.

Hyvonen, P. T. (2011). Play in the school context? The perspectives of Finnish teachers. *Australian Journal of Teacher Education, 36*(8). Retrieved from http://ro.ecu.edu.au/ajte/vol36/iss8/.

Hyson, M., Horm, D. M., & Winton, P. J. (2012). Higher education for early childhood educators and outcomes for young children: Pathways toward greater effectiveness. In R. Pianta, L. Justice, S. Barnett, & S. Sheridan (Eds.), *Handbook of early education* (pp. 553–583). New York, NY: Guilford Press.

Jacobs, E., & Adrien, E. (2012). Canadian child care regulations regarding training and curriculum. In N. Howe & L. Prochner (Eds.), *Recent perspectives on early childhood education and care in Canada,* (pp. 109–146). Toronto, ON: University of Toronto Press.

James, A. (2013). Lego serious play: A three-dimensional approach to learning development, *Journal of Learning Development in Higher Education, 6*(6), p. 18.

James, A. & Brookfield, S. (2014). *Engaging imagination: Helping students become creative and reflective thinkers.* San Francisco, CA: Jossey Bass.

James, A., &, Nerantzi, C. (2019). *The power of play in higher education: Creativity in tertiary learning.* London, UK: Palgrave Macmillan.

Johnson, J. E. (2016). Play and early childhood education. In D. Couchenou & J. K. Chrisman (Eds.), *The SAGE Encyclopedia of Contemporary Early Childhood Education* (Vol. 3, pp. 1017–1024). Thousand Oaks, CA: SAGE. Retrieved from https://doi: 10.4135/9781483340333.

Johnson, J. E. (2014). What is the state of play? *International Journal* of Play, *3*(1), 4-5. https://doi.org/10.1080/21594937.2014.891359.

Kaynardağ, A. Y. (2019). Pedagogy in HE: Does it matter? *Studies in Higher Education, 44*(1), 111-119. http://dx.doi.org/10.1080/03075079.2017.1340444.

Kemple, K. M., Oh, J. H., & Porter, D. (2015) Playing at school: An inquiry approach to using an experiential play lab in an early childhood teacher education course. *Journal of Early Childhood Teacher Education, 36*(3), 250-265. http://dx.doi.org/10.1080/10901027.2015.1062830.

King, N. (1986). When educators study play in schools. *Journal of Curriculum and Supervision, 1*(3), 233–246.

King, N., & Horrocks, C. (2010). *Interviews in qualitative research.* London: Sage.

Kinzie, J. (2011). Student engagement and learning: Experiences that matter. In J. C. Hughes, & Mighty, J. (Eds.), *Taking stock: Research on teaching and learning in higher education,* (pp. 139–154). Kingston, ON: Queen's University, School of Policy Studies.

Kolb, A. Y. & Kolb, D. A. (2010). Learning to play, playing to learn: A case study of a ludic learning space. *Journal of Organizational Change Management, 23* (1), 26–50.

Lewis, P. J. (2017). The erosion of play. *International Journal of Play*, 6(1), 10–23. http://dx.doi.org/10.1080/21594937.2017.1288391.

Lobman, C. (2005). "Yes and": The uses of improvisation for early childhood professional development. *Journal of Early Childhood Teacher Education, 26*(3), 305–319.

Lobman, C. & Perone, T. (Eds.) (2018). *Big ideas and revolutionary activity: Selected essays, talks and articles by Lois Holzman*. New York: East Side Institute.

Lock, J., Kim, B., Koh, K., & Wilcox, G. (2018). Navigating the tensions of innovative assessment and pedagogy in higher education. *The Canadian Journal for the Scholarship of Teaching and Learning, 9*(1). https://doi.org/10.5206/cjsotl-rcacea.2018.1.8

Lord, A., & McFarland, L. (2010). Pre-service primary teachers' perceptions of early childhood philosophy and pedagogy: A case study examination. *Australian Journal of Teacher Education, 35*(3), 1–13.

Marton, F. & Säljö, R. (1976). On qualitative differences in learning I: Outcome and process. *British Journal of Educational Psychology, 46*, 4–11.

Meyer, E. (2010). *From workplace to playspace: Innovating, learning, and changing through dynamic engagement*. San Francisco, CA : Jossey-Bass.

Miller, E., & Almon, J. (2009). Crisis in the kindergarten: Why children need to play in school. *The Educational Digest, 75*, 42–45.

Moyles, J. (Ed.). (2010). *The excellence of play* (3rd ed.). Berkshire: Open University Press.

Nell, M. L. & Drew, W. F. (2013). *From play to practice: Connecting teachers' play to children's learning*. Washington, DC: NAEYC.

Nicholson, J., Shimpi, P. M., & Rabin, C. (2014). If I am not doing my own playing then I am not able to truly share the gift of play with children: Using poststructuralism and care ethics to examine future early childhood educators' relationships with play in adulthood. *Early Child Development and Care, 184*(8), 1192–1210.

Nørgård, R. T., Toft-Nielsen, C. & Whitton, N. (2017). Playful learning in higher education: Developing a signature pedagogy. *International Journal of Play, 6*(3), 272–282. http://dx.doi.org/10.1080/21594937.2017.1382997

Patte, M. (2012). Implementing a playful pedagogy in a standards-driven curriculum: Rationale for action research in teacher education. In L. E. Cohen & S. Waite-Stupiansky (Eds.), *Play: A polyphony of research, theories, and issues: Play and culture studies*, Vol. 12, (pp. 67–89). Lanham, MD: University Press of America.

Pyle, A., & Danniels, E. (2016). A continuum of play-based learning: The role of the teacher in a play-based pedagogy and the fear of hijacking play. *Early Education & Development*. http://dx.doi.org/10.1080/10409289.2016.1220771

Ranz-Smith, D. J. (2007). Teacher perception of play: In leaving no child behind are teachers leaving childhood behind? *Early Education & Development, 18*(2), 271–303. *3*(1), 63–77. http://dx.doi.org/10.5278/ojs.jpblhe.v3i1.1203

Saracho, O. (2012). *An integrated play-based curriculum for young children*. New York, NY: Routledge.

Scott, C. L. (2015). *The Futures of Learning 3: What Kind of Pedagogies for the 21st Century?* (ERF Working Papers Series, No. 15). Paris: UNESCO Education Research and Foresight.

Thorsted, A. C., Bing, R. G., & Kristensen, M. (2015). Play as mediator for knowledge-creation in Problem Based Learning. *Journal of Problem Based Learning in Higher Education*, 3(1), 63–77.

Trawick-Smith, J. (2012). Teacher-child play interactions to achieve learning outcomes in preschool: Risks and opportunities. In R. Pianta, S. Barnett, L. Justice, & S. Sheridan (Eds.), *Handbook of Early Childhood Education*. New York: Guilford.

Universities Canada (2018). Investing in skills and talent to build a better Canada. Retrieved from: https://www.univcan.ca/media-room/publications/investing-in-skills-and-talent-to-build-a-better-canada/jj

Vu, J. A., Han, M., & Buell, M. J. (2012). Preserving play in early childhood classrooms: Suggestions for early childhood teacher education and policy. In L. E. Cohen & S. Waite-Stupiansky (Eds.), *Play a polyphony of research, theories, and issues: Play and culture studies*, Vol. 12, (pp. 207–221). Lanham, MD: University Press of America.

Whitton, N. (2018). Playful learning: Tools, techniques and tactics. *Research in Learning Technology, 26*. http://dx.doi.org/10.25304/rlt.v26.2035

Wood, E. A. (2014). The play–pedagogy interface in contemporary debates. In L. Brooker, M. Blaise, & S. Edwards (Eds.), *The Sage handbook of play and learning in early childhood* (pp. 145–156). Los Angeles, CA: Sage.

Wood, E., & Attfield, J. (2005). *Play, learning and the early childhood curriculum* (2 ed.). London: Paul Chapman.

Yogman, M., Garner, A., Hutchinson J, Hirsh-Pasek, K, & Golinkoff, R. M. (2018). The power of play: A pediatric role in enhancing development in young children. *Pediatrics. 142*(3). Retrieved from: http://pediatrics.aappublications.org/content/142/3/e20182058

APPENDIX:
LIST OF QUESTIONS AND INTERVIEW PROTOCOLS

Demographic Questions and Questions about How People Learn

Written responses to the following questions were collected prior to the first semi-structured interview:

1. Gender? Age?
2. What is your history of employment within the field of ECEC? Please elaborate.
3. Where are you currently employed?
4. What is your title?
5. How long have you been working in a post-secondary ECE program?
6. Do you have a teaching role within the post-secondary institution?
7. What courses are/have you taught?

8. Where did you receive your formal training in ECEC? Please describe your training (length, focus, type of program).
9. What are your views on how children learn?
   Do children learn in different ways? Please describe how.
   What do you think is most important when working with young children?
10. What are your views on how adults learn?
    Do adults learn in different ways? Please describe how.
    What do you think is most important when working with adult learners?

INTERVIEW PROTOCOL:
INTERVIEW 1 (BELIEFS ABOUT PLAY AND LEARNING)

To help get to know you a bit better, let us take a few minutes to go over the questions you had answered prior to this interview. Please feel free to add anything or correct me if I have misinterpreted anything.

Now, as we had previously discussed, you were asked to select two images for this conversation. These images will be the basis of our discussion about your beliefs about play and learning.

Part A. Image–beliefs about play and learning for children in Early Childhood Education and Care (ECEC) settings

1. Tell me about the image you have selected.
2. Why did you select this particular image?
3. What is it about the image that specifically speaks to you about play and learning with children in ECEC settings?

Possible prompts (if needed)

- time and opportunity for children's play and learning
- access for children's play and learning
- space for children's play and learning
- materials/equipment for children's play and learning
- children's choice/initiative in play and learning
- the early childhood educator's role in promoting children play

4. How do you see the difference between play versus playful, playfulness, or playful practice?
5. Is there anything else you would like to add?

Part B. Image–beliefs about play and learning for adult learners in post-secondary Early Childhood Teacher Education (ECTE) settings

1. Tell me about the image you have selected.
2. Why did you select this particular image?
3. What is it about the image that specifically speaks to you about play and learning with adult learners in Early Childhood Teacher Education settings?

Possible prompts (if needed)

- time and opportunity in regard to play and adult learning
- access in regard to play and adult learning
- space in regard play and adult learning
- materials/equipment in regard to play and adult learning
- adult learners' choice/initiative in play and learning
- the instructor (faculty)'s role in adult play and learning

4. Is there anything else you would like to add?

Part C–Overall reflections on play and learning

I notice (similarities/differences) between the two images you provided . . .

1. Tell me more about how you see place and learning for children in ECEC (vs./and) for adult learners in ECTE settings.
2. Anything else you would like to add?

Before our second interview I would like you to write a short narrative about how you put your beliefs into practice when teaching upcoming early childhood educators in the post-secondary ECTE program in which you work.

INTERVIEW PROTOCOL:
INTERVIEW 2 (PLAY-BASED PRACTICES IN ECTE)

During our last conversation we looked at images you had selected and discussed your beliefs about play and learning. We are now going to talk about your teaching practices. In preparation, you were asked to reflect upon our last discussion and write a short narrative about how you put your beliefs into practice when teaching upcoming early childhood educators in the post-secondary ECTE program in which you work.

1. Tell me about what you have written.
2. Can you give an example of how you implemented your beliefs about play and learning in one of your classrooms?
3. I would like to hear more. Tell me more details.

Possible prompts (if needed):

- What was your role? What did you do?
- What did your students do?
- What kind of materials/equipment were used?
- What kind of space was created to encourage this?
- Is this what you had initially intended?
- How did it turn out? Did you meet your goals? Why or why not?
- Is there anything you would do differently?
- How does this reflect your beliefs about play and learning for children or adult learners (or both)?

4. Can you think of any factors that help you put your beliefs about play into practice when teaching upcoming early childhood educators?
5. Can you think of any factors that hinder the implementation of your beliefs?
6. What kinds of professional development opportunities about play and ECEC have you been involved in?
7. Would you find it beneficial to have professional development initiative specific to play for faculty working in Early Childhood Teacher Education programs? If so, what could these initiatives focus on? What would you include and how would you structure it?

Once these interviews have been transcribed, they will be sent back to you along with your narrative. At that time, if there is anything you would like to add or change you will have an opportunity to do so.

Chapter Eight

Learning, NOT Playing

Mixed Method Analysis of Early Childhood Preservice Teachers' Perceptions on Children's Play

Ilfa Zhulamanova

An extensive body of research suggests that play offers a multi-faceted educational impact and educates children intellectually, emotionally, socially and physically (Bergen, 2009; Prager, Sera, & Carlson, 2016; Thibodeau, Gilpin, Brown, Brooke, & Meyera, 2016; Wood & Attfied, 2005). However, play in early childhood education is on a decline. For example, comparing public school kindergarten classrooms between 1998 and 2010 using two large, nationally representative data sets, Bassok, Latham, and Rorem (2016) found that, in the later period, kindergarten teachers emphasized advanced literacy and math content, teacher-directed instruction, and assessment and considerably less time spent on art, music, science, and child-selected activities. As kindergarten has become heavily focused on teaching literacy and other academic skills, "preschools are rapidly moving in that same direction" (Miller & Almon, 2009, p. 7).

Researchers maintain that the majority of the early childhood teachers believe in play and the advantages it offers (Lynch, 2015; McLane, 2003; Nicolopoulou, 2011; Sisson & Kroeger, 2017). However, constraints of time and resources in combination with the pressure of accountability and testing seem to compel teachers to return to a back-to-basics curriculum and to focus on narrowly defined outcomes (Lynch, 2015; Nicolopoulou, 2011). To reverse this negative tendency, early childhood teacher educators in many universities work diligently to teach preservice teachers about the importance of play during a child's early years. Yet, when placed in schools for their student teaching fieldwork, many pre-service teachers align their perceptions about play with the reality they observe, in which play is devalued (Jung & Jin, 2014; Jung & Jing, 2015). Therefore, the challenge today is to prepare pre-service teachers for the education field in which, "child-initiated play-based curriculum, standards-based curriculum, and accountability issues frequently collide" (Jung & Jin, 2014, p. 358).

TEACHER EDUCATION AND PLAY

Although there has been considerable evidence supporting the effectiveness of learning through play, scholarly discussion of play in teacher education is still limited (Miller & Almon, 2009, Jung, Zhang & Zhang, 2016). Close examination of existing studies on preservice teachers' beliefs on play indicates that play, as a concept, does not have a shared meaning. Multiple meanings and contradictions present within the preservice teachers' beliefs about play highlight the challenges of defining and conceptualizing play within teacher education (Klugman, 1996; Sherwood & Riefel, 2010;). Yet, it is important to understand how preservice teachers perceive play since, as research shows, the perspectives they hold as future educators before beginning intensive instruction will have a vital role in how they will be able to link play and curriculum in an early childhood setting (Jung & Jing, 2014; Klugman, 1996; Jung, Zhang, & Zhang, 2016).

In this study, "preservice teachers" specifically refers to those individuals seeking initial licensure in a four-year higher education program leading the students to a Bachelor of Science in Education degree in Early Childhood Education (ECED) preparing teachers for preschool through third grade. All students complete field and practicum experiences with students at earlier stages of the program being paced in toddlers, preschool and kindergarten and primary grades classrooms as they move up within the program.

As for the concept of play, in the context of school, play is best viewed as a continuum with guided play on one end and free play on the other (Miller & Almon, 2009). Typically, playful learning includes both guided play and free play (Bodrova & Leong, 2010; Reed, Hirsh-Pasek, & Golinkoff, 2012). Usually play is described as an intrinsically motivated, enjoyable, process-oriented, non-realistic, and self-chosen activity (Hirsh-Pasek Golinkoff,Berk, & Singer., 2009; Krasnor & Pepler, 1980). Play as "playful learning" is a focus of this study.

The concept of perception, according to Leibniz is "the expression of many things in one" (as cited in Kulstad, 1982, p. 66); in other words, a sensation along with an image. In its relevance to this study, perception includes the meanings of knowledge, beliefs, attitude, value, feeling, thinking, and implicit theory.

DESCRIPTION OF THE STUDY

The study is a part of a larger participant-selection model mixed methods investigation. Participant-selection model is a variation of the sequential explanatory mixed methods research design that prioritizes the qualitative phase of the study instead of the initial quantitative phase (Creswell & Plano Clark, 2007). The study was conducted at one of the Midwestern universities' early childhood undergraduate education programs in the United States. Within the program, 241 students at different stages, Cohort I (second semester, sophomore year), Cohort II (first semester junior year), Cohort III (second semester junior year), Cohort IV (first semester senior year), and Cohort V (second semester senior year), completed two online surveys–Instrument I (Part A & B) and Instrument II (Future Professionals' Survey). The results of the surveys were used for the selection of 10 participants for the qualitative segment of the study. The participants were selected from the sample pool of 71 survey respondents, who provided contact information and also indicated that they were willing to participate in a follow up interview. The criteria for the inclusion was the "extreme or outlier cases" (Creswell, 2014). Thus, two participants from each cohort, one demonstrating the most positive attitude (highest mean score on the survey) and the least positive attitude towards play (lowest mean score on the survey) were selected and interviewed for the qualitative part of the study.

The study utilized mixed method. The quantitative question aimed to explore how the preservice teachers' attitudes towards play and the role of play in learning and curriculum differ among five cohorts of students. The qualitative inquiry focused on preservice teachers' beliefs about play and the factors that contributed to their understanding of play. Finally, the mixed methods segment was designed to explain perspectives on how play contributes to children's learning by comparing and contrasting the qualitative findings with the quantitative results.

QUANTITATIVE STUDY

Participants

Normally, within an Early Childhood Education program, students form a cohort to complete a five-cohort sequence of courses, while gaining teaching experiences linked to coursework. The participants in this study included 241 students (Cohort I–second semester sophomore year; Cohort II–first semester junior year; Cohort III–second semester junior year, Cohort IV–first semester senior year, and Cohort V–second semester senior year) were taking courses for their major in early childhood education.

Demographic questions, including those related to age, gender, ethnicity, and education levels (Cohort) , were asked in a separate section of the survey research. Of the 241 participating students, 233 (96.7 percent) were female and 8 (3.3 percent) were male. Additionally, there were 54 students (22.4 percent) in Cohort I, 41 (17 percent) in Cohort II students, 61 (25.3 percent) in Cohort III, 44 (18.3 percent) in Cohort IV and 41 (17 percent) in Cohort V who completed the study surveys. Participants' ages ranged from 19 to 38 with an average age of 21.1 ($SD = 1.795$). Of the group, 231 students were White, 10 (4.1 percent) were nonwhite. 239 students were born in the US.

Data Collection

The quantitative data were collected using two Likert Scale instruments–Instrument I (Part A & B) and Instrument II (Future Professionals' Survey). For the purposes of the present study, only Instrument II is described.

Future Professional's Survey (FPS) Likert scale, developed and tested previously by Jung and Jin (2014), was used in this study to measure participants' understanding of play and the role of play in learning and curriculum. The survey questions design was guided by conceptual and educational literature. Participants' responses were rated on a scale from 1 (strongly disagree), 2 (disagree), 3 (somewhat agree), 4 (neutral), 5 (agree), to 6 (strongly agree).

The survey questions are presented below:

1. Play will continue to be important in educational settings.
2. Play is important to the development of social skills in children.
3. Play is important to the development of emotional skills in children.
4. I do not believe the use of play in teaching would support students' learning.
5. Integrating play in teaching will help my future students' learning.
6. Play helps children to learn effectively.
7. Use of play promotes learning.
8. Play is important to the development of cognitive skills in children.
9. Using play stimulates interest in subject matter.
10. The play-based curriculum is confusing to me.
11. Children learn better from classrooms with standards-based curriculum than play-based curriculum.

Data Analysis

For analysis purposes, the 11 survey items were classified into three main groups–Importance of Play in Classroom, Role of Play in Learning, and Role of Play as Curriculum–identified by previous researchers (Jun & Jing, 2014), in the following manner: Importance of Play in Classroom (Play will continue to be important in educational settings, Play is important for development of social skill in children, Play is important for development of emotional skills in children, I do not believe the use of play in teaching would support students' learning), Role of Play in Learning (Integrating play in teaching will help my future students' learning, Play helps children to learn effectively, Use of play promotes learning, play is important to the development of cognitive skills in children, Using play stimulates interest in subject matter), Role of Play as Curriculum (Play-based curriculum is confusing to me, Children learn better from classrooms with standards-based curriculum than play-based curriculum).

Results

The scores of items on each scale were averaged for mean values of the data. Descriptive information about these ratings, including means, standard deviations are presented in Table 8.1.

Table 8.1. Descriptive Statistics for Items on Importance of Play in Learning and Curriculum

	Mean	SD	Alpha
Importance of Play in Classroom			.685
Play will continue to be important in educational settings	5.51	1.033	
Play is important to the development of social skills in children	5.85	.681	
Play is important to the development of emotional skills in children	5.80	.758	
I do not believe the use of play in teaching would support students' learning	5.66	.899	
Role of Play in Learning			.934
Integrating play in teaching will help my future students' learning	5.67	.778	
Play helps children to learn effectively	5.63	.759	
Use of play promotes learning	5.69	.789	
Play is important to the development of cognitive skills in children	5.76	.677	
Using play stimulates interest in subject matter	5.71	.687	
Role of Play as Curriculum			.522
Play-based curriculum is confusing to me	4.65	1.333	
Children learn better from classrooms with standards-based curriculum than play-based curriculum	4.44	1.454	

On this instrument, the "Play is important to the development of social skills in children" item indicated the highest level of agreement among the five cohorts ($M = 5.85$), followed by "Play is important to the development of emotional skills in children" ($M = 5.80$) and "Play is important to the development of cognitive skills in children" ($M = 5.76$) items. Two reverse-coded items, "Play-based curriculum is confusing to me" ($M = 4.65$) and "Children learn better from classrooms with standards-based curriculum than play-based curriculum" ($M = 4.44$) had lower means, indicating a lower level of agreement among the five groups. These two items under the third category of the survey had larger standard deviation. High standard deviation indicates that the data points are spread out over a wider range of values indicating considerable variability in views among the participants on these two items.

Results of inferential statistics. Due to violations of the assumption of homogeneity of variance on Levene's test, the Kruskal-Wallis, nonparametric statistical test was used to examine a difference in preservice teachers' (Cohort I, Cohort II, Cohort III, Cohort IV and Cohort V) levels of agreement with the three scales: Importance of Play, Role of Play in Learning, and Role of Play as Curriculum.

According to the Kruskal-Wallis test results, the Role of Play as Curriculum scale had significant differences in the mean scores. According to Post Hoc test results, significant difference in mean scores was found between Cohort III and Cohort V on this scale ($p = 002$, $p < .01$). Cohort III students had a significantly more positive attitude towards the Role of Play as Curriculum (items included "Play-based curriculum is confusing to me" and "Children learn better from classrooms with standards -based curriculum than play-based curriculum") than Cohort V participants. In order to understand further about the differences between these two cohorts (III and V), the following qualitative study was conducted.

QUALITATIVE STUDY

Participants

The survey results were used to select participants for the qualitative part of the study. The selected participants for semi-structured interviews, two from each group (Cohort III and Cohort V), were invited to elaborate and explain the responses they gave on the survey. The Cohort III students' coursework relates to subjects including Phonics, Mathematics, online course IB-Primary Year Programme, Home-School Community Partnerships and Integrated Social Studies. They usually spend two days a week in kindergarten or primary classrooms with additional focus fields in math and literacy. The Cohort

V students teach in a kindergarten or primary class for five days a week throughout the length of one semester (15 weeks) and take a Student Teaching Seminar class.

Data Collection

The qualitative data were collected through semi-structured individual interviews during which the participants were invited to elaborate and explain the responses that they gave on the survey. During the interview, in order to elicit the earlier pre-existing perceptions on play, the participant were asked, to draw in three to five minutes the specific play activities they engaged in childhood. These drawings were used a starting point for the conversation to ask open-ended questions like tell me about what is going on in your drawing, how old are you in that picture, was it outside or inside, was it imaginative play or physical, how is that play, what other kinds of play do you remember from your own childhood, what types of play do you remember from school. Other questions were designed around information gleaned from individual responses on the survey. Qualitative data were then analyzed and compared with the survey results.

Analysis

Data collection and analysis are not separate processes but are interconnected and simultaneous (Hesse-Biber & Leavy, 2006). Inductive analysis (Hatch, 2002) that promotes proceeding from specific to general was used to analyze and gain insight into the interview data. Thematic coding was used for gaining insight into the interview data to identify influences impacting preservice teachers' perceptions of play and thus casted light on the numerical data.

Findings

Interview participants defined play as a creative, imaginative, engaging, fun, enjoyable, self-chosen and child-driven activity which is essential for learning, and pointed out that in play, children naturally learn numbers, patterns, and classifications. Through play, in their views, children also easily acquire content knowledge of subjects such as math, literacy, or science and develop socially, emotionally, cognitively, and physically.

Close examination of these four interview participants' perceptions of play revealed, however, that while they agreed on some qualitative aspects of play, there is not one common definition of play among this group and not one respondent defined play the same as a peer did. For example, during her interview, Mary (Cohort III) from the lower end of the play attitude spectrum, shared that she was the youngest of three children in her family. As a child, she liked to play outside, explore nature, play with rocks, swim, skate on her rollerblades, and play in the basement of her friend's home. She liked to watch Disney movies and to reenacting the roles allowed her to show "what we wanted to be when we grew up . . . even . . . just fantasy of . . . I'm a princess, I'm important . . . " Mary also recalled playing volleyball and soccer with her older brother and a lot of playing board games with her family. In response to, "What is play?" Mary stated:

> *I think just getting their energy out, a lot of the times, and using their creative side of what they're wanting to do. Without . . . being forced into . . . a structure play, or . . . maybe not structured play, but being forced into . . . their school-work or anything, it's their time to do their own thing, and . . . feel . . . they have control of what they're doing.*

From these lines, it is evident that for Mary, play activity should be completely unstructured, not related to any type of schoolwork, creative and owned and driven by children. When asked if she would consider reading a book and singing ABCs as play, Mary stated that she would not consider reading a book as play because: "I feel a lot [of times] when I was younger, reading was forced upon me, so I never thought of reading as play." She did consider singing ABC as play, however, because she liked to sing as child and remembered doing musicals and performances. Thus, Mary's definition of play demonstrates the influence of her individual and personal experiences.

The second participant from Cohort III, Danielle, who had higher scores on the play attitude spectrum than Mary, came from a family of four children. She remembered playing in the park and swinging on the swings on her way from school. When she was young, Danielle liked riding bikes, scooters, rollerblades, swimming in a pool, playing tag, playing outside and engaging in different games with her siblings. She also liked to play with dolls like Bratz and American dolls and building Legos and Lincoln Logs.

When asked how she would define play, Danielle said, "I would say engaging and . . . using your imagination to create a world even, or something you want to be in or something that you like to do." While Mary and Danielle's definition of play overlap in terms of freedom, intrinsic motivation, and structure, noticeably the creative aspect of play is very important for Danielle. Such personal perception shapes her understanding. Danielle's response to whether she would consider reading a book as play was, "Yes, just because it's so creative. . . . Someone is telling a story and you can dive into a book and figure out what someone else was thinking or what they want you to see or even what you are creating in your mind." Thus, while both Mary and

Danielle define play is similar ways, their personal childhood experiences with play seem to shape their understandings and perceptions of what constitutes play.

The difference in perceptions is also evident between two Cohort V participants, Lily and Holly. During her interview, Lily, who was chosen from the lowest end of the play attitude spectrum, said that in her childhood she liked to play with dolls, stuffed animals, puzzles, and Legos. Lily also liked reading, board games, taking on roles or dressing up, watching TV shows, riding bikes, and playing outside in her neighborhood. Lily loved to engage in imaginative play activities with her younger sister. She defined play in the following way:

> I think it's an imaginative kind of thing. I think play is children creating characters, or creating . . . structures using different materials, and creating storylines with it. Play could even be . . . children painting or creating a picture, and telling a story about it, or putting their own ideas out there. Rather than just sitting.

Clearly Lily's definition of play is very broad. As did Mary and Danielle, she perceived play as an imaginative and creative activity used by children to express themselves. Lily, unlike Danielle, did not oppose the idea of considering reading a book as play but she was not completely open to it either. Additionally, Lily was fully opposed to considering a scientific experiment as play because, "science is a content part of the day and is therefore seen solely as education, not play." Thus, it is evident that even at the last stage of the program Lily still holds on to her own definition of play and views play and schooling as two separate concepts.

Holly, a Cohort V student from the positive end of the play attitude spectrum, considered reading a book and doing a scientific experiment as play. During the interview she recalled playing mostly in dramatic play. She also enjoyed engaging in free play using dolls and open-ended natural materials, reading, and making stories. As she reflected, ". . . I would read book by making up the stories. . . . And I would also play the stories out through dramatic play. That was my favorite thing to do." Holly came from a family with three children including a twin sister who rarely played with her. To try to stimulate her imagination, Holly's parents did not buy many toys for their children which encouraged Holly to use other objects in a symbolic way. She remembers turning a shelf into a doll house, playing on her own for hours and hours. After relating such experiences, Holly defined play in this way:

> It's not just a sport . . . and it's not just dramatic play, and it's not just . . . drawing . . . it's many things . . . especially as a child, it's how you express yourself, and learn and grow . . . You have all these different modalities . . . drawing,

reading . . . creating and working through your questions and your life. It's different for everyone. Like for me, it was a lot of drawing and a lot of creating of stories. But that's just where my interests were . . . for someone [else] it might be different.

Similar to Lily, Holly's definition of play is broad and includes a variety of activities and experiences of young children. Holly realizes that play can be defined differently by others. Her understanding stemmed from her experience with her twin sister, who engaged in and enjoyed completely different activities.

All four participants' definitions of play overlapped in some respects, viewing play as an open-ended, free, unstructured, creative, imaginative exploration that is driven and owned by children. However, their perceptions of play also varied. Each participant assigned her own meanings to play based on her childhood play experiences. Accordingly, these two pairs of participants, with relatively similar backgrounds and going through the same teacher education program defined play differently and expressed different understandings.

MIXED METHODS FINDINGS

Mixed methods analyses examined how the qualitative findings explained the quantitative results about the participants' perceptions on play and the role of play in learning and curriculum. The quantitative results showed that Cohort III students, compared with Cohort V students, had more positive responses on the Role of Play as Curriculum scale items which included "Play-based curriculum is confusing to me" and "Children learn better from classrooms with standards-based curriculum than play-based curriculum" than did Cohort V participants demonstrating positive attitude towards role of play in classroom curriculum. Both survey items were reverse-coded.

However, the four interview participants' opinions on these two statements were somewhat divided. For example, while Lily (Cohort V) and Danielle (Cohort III) disagreed with the statement, "Children learn better from classrooms with standards-based curriculum than play-based curriculum," Mary (Cohort III) and Holy (Cohort V) strongly agreed with the statement.

Mixed together, the quantitative results and qualitative data help to understand the difference between these two cohorts' responses, adding light to the quantitative data results. While Cohort III participants scored higher on the Role of Play as Curriculum scale demonstrating positive attitude towards role of play in classroom curriculum and Cohort V participants scored lower on this scale, the interviewees narratives reveal a lack of clarity about how play relates to child development, learning and curriculum making in early childhood classrooms. This confusion holds for both groups. For example, Mary (Cohort III): "I know it does [play stimulates cognitive development] just from my courses. But I can't think of, like, specifically how it does . . . " (Mary's interview). Similarly, on question about play and curriculum in early childhood classroom, Lily (Cohort V) states: "I know we get taught about it [play-based curriculum]– but I feel like it needs to be more in-depth of what exactly that it means and what you could be doing for it, because I know a lot of the field sites that we're placed in are not play-based at all, so it's tricky to be taught it and then not see it in practice" (Lily's interview).

These lines show that while both interviewees, at different stages within the program, strongly believe in the importance of play for learning and there is an emerging understanding of the connection between play and learning, the confusion is still present. For seniors, Cohort V, who have been in the field for many hours many and become fully aware of issues of accountability in schools, this gap in knowledge affects their perspectives and creates uncertainty toward play.

DISCUSSION

Results indicate that participants strongly believed in the importance of play and play-based education in early childhood classrooms. However, among the survey items, two items "Children learn better from classrooms with standards-based curriculum than play-based curriculum" and "Play-based curriculum is confusing to me" indicated the lesser level of agreement among the five cohorts.

The highest agreement was on the item, "Play is important to the development of social skills in children," and resembles previous research findings (Klugman, 1996). It may imply that while the participants understand the relationship between play and social development, there is a lack of clarity in their mind on how play contributes to children's cognitive and intellectual development. Exploring seven preservice teachers' perspectives on play Sherwood and Riefel (2013) also found that their understanding of play is closely related to the concept of play. Therefore, the ambiguity in preservice teachers' thinking about this term results in the confusion to connect play with learning and development. Sherwood and Reifel (2013) write that, "even though the preservice teachers could describe a range of learning opportunities offered by individual play and not-play activities, when they discussed play and not-play in more general terms they presented a narrower vision of how each one affects learning" (p. 272). Therefore, the preservice teachers believed that the "form of learning that children undergo during play do not encourage the "essential" types of cognitive development that occur in not-play activities" (p. 279).

Furthermore, in the present study, Cohort V participants had statistically significantly (p < .01) lower scores on the Role of Play as Curriculum scale ("Play-based curriculum is confusing to me" and "Children learn better from classrooms with standards-based curriculum than play-based curriculum") than did Cohort III participants. The difference in mean scores suggests that Cohort III participants have significantly more positive attitudes towards play-based curriculum than did Cohort V participants. Previous research findings (Jung & Jin, 2014) support these results, with juniors being more positive and seniors being more negative toward these statements.

One possible explanation of these results could be the participants' coursework and field placements. In their course work, the students learn how to plan lessons based on subject related standards and think about goals, objectives, and outcomes that are measurable and observable. The current test-driven environment in schools, where play is generally not much in practice, supports this type of practical orientation to teaching and learning. Thus, it is possible that seniors value play but also developed a more balanced or practical approach to learning and teaching compared to students at the earlier stages of their studies. It may also imply that students who approach their senior year in school might feel play is important, but they are not sure if they can continue to hold the same beliefs about the place of play in learning or in the curriculum. The difference in seniors' perceptions compared to earlier cohorts' perceptions may indicate that seniors may be facing a problem in integrating a play-based curriculum with the standard-based curriculum in a current test-driven educational environment of early childhood classrooms.

The interview participants' perception of play as creative, imaginative, engaging, fun, enjoyable, self-chosen, and child-driven activity is analogous with the widely accepted definition of play as an intrinsically motivated, enjoyable, process-oriented, non-realistic, and self-chosen activity (Hirsh-Pasek et al., 2009; Krasnor & Pepler, 1980). Along with the consensus in participants' perceptions, there was a disagreement within the group on a definition of play. Interestingly their responses became scattered when it came to specific play activities. For example, reading a book was considered by one participant as play and was not considered as such by another. Sherwood and Riefel's (2010) further complicate this issue stating that even when participants identify the same activities as play, their reasons for doing so vary. The participants in this study used their personal experiences with reading as a rational considering this type of activity as play or not play.

The lack of shared definition of play among this group of participants supports the idea that the construct of play is a "roomy subject, broad in human experience, rich and varies over time and place" (Eberle, 2014, p. 214). The absence of unanimity among participants on a single definition of play also shows that preservice teachers possess vastly different opinions about what does and does not constitute play. Previous researchers' findings (Lewis, 2014; Sherwood & Reifel, 2010) reflect this fact and indicate pre-service teachers' diversity of beliefs and opinions about play.

Moreover, both the survey results and interview findings revealed that study participants strongly believed in the importance of play for children's learning and development. These results are consistent with the inquiry and play-based constructivist approach to early childhood education that is emphasized by the teacher education program in which the students were enrolled. Most recent research findings fall in congruence, indicating that intentional and purposeful teaching of play at the college level positively impacts preservice teachers' perceptions on play and their intention to use play in their future classroom practices (Cevher-Kalburan, 2015; Charko, Fraser, Jones, & Umangay, 2016; Jung & Jin, 2014; Jung & Jin, 2015; Nicholson & Shimpi, 2015; Nicholson, Shimpi, & Rabin, 2014; Ridgway & Quinones, 2013; Van der Aalsvoort, Prakke, Howard, König, & Parkkinen, 2015).

However, based on mixed methods results, it can be concluded that while the participants realize that play significantly contributes to children's learning, a confusion on the relationship between play and learning seemed present. Deep-seated beliefs about play that originated in childhood may not have been fully challenged creating barriers for understanding. Unfortunately, such beliefs about play are difficult to dislodge (Leaupepe, 2009). Thus, the concepts of play and learning seemed not fully integrated in participants' minds; consequently, a fundamental link between play and learning may not have been established. Therefore, as researchers have suggested, while students might gravitate toward the progressive college agenda that emphasizes constructivist and inquiry play-based learning and teaching during their college training, it is unclear whether they will apply the gained knowledge on play in teaching and curriculum making in their future classrooms (Ahn, 2008; Jung & Jin, 2015; Jung, Zhang & Zhang, 2016).

IMPLICATIONS FOR POLICY AND PRACTICE

Although the National Association for the Education of Young Children (NAEYC) continues to emphasize the critical importance of play in children's lives and education (Copple & Bredekamp, 2009), the findings of this study illustrate the difficulty of defining and conceptualizing play in early childhood education. The absence of a shared definition of play makes it challenging to incorporate it into the teacher education program to teach students effectively. Therefore, in the light of these findings, it is suggested to re-direct the focus of early childhood teacher education program from teaching play to teaching learning.

The results of the study show that prospective teachers do have a good sense of play concept, even though their perceptions vary. What should be clarified for future teachers is the complexity of young child's cognition that is deeply rooted in sensory processes, physical development, the psyche, the social world, and linguistic experiences. When teachers have a clear understanding of how children learn, play-based instruction will occur naturally. This fundamental knowledge, hopefully, will help solve the widespread problem of academization in early childhood education as well as problems of teaching diverse learners (English language learners, children with special needs, children with trauma, low-income population children, etc.).

Learning in early childhood education cannot be limited to seeing it as "increasing quantity of (surface) knowledge and skill" (Niikkoa & Ugaste, 2019, p.48). Thus, leading organization such as NAEYC should clearly define the concept of learning in its main documents and standards, approaching it broadly and holistically. It should be defined distinctively within and between ages and stages. These changes will hopefully result in new understanding of teaching in early childhood that meets the needs of a whole child who learns, develops and constructs knowledge through play.

CONCLUSION

Overall participants generally perceived play in early childhood classrooms as important to children's learning and development. The students at earlier stage of the early childhood teacher education program held positive attitudes toward play and play-based curriculum. These perceptions were different from those of the students approaching graduation. Many seniors seemed uncomfortable about incorporating play in their classrooms. Another major finding was that play as a concept did not have a shared meaning. Preservice teachers apparently come to college with deeply seated understandings and beliefs about play—possibly gained from life and school experiences. These preconceived notions can create barriers for connecting the concept of play to learning and development. Encounters with the "realities" in the field, where play is not commonly in practice, can further deepen their confusion. Thus, preservice teachers leave teacher education programs with mixed beliefs and understandings about how play relates to teaching, learning, and curriculum-making in early childhood classrooms. The essential question about how exactly play contributes to children's learning seems left open. It can be predicted that it is more likely that preservice teachers will align their perspectives with those in the field and continue to perpetuate the existing practice in which play is devalued.

In addition to not having longitudinal data there were other limitations in this study related to reliability, homogeneity of variance and potential bias. The survey instrument used in this study had previously reported Cronbach's alpha values in the acceptable range. The widely accepted threshold for scale reliability is $\alpha > = .70$ (Nunnally, 1978). In this study, while the alpha coefficient for Importance of Play in Classroom scale was relatively close to .70, for the other two scales on the Future Professional's Survey, the alpha coefficients were well below or above the acceptable threshold of reliability (see alpha on Table 8.1). A potential source may be the limited number of items on these scales and adding more items to these two scales might significantly improve its reliability.

With the qualitative data collection process there could be a potentially unknown bias (Vogt, 2007) because the sample was purposefully selected and limited to only one early childhood education college program in the United States. Therefore, the findings represent the characteristics of the specific sample and the culture of only one program. Another limitation is that the sample population is relatively homogeneous in terms of race, gender, and age.

This research is important because every generation of preservice teachers experience differences in childhood culture and in the social structure that supports childcare and education caused by economic, political, social, technological changes in the society. Thus, it is essential to account for these varied experiences in planning programs and college-level courses (Klugman, 1996). Moreover, learning about the factors that influence preservice teachers' perceptions on play may potentially provide for teacher educators strategies on how to interrogate preservice teachers' deeply held beliefs internalized during their childhood that are not available for reflection (Leaupepe, 2009). Future researchers should conduct longitudinal studies following the same group of preservice teachers from the beginning of the teacher education program to the very end. It would be valuable to do similar studies at different colleges or universities with diverse student bodies in terms of personal and demographic background characteristics.

REFERENCES

Ahn, S. Y. (2008). Exploring constructions of the meanings of play among Korean preservice kindergarten teachers. (Dissertation thesis) Retrieved from https://search-proquest-com.proxy.library.kent.edu/docview/304183557?accoun tid=11835 (Order No. 3347872).

Bassok, D., Latham, S., & Rorem, A. (2016). Is Kindergarten the New First Grade? AERA Open. https://doi.org/10.1177/2332858415616358

Bergen, D. (2009). Play as the learning medium for future scientists, mathematicians, and engineers. *American Journal of Play*, 1 (4), 413–428

Bodrova, E., & Leong, D. J. (2010). Curriculum and play in early child development. In *Encyclopedia on Early Childhood Development.*

Cevher-Kalburan, N. (2015). Developing pre-service teachers' understanding of children's risky play. *Journal of Adventure Education and Outdoor Learning*, 15 (3), pp. 239–260.

Charko, L., Fraser, C., Jones, D., & Umangay, U. K. (2016). Faculty, candidates, and children at play: Perceptions and dissonances. In T. Brabazon & T. Brabazon (Eds.), *Play: A theory of learning and change* (pp. 55–70). Cham, Switzerland: Springer International Publishing.

Copple, C. & Bredekamp, S. (2009). *Developmentally appropriate practices in early childhood programs serving children from birth through age 8.* (3rd ed.). Washington, DC: NAEYC.

Creswell, J. W. (2014). *Research design: Qualitative, quantitative, and mixed methods approaches.* Los Angeles, CA: SAGE

Creswell, J. W., & Plano Clark, V.L. (2007). *Designing and conducting mixed methods research.* (2nd. ed.). Thousand Oaks, CA: SAGE Publications. Inc

Eberle, S.G. (2014). The elements of play: Toward a philosophy and a definition of play. *American Journal of Play,* 6(2), 214–233.

Hatch, J. A. (2002). *Doing qualitative research in education setting.* New York, NY: State University of New York Press.

Hesse-Biber, S. N., & Leavy, P. (2006). *The practice of qualitative research.* Thousand Oaks, CA: Sage Publications.

Hirsh-Pasek, K. Golinkoff, R.M., Berk, L.E., & Singer. D.G. (2009). *A mandate for playful learning in preschool: Presenting the evidence.* New York, NY: Oxford University Press.

Jung, E., & Jin, B. (2015). College coursework on children's play and future early childhood educators' intended practices: The mediating influence of perceptions of play. *Early Childhood Education Journal*, Vol. 43, pp. 299–306.

Jung, E., & Jin, B. (2014). Future professionals' perceptions of play in early childhood classrooms. *Journal of Research in Childhood Education,* 28, pp. 358–376.

Jung, E., Zhang, Y., & Zhang, Y. (2016). Future professionals' perceptions of play and intended practices: The moderating role of efficacy beliefs. *Early Childhood Development and Care.*

Klugman, E. (1996). The value of play as perceived by Wheelock college freshmen. *Playing for Keeps: Supporting Children's Play,* 2, 13–32.

Krasnor, L. R., & Pepler, D. J. (1980). The study of children's play: some suggested future directions. In K. H. Rubin (ed.). *New Directions for Child Development: Children's Play*, San Francisco: Jossey Bass.

Kulstad, M. (1982). Some difficulties in Leibniz's definition of perception. In Hooker, M. (Ed.), *Leibniz: Critical and Interpretive Essays* (pp. 65–79). Minneapolis, MN: University of Minnesota Press

Leaupepe, M. (2009). Changing student teachers' beliefs: Experiences from Pacifica early childhood teacher education in New Zealand. *Journal of the Pacific Circle Consortium for Education*, 21 (2), pp. 55–63.

Lynch, M. (2015). More play please: The perspective of kindergarten teachers on play in the classroom. *American Jornal of Play*, 7 (3), 347–369.

Lewis, M. E. (2014). *Early childhood education pre-service teachers' concepts of play* (Master's thesis). Oklahoma State University, Stillwater, Oklahoma.

McLane, J. B. (2003). "Does not." "Does too." Thinking about play in the early childhood classroom. *Erikson Institute Occasional Paper*, 4. Retrieved February 25: 2017 from http:// fwww.erikson.edu/files/nonimages/mclaneoccasional paper.pdf.

Miller, E. & Almon, J. (2009). *Crisis in the Kindergarten: Why children need to play in school.* Alliance for Childhood. College Park, MD: Alliance for Childhood

Nicholson, J., Shimpi, P. M., & Rabin, C. (2014). "If I am not doing my own playing then I am not able to truly share the gift of play with children": using poststructuralism and care ethics to examine future early childhood educators' relationships with play in adulthood. *Early Child Development and Care*, 184 (8), 1192–1210.

Nicholson, J., & Shimpi, P. M. (2015). Guiding future early childhood educators to reclaim their own play as a foundation for becoming effective advocates for children's play. Early Child Development and Care, 185 (10), 1601–1616.

Nicolopoulou, A. (2011). The alarming disappearance of play from early childhood education. *Human Development,* 53(1), 1–4.

Niikko, A. & Ugaste, A. (2019) Estonian and Finnish preschool teachers' conceptions of learning, *European Early Childhood Education Research Journal*, 27 (1), pp. 40-52, DOI:10.1080/1350293X.2018.1556533

Nunnally, J. C. (1978). *Psychometric theory* (2nd ed.). New York: McGraw-Hill.

Prager, E.O., Sera, M. D., & Carlson, S. M. (2016). Executive function and magnitude skills in preschool children. *Journal of Experimental Child Psychology, 147, 126–139*

Reed, J., Hirsh-Pasek, K., & Golinkoff, R. M. (2012). A tale of two schools: The promise of playful learning. In B. Falk (Ed.), *Defending childhood: Keeping the promise of early education.* 24–47. New York: Teachers College Press.

Ridgway, A., & Quinones, G. (2013), How do early childhood students conceptualize play-based curriculum? *Australian Journal of Teacher Education*, 37 (12), pp. 46–56.

Sherwood, S. A., & Reifel, S. (2010). The multiple meanings of play: Exploring preservice teachers' beliefs about a central element of early childhood education. *Journal of Early Childhood Teacher Education*, 31, 322–343.

Sisson, J. H., & Kroeger, J. (2017). "They get enough of play at home": a Bakhtinian interpretation of the dialogic space of public school preschool. *Early Child Development and Care,* 187:5-6, 812-826, DOI: 10.1080/03004430.2016.1252533

Thibodeau, R. B., Gilpin, A.T., Brown, M. M., & Meyer, B. A. (2016). The effects of fantastical pretend-play on the development of executive functions: An intervention study. *Journal of Experimental Child Psychology,* 145, 120–138.

Van der Aalsvoort, G., Prakke, B., Howard, J., König, A. & Parkkinen, T. (2015). Trainee teachers' perspectives on play characteristics and their role in children's play: An international comparative study amongst trainees in the Netherlands, Wales, Germany and Finland. *European Early Childhood Education Research Journal,* 23 (2), 277–292.

Vogt, W. P. (2007). *Quantitative research methods for professionals.* Boston, MA: Pearson Education.

Wood, E. A., & Attfield. J. (2005). *Play, learning and the early childhood curriculum.* (2nd ed.). London, Great Brittan: Paul Chapman Publishing.

Chapter Nine

Games at College

Furthering Pedagogical and Co-Curricular Goals through Play

Abby Loebenberg, Robert Mack, and Laurel Bongiorno

In this chapter, comprised of three case studies each written by one of the authors, we describe a theoretical framework that will consider the neurological and social basis for academic success in the college classroom. We argue that hypothetical neurological links between play and executive function, as well as the generally supportive role of play in brain development, are important at the college level as these students' brains are still developing and should be supported appropriately in the classroom.

In the first case study, written by Loebenberg, the use of the role-playing game GURPS (Generic Universal Role Playing System) is explored as a pedagogical tool for teaching ethnographic writing to undergraduate university students. GURPS is an open-ended role-playing game, which is similar to Dungeons & Dragons, but with more flexibility. In the case study, Loebenberg describes the characteristics that make GURPS particularly well-suited to teaching ethnography and she compares this to other current methods of using play in the classroom. In the second case study by Mack, he addresses the use of design elements from contemporary Eurogame board games in the creation of collegiate learning activities (in this case, seminar discussion). Mack considers the enduring appeal of these elements before providing some examples of how they might translate to the classroom context. In the final case study by Bongiorno, she addresses how a classic family board game, *The Game of Life*, can be used to teach to undergraduates fiscal responsibility and post-college planning.

In sum, the case studies in the chapter demonstrate that role-playing games and adaptations of classic board games are all excellent scaffolds to engage students in an experimental, yet effective new class or student support structure. We argue that, understood on a deeper level than simply mechanically, play can be effectively used in higher education to create new pedagogies that allow for students to explore concepts rather than content. We argue this in order to make sure that we are engaging students not just mechanistically as they may have been in the past, but in a way that organically supports their psycho-social development. Furthermore, all three cases hold that goal attainment as a form of executive function, and as it is supported by the complex actions surrounding play, is not simply a matter of individual development, but entails socio-cultural processes too.

LITERATURE REVIEW

The study of the brain in education first appeared in the 1970s and became popularized through self-help books for adults such as *Use Both Sides of Your Brain* (Buzan, 1974) and *Drawing on the Right Side of the Brain* (Edwards, 1979), both based on the research of Nobel Laureate Roger Sperry. Moreover, during the 1980s and 1990s popular texts for classroom pedagogy such as Gardener (1983) and Caine & Caine (1991) took research done in cognitive neuroscience and started applying it to classroom practice. It became apparent that if educators ignored the development of students' brains they could impair students' learning. However, with further research, certain models like the left/right brain model of creativity, despite their ongoing popularity, proved to be over-simplified. We all mostly use all of our brains, most of the time (Jensen, 2008).

In fact, more contemporary educational approaches to the brain need to account for a host of complex phenomena, especially in relation to changes throughout the life cycle. The adolescent (through age 20) and young adult years (age 21–39) are still a time for maturation and change in the brain (Bergen, Schroer & Wooden, 2018). Particularly for the teenage group, there is a tendency for risky behavior, thrill-seeking and emotionally charged experiences to be sought out as this group is still developing the part of their brain known as executive function. Adults have roughly half of the neurons found in the brain of a two-year-old (Jenson, 2008), while young adults see a decline in the gray matter even as white matter in the brain continues to increase until around the age of 40, after which it drops off quickly (Bergen *et al.*2018).

One educational approach to the brain that might help account for such changes involves play. Bergen et al. (2018) have argued that it is difficult to pinpoint any positive correlations between play and brain research because no studies have been able to prove causality between what is a complex set of social and/or physical actions and specific neurological consequences. However, they do argue that game playing, in particular, fosters skills like pretend-play, self-regulation, and problem-solving which can be hypothetically related to brain research, and some research does demonstrate connections between these skills and areas of the brain. Thus, focusing on areas of brain research allied to play, such as these skills, is particularly important in establishing the relevance of play to the adolescent brain, or any age group (Bergen, 2009; Bodrova & Leong, 1995, 2006; Singer, Golinkoff & Hirsch-Pasek, 2006).

Two studies argue that streamlined neuron pathways and brain organization lead to perceptions of intelligence (Miller & Cohen, 2001; Cole, Yarkoni, Repovs, Anticevic, & Braver, 2012). Further evidence shows that the role of the lateral prefrontal cortex (LPFC) is critical in areas of brain function and development such as inhibition, moving between ideas, and working memory that collectively help to control thought and behaviors, the aforementioned "executive function" that is also important to success in learning. Further, the LPFC acts as a "global hub" (Cole et al., 2012, p. 8988) in controlling the neurological processes that are vital to academic success. Although neurological pathways develop and are discarded all through our lives, even into adulthood, the high points of this brain activity coincide with an intensification of REM sleep and, of interest for the purpose of this chapter, play (Brown & Vaughan, 2010)—an activity documented to be both pleasurable and typified across species as evolutionarily adaptive, pushing boundaries in non-life-threatening situations (Spinka et al., 2001).

As play is a preferred behavior for children and young adults, as well as essential to the hub of the brain that deals with intelligence processes, it is reasonable to associate increased pedagogical use of play with increased (or perceived increased) support for skills such as goal attainment/executive function, a skill vital to academic success not only in the classroom, but for deferring gratification outside of the classroom (e.g., in order to complete homework and so on). However, almost no emphasis is placed on the pedagogical value of play in the classroom in secondary and higher education.

Henricks (2015) underscores this absence by noting the pervasively social element of play. In addition to associating play with Mikhail Csikszentmihalyi's "flow" states argument (1990), Henricks points out that play is a community (rather than individual) construction. This point is particularly salient as we consider the case studies in this chapter, as not only do all three of these games occur in a community setting but with adolescents, people who are often highly motivated by social approval and interaction. Furthermore, bearing the sociality of play in mind is important from a socio-biological point of view. While neurological studies might be useful when advocating for the value of play for adolescents in a college setting to administrators or others who are skeptical about outcomes and benefits, they perhaps encourage us to think too much about the individual value of play, rather than the group. Henricks' work can remind us that learning communities are first-and-foremost social ones.

CASE 1: ANTHROPOLOGY
EXPERIMENT WITH ROLE-PLAYING GAMES

For teenage students to substantially "be playful" they require more than just the injunction to do so, although often just an opportunity is enough. Rather, as Vygotskian education theory states, the students need a *scaffold* (Faulkner, Littleton & Woodhead, 2013). This is an activity that allows students to build a framework allowing for a substantial task to be accomplished. Vygotsky (1978) describes an area of achievement between what a learner can and cannot do as the *Zone of Proximal Development* or ZPD, often seen to be the area of understanding that students can be guided to by a facilitator, and the scaffold is seen to be the framework that facilitates the construction of this zone. Thus, in the sense of the "play," the scaffold might be some type of structure, activity or facilitation method that primes the students to produce play, in our case a role-playing game (RPG) simulation using the Dungeons & Dragons-style role-playing system GURPS.

GURPS[1] has the advantage of a relatively simple and quick-to-teach rule set that allows players to generate a flexible character quickly, without needing to know about in-game character archetypes. Rather, the character creation process focuses on what the character can do within the game, leaving the more thematic aspects such as motivation and game-world integration up to the player or even allowing them to be added on to, or removed, during the game, perhaps as a reward or punishment. Unlike Dungeons & Dragons, GURPS does not constrain students to fixed character archetypes like barbarian, mage and so on; they can be anyone or anything they choose. Right from the initiation of the game the students need to accept the idea that the game world both has no constraints (few rules) and that the rules of what will be fun will come from how their character will successfully interacts with those in their play-group, how they will set challenges for that character (and themselves - and that those things may be different), and that they will need to manage or negotiate emotional moments in which they might not find themselves in everyday life. All of these unpredictable moments that are presented through complex role-play suggest the involvement of higher order cognitive functions.

In contrast to other in-class game systems, including the very popular general studies class substitute *Reacting to the Past* (Carnes, 2014), which uses pre-set roles and scenarios to feed closed-ended goals such as essay-writing and speech making, I selected GURPS precisely to harness two major aspects of RPGs: their ability to be open-ended, and their natural connection to that human universal, storytelling. The anthropological imperative to position our personhood through narrative is an element not only common to play but to the creation of ourselves in the stories of our lives, our families and our social groups. While participating in an RPG might not be something everyone does by choice, this resonance with the natural act of storytelling does make it simple for students to engage with the instinctive level of the task. It is in responding to the reactions of others, or of random circumstances (represented by dice), and in trying out new strategies as a group that the game is successfully played and goals are met or failed. The development of a sophisticated working memory to remember the plot points from other players and ability to creatively solve abstract problems presented by a Game Master inherently improves an RPG game; these are two areas of executive function connected to the lateral prefrontal cortex, the hub of intelligence processes in the brain.

I would clearly distinguish this type of pedagogy from what has become known as *gamification*, a form of incentivizing of either syllabus, assignments, or both, that apply the principles of games, often video games, to high school and college-level classes. Commercial development of gamified teaching software such as Classcraft.com would seem to support this increase in the use of games as a teaching strategy, but winning and losing, scoring points (which equate to grades) such as Carnes (2014) describes, and "levelling" (also equated to grades) such as Jackson (2009) describes, do not have to be the sole vehicle of bringing play into the classroom. It can be stated that games in general are successful in engaging students in part because they allow students to get into what Csikzentmihalyi (1990) calls "flow," that is the loss of a sense of time that comes through absorption in an activity, distinct from their use of points for grades, or other types of transaction. Although the use of GURPS as a pedagogical tool draws on many of the benefits of gamification in terms of motivating students to tasks that they would otherwise avoid, or only minimally address, building the game aspects into the entire structure of the course helps to extend the coursework into the realm of performance, play and creativity as discussed by Huizinga in his classic *Homo Ludens* (1949).

Outside of the classroom context, there are a number of ethnographic studies of role-playing games, from Gary Fine's benchmark *Shared Fantasy* (1983) to Dennis Waskul (2006) and Sarah Bowman (2010). However, the point of my research is not to show that an ethnography (the reporting mode of anthropology and sociology) can be written of a role-playing game *per se,* as that is evident; it is to create an effective scaffold for non-specialist undergraduates who can be taught to write ethnographically through this process. Through it, they gain a useful skill that they can apply to their interdisci-plinary education and perhaps use going forward to a potential thesis project (one of the parts of the curriculum at this institution). The very nature of the class is an ongoing role-playing game, albeit a challenging and open-ended one, so the students are caught in a 'flow' and enjoy the class. Ultimately, it is a fun class and non-anthropology majors want to enroll in it, which gives a platform for spreading awareness out about the benefits of cross-cultural knowledge as part of an undergraduate education that often does not include experience in qualitative research methods. In addition, the instructor can ef-fectively teach ethnographic techniques while obviating most of the obstacles and risks inherent to "real" fieldwork, such as potentially extensive amounts of IRB paperwork, the ethical concerns of whichever groups they are sent to interact with, and the safety risks to the students themselves.

The class takes the form of a GURPS-based one-credit honors course on ethnographic writing, a form of anthropological writing that is characterized by long-form narrative, or excerpts of fieldnotes, grouped into patterns of cultural behaviors combined with comparative or cross-cultural analysis of similar patterns moving towards a line of logical argument. A major dif-ficulty of teaching this form of writing is finding an environment where the student can safely and ethically perform the research that is to be described. Classically, at least a year in the field is recommended, but this is not practi-cal for undergraduate teaching; the GURPS narrative/game is therefore used to generate this "field site" environment, although of course with the idea that this is in the space of the classroom and not real, and the "people" with whom the writer must interact are sometimes characters. Inherently, this adds an element of challenging unreality to the class, which arguably skills emerg-ing from higher order functions are necessary to mediate. On the other hand, the simple premise of the students' work is that they use anthropological writing and note-taking techniques as they play the game to document their "in-game" and "out-of-game" experiences, mirroring the participant-observer dynamic. This is a way to think about their active role in shaping and produc-ing the game world, but also the peculiarities of the passive cultural aspects of the game world they were co-creating.

The class ran twice, first with a theme based on Ancient Greece and the second time based on Ancient China. It was configured into 12 one-hour ses-sions with 4-5 students per group. I tried to keep the groups at roughly simi-lar ability levels and assigned more experienced volunteers to act as Game Masters. The first class of the semester involved character creation, as well as a few other presentation and discussion sessions during the semester. I also asked students' permission to publish their work anonymously and collected these consent forms on the first day of class. The following classes were all dedicated to group gameplay.

In the first iteration, the students used material from a game called *Caravan to Ein-Arris* (Steve Jackson Games) which was adapted thematically to fit the Ancient Greek theme. This was chosen because all first-year students in the Honors College take a mandatory seminar where Ancient Greece is covered, and so the students would all have some basic familiarity with this time period. Because this adapted version had far too much material for the students to cover in one semester, a student volunteered to write a custom game for the next run of the class set in Ancient China during the book burnings (which prove to be a central theme of the game).

All the groups more or less ended up in the same place at the end of the game, and then from their collection of "field notes" that they had written over the semester they had to (re)create a journal of their character's experience, crafting a voice for their character and filling in the details of the place as they had seen it in their mind's eye. Some students created artworks, maps or photography projects, but most created creative non-fiction-style writing projects or formal essays as their final projects. A combination of the students' fieldnotes, their participation, and this final project was used to assign their final grade in the class.

Successful writing that emerged from this class seemed to be due to students' willingness to pay attention to the nuances of the dynamics between people and the game and from feedback I gave them on their notetaking, asking them to pay closer attention to the details between participation and observation, or perhaps asking for more specific detail in social interactions. As students started to reflect on the class as a social learning experience as well as a knowledge production experience (Loebenberg, 2019), their insights became more profound. Because they were playing and were often quite competitive and whimsical or chaotic (even violent) in their play, but then had to reflect and document this process, they had to reflect on questions about what kinds of things they knew, or what their character knew, why they would make one strategy choice over another, what the probability for a certain outcome was, and so on. Ultimately, the final projects and essays offered many reassessments and reflections, for some students, on their ideas of what knowledge production might be and where they might be located. This highlights the parallels between the play behaviors of challenging themselves to achieve the goals of the game while dealing with the consequences of some silliness and violence and the idea of learning through productive knowledge, that is through trial and error.

From conducting these two classes it is clear that games are not only something that is valuable intellectually, as these students showed by using role-playing games to develop a final project in a class, but that they can also be useful pedagogically, and for students as a tool to develop knowledge that through scaffolds that can be clearly connected to higher cognitive functions, and to other complex phenomena including, most obviously, creativity and play. In an intellectual and economic climate where pre-professional and professional degree courses seem safer and more relevant to students than, as specifically discussed here, the social sciences, demonstrating relevance in a way that is also engaging to students is a challenge.

CASE 2: THE EUROGAME
SENSIBILITY IN THE COLLEGE CLASSROOM

German-style board games—often called "Eurogames" by those who play and collect them—have achieved remarkable worldwide popularity in the last three decades. Some of the better-known examples in this genre include *The Settlers of Catan, Carcassonne*, and *Ticket to Ride*. Donovan (2017) attributes the ascension of the genre to its captivation of children and adults alike. Unlike more mainstream or juvenile titles like *Sorry!* and *Monopoly*, Eurogames broaden "tabletop gaming's appeal to those who want to keep playing after childhood with new experiences and themes that connect with adults better" (p.255). As such, in this second case study I will explore how the principles of modern Eurogame design can be adapted to the classroom to facilitate enjoyable learning experiences for a population caught precisely between childhood and adulthood: first year college students.

Woods (2012) identifies a number of formal elements that distinguish Eurogames from other kinds of board games. Eurogames typically feature a simple set of rules that nevertheless lend themselves to strategic play. Much of this simplicity involves restricting player choices so that they have only "a relatively small number of actions to take on a given turn" (p. 86). These actions remain meaningful because Eurogames tend to avoid chance and instead privilege the direct effects of player decisions. In addition, these games often stress constructive player interaction and indirect conflict; in general, there is more opportunity for interaction through negotiation or trade than through direct attack. This emphasis means that most Eurogames also avoid mechanisms that might eliminate players before the conclusion of the game, and games themselves often only last for a predetermined number of turns—a stark contrast to more day-consuming titles like *Risk* or *Alix & Allies*. Finally, while Eurogames typically feature historical and economic themes, these themes are largely secondary to the underlying game mechanics, serving as heuristics that help players make sense of the rules rather than opportunities for highly immersive experiences. This quality has led many players to frame the genre as "largely abstract games with themes that are applied late in the design process" (p.106), with new games often recombining mechanics of previous titles.

The abstraction of Eurogames extends as well to their physical components, which are typically of high quality but feature minimal narrative specificity/richness. As Wilson (2015) notes of the livestock tiles in the popular Eurogame *The Castles of Burgundy*, "these animals can be interpreted as companions, wards, ornaments, or consumable resources" (p. 48). The element of interchangeability is especially apparent in the ubiquity of small, colorful, wooden cubes that appear in many Eurogame titles. In some instances these cubes represent influence (as they do in the game *Tigris and Euphrates*), and in other instances they stand for population (in *Eclipse* and *El Grande*). Most often they represent trade goods or resources. In the game *The Traders of Genoa*, for example, players exchange cubes of eight different colors that represent merchandise like copper, rice, and silk. Only occasionally does the color of the cube play a deeply thematic role in these designs. *Fresco*, a game where cubes represent different colors of paint that players acquire and use to adorn the ceiling of a church, is a notable exception within the genre.

Both the formal features and the components of Eurogames are sources of enjoyment for those who play them. Game designer Luke Laurie (2016) identifies a number of ways that multi colored cubes can contribute to the pleasure of a game. They stack and organize easily, and their simultaneous diversity and uniformity help players process information quickly in order to optimize strategy. They are also particularly well-suited for physical exchange. "Grabbing cubes is easy because of their corners, edges and right angles," he writes. "Some of the cool, fancy substitutes for cubes . . . can be tricky to pick up and move around with ease." By comparison, the appeal of these games' formal features can be harder to articulate. The emphasis on interaction and keeping all players active may be evident sources of allure, but the focus on limited action, time, and luck might strike the uninitiated as more puzzling sources of enjoyment. Erway (2018) clarifies this matter when he argues that these elements are ultimately appealing because of how they mimic life broadly:

> The Eurogamer specifically enjoys the game to the degree it captures the fundamental position we all find ourselves in: given what we have, how can we best act within the ever-present constraints imposed by our limited resources? The Eurogamer wants strategy and skill to overcome random chance in deciding the outcome. A deep, evolutionary pleasure is hardwired in us when we meet such challenges well (p. 35).

Though these enjoyments are often discussed in relation to the diehard aficionados of Eurogames, it is possible for those who do not play these games regularly to experience them as well—even in contexts outside of gaming proper. As a fan of these games myself, I have found that incorporating their mechanisms and materials into the classroom can help students develop skills tied to mental executive function in enjoyable ways. Most of my current teaching involves working with first year honors students in small, critical discussion seminars organized around exploring topics in the humanities. Many students arrive to the honors program with little to no experience with seminar classes, and as a result some of them are initially ill-prepared to manage the rigor of initiating, maintaining, and especially leading the bulk of the in-class discussion. Naturally, some also possess a dispositional shyness or reticence that they find difficult to overcome in the classroom context. Activities that intersect with the principles of Eurogames seem to yield especially positive results in helping these students build effective discussion skills.[2]

To facilitate these activities I have invested in a set of square-inch cubes made of dense foam in six different colors: Blue, red, green, orange, yellow, and purple. The set contains approximately 35 cubes of each color, with which I have found a sufficient number to implement a wide variety of activities. Though manipulatives broadly conceptualized have a longstanding history as a pedagogical tool, student behaviors that I have witnessed over the last three years suggest that there is something special about the specific use of these cubes in this context. Many students show signs of immediate interest when I distribute them in class. Most do not expect such colorful, toy-like objects to appear in a college classroom. In addition, though I typically do not tell students what to do with the cubes beyond some basic instructions, I have witnessed numerous students over the years instinctively arrange them to their liking in their personal areas. They often stack them into towers or pyramids, exemplifying Laurie's (2016) discussion about the inherent appeal of the shape. Furthermore, the cubes' foam exterior means that some students over the years have written on or poked holes in them. This annoyed me at first (and prompted me to replace the most battered examples), but I soon came to see these marks as remnants of students' clear engagement with the cubes' materiality. In some ways the marks are a testament to the benefits of using physical objects over more insubstantial approaches to instruction.

The most basic activity that I carry out with the cubes communicates the importance of balancing perspectives in a critical discussion. Each student receives a purple cube and an orange cube at the start of the seminar. I tell students that during the ensuing discussion, once they have contributed something of substance to the group's evolving analysis, they should toss their purple cube into the center of the discussion circle. They then cannot share again until each of their peers have also "used" their purple cube. The same rules apply once everyone has only the orange cube in front of them. Once all cubes have been tossed into the center, I challenge them to keep up the balance in contributions on their own. Though the forced nature of this activity may strike some instructors as punitive, students regularly carry out remarkable discussions with this system. Previously quiet students participate with perceptive insights. Those who tend to dominate conversation remark afterward how much they learned from sitting back and listening to their peers. I believe that this activity works well in part because it embodies many design elements of contemporary Eurogames: Though students have only a simple decision to make at any given moment (use their cube or not), their decisions constructively affect others' decisions and keep everyone actively involved throughout the experience. The use of only two cubes also helps instantiate a definitive length to the activity, which I believe helps students rationalize and undertake a different behavior than they might otherwise exhibit during discussion. These elements thus assist in prompting and shaping executive function behaviors like group deference and small goal setting that can be crucial to the future academic success of these young students.

In the same way that Eurogames emphasize game mechanisms over theme and thus grant the genre a kind of endless, recombinant flexibility, the above framework is adaptable for classes requiring extra assistance in carrying out deep and sustained discussions. For seminars whose members struggle with *what* to say, for example, I assemble a mixture of cubes with colors and amounts keyed to the basic behaviors of a successful discussion: Asking a question (yellow), providing evidence (green), extending an idea (blue), challenging an idea (red), or "wild" (purple). Students then draw four of these cubes randomly from a bag at the start of class, and it becomes their goal to "use" their cubes by contributing in the related fashions before the end of the discussion. This activity builds upon the Eurogame-inspired logic of the previous one but narrows decision-making considerably. The random draw might mean, for instance, that a given student need only focus on contributing evidence twice, as well as posing one question and challenging one peer during the entire discussion. Such distinctions can help students practice making different kinds of thoughtful contributions than they might otherwise audition, with the eventual goal of cultivating ability in each of these behaviors.

A more common adaptation that I utilize for some groups highlights the portability of the cubes rather than their color. Here students again begin with two cubes, and they again remain silent when they no longer possess any. In this case, however, instead of tossing a cube into the center upon making a contribution, I ask students to pass the cube to their right-hand neighbor. I draw explicit attention to the ways in which the cubes here help model the interconnection of a discussion: One students' contribution quite directly authorizes another to speak. In addition to the restricted but meaningful decisions present in the previous activities, then, this version draws inspiration from the mutually beneficial interaction, negotiation, and trade that so many enjoy in Eurogames. It also illustrates how the communal nature of play can help underscore executive function behaviors like coordination and shifting between ideas. In fact, I have had seminars in which students who find themselves slumping in the quality of their discussions request this activity as a refresher on the importance of hearing from every member.

In drawing these connections between my pedagogy and Eurogames, I am not suggesting that all students find these activities enjoyable, nor that their effectiveness is solely a product of the activities' resonance with game design. There is enough of an overlap between these various fields, however, to think seriously about how the intentional import of a "Eurogame sensibility" into the college classroom might spark learning opportunities that are appealing and effective in cultivating executive function for academic success. Central to this sensibility is the use of simple, restricted rules that still allow for consequential decisions in constructive group interaction. The use of small, colorful cubes can help generate instinctive interest, expedite collaboration, and signify a variety of resources within a familiar framework. (Indeed, after my students realized that the cubes represent their individual contributions, it is much easier for the cubes to signify the idea of group interdependence.) I have discussed how this sensibility might function in relation to critical discussion skills here, but there is no reason to believe that they are only useful for this subject matter. History and economics—the secondary but pervasive themes of so many Eurogames—might also represent educational areas that could benefit from contemplating this sensibility at greater length.

CASE 3: A BOARD-GAME
SIMULATION CO-CURRICULAR ACTIVITY

In addition to what can be learned from early childhood researchers, much can also be learned from game design theory and the development of serious games. Flanagan (2010) describes the challenges of games that move towards social, political, aesthetic, or educational aims, and makes a connection between real world issues and play. Many games have been designed to address social challenges and to offer learning opportunities for players. There are lessons to be learned in the higher education landscape about motivating students to try, fail, and try again. Curricula can be developed to be engaging, such as play simulations, to promote opportunities for learning through experience.

The *Game of Life* has been part of Champlain College's co-curricular programming since Fall 2012. The game, based on Hasbro's popular board game, was originally conceptualized by the Federal Deposit Insurance Company (FDIC), implemented at Brockton High School in Brockton, MA, and Champlain received permission to replicate and adapt the program. Since then, Champlain has developed the program to become one of the most unique financial education experiences for first-year students during their college tenure. The simulation is part of a career decision-making exercise designed to help students evaluate their needs, values, and options, one of the reasons the program is managed through the Champlain College's Career Collaborative, our career center.

As a required element of their co-curricular program, *InSight*, a total of 379 of this year's (the year of 2018) first-year students participated in the in-person game simulation. Each session included more than one hundred students spending 90 minutes on a Saturday afternoon playing a simulation game of their financial life after college. Every student received a customized budget based on starting salary for the state of Vermont, aligning with their major, and on a benefits package.

Students visited 15 booths including transportation, housing, utilities, electronics, entertainment, food, clothing, personal care, insurance, savings, retirement, philanthropy, and student loans. In addition, they spun a *wheel of fortune* representing random, surprise financially related life events, including the potential of *winning the lottery, taking part in a friend's wedding, repairing a car issue*, and being named *"employee of the month" and earning a bonus*. They also visited a booth with a cost-of-living analysis that adjusted their anticipated Vermont salary to prospective salaries in other states, in case students decide to live in San Francisco or New York, for example. Students could also decide if they could afford a pet or a fitness center membership, or if they needed a roommate to help balance their budget.

After visiting all 15 booths, they completed their budget sheets and met with volunteer mock financial counselors to collaboratively discuss their budget spending and financial decision making. They used a debrief worksheet that they could take with them to recall the simulation experience.

I interviewed a dozen students as they waited in line for their financial counselor session. First, all students interviewed reported familiarity with the board game. One Social Work major indicated that she went through the simulation with a friend majoring in Data Analytics. She told me that she learned she had better plan to share an apartment with her friend when they graduated since her friend would make a lot more money than she would. Several students indicated their biggest surprise from the simulation was that they could not even afford a fitness center membership. From the program's data collection, of the students who participated in Fall 2018, an overwhelm-ing number, 253 of the 379, reported that as a result of the experience they would save more, spend less, or budget better.

With an understanding that this stimulation was not purely play with its required nature and intentional outcomes (Stotz, 2008), I asked the students whether they had fun. Most indicated that it was much better than a class or a workshop. They found it "sort of" fun. All of the students interviewed believed they had learned something from the experience: the cost of school loans, how little insurance cost, how quickly their money was spent, how expensive food was, and for the Social Work major, disappointment that she could not be more philanthropic.

The manager of the program explained that the foundational learning she hopes students take with them each time they play the *Game of Life* is to make intentional decisions in regard to their personal finances: "Sometimes those decisions require sacrifices, but as long as our true priorities are guiding those decisions, budgeting and managing our money becomes less intimidating and more conquerable." The manager also believes that personal finance is a topic that can be emotional. She believes by incorporating play, the students' anxiety is lowered so they are more open to learn and practice behaviors that hopefully take them closer to healthy financial habits.

CONCLUSION

Three case studies provide resources for scholars and teachers resisting those who assume that games and play are things of childhood and unsuitable for use in higher education. The first case study shows that while it is almost impossible to 'sell' classes on research methods to undergraduates, despite the advantages that early exposure can provide to later studies, classes on games can be filled with ease, precisely because students want to take some-thing different and fun. The research on RPGs in the Honors College context demonstrates that games can be challenging, and worthwhile pedagogy, for even the most difficult to challenge students. The second case study on Euro-games as pedagogy for seminar facilitation demonstrates that it is not simply the physical use of cubes that makes for effective pedagogical intervention, but the mechanical and structural understanding of the game mechanisms behind their use that makes the experience a useful structure to assist students to improve their discussion skills. Lastly, the third case study demonstrates that ready-made games such as *The Game of Life* can be used to teach stu-dents how to engage with the post-college experience and visualize future outcomes through a familiar simulation. Together the case studies support the notion that games might be particularly effective means for students to practice executive function behaviors like short and long term planning, intellectual coordination, and impulse inhibition so central so academic success in the contemporary collegiate environment. Students in all three of these cases certainly built knowledge, but through the scaffold of these games they more importantly begun to learn *how* and *where* knowledge production is situated while simultaneously exploring their role as active participants in their own learning.

NOTES

1. The Generic Universal Role-Playing System, first published by Steve Jackson Games in 1986.

2. Importantly, I do not lay claim to these activities as wholly original creations. Many are adaptations of activities passed along to me by colleagues, or ones that I discovered in pedagogical research. As such, rather than present them as revolutionary ideas, my goal here is to think about why they might particularly appeal to students and work to advance educational goals.

REFERENCES

Bergen, D. (2009), Play as a learning medium for future scientists, mathematicians and engineers. *American Journal of Play*, 1(4), 413–428.

Bergen, D., Schroer, J., & Woodin, M. (2018). *Brain research in education and the social sciences: Implications for practice, parenting, and future society*. New York, NY; Abingdon, Oxon: Routledge

Bodrova, E.& Leong, D. (1995). *Tools of the mind: A Vygotskian approach to early childhood education*. Boston, MA: Twayne Publishers.

Bowman, S. L. (2010). *The functions of role-playing games how participants create community, solve problems and explore identity*. Jefferson, NC: McFarland.

Brown, S. L., & Vaughan, C. C. (2010). *Play: How it shapes the brain, opens the imagination, and invigorates the soul*. New York: Avery.

Buzan, T. (1974). *Use both sides of your brain*. New York, NY: E.P. Dutton.

Caine, G., & Caine, R. (1991). *Making connections: Teaching and the human brain*. Alexandria VA: Association for Supervision and Curriculum Development.

Carnes, M. (2014). *Minds on fire: How role-immersion games transform college*. Cambridge, MA: Harvard University Press.

Cole, M. W., Yarkoni, T., Repovs, G., Anticevic, A., & Braver, T. S. (2012). Global connectivity of prefrontal cortex predicts cognitive control and intelligence. *Journal of Neuroscience,32*(26), 8988–8999.

Csikszentmihalyi, M. (1990). *Flow: The psychology of optimal experience*. New York: Harper Collins.

Donovan, T. (2017). *It's all a game: The history of board games from Monopoly to Settlers of Catan.* New York: St. Martin's Press.

Edwards, B.(1979). *Drawing on the right side of the brain.* Los Angeles, CA: J.P. Tarcher.

Erway, S. (2018). *Loving Eurogames: A quest for a well played game.* Carnation, WA: Griffin Creek Press.

Faulkner, D., Littleton K., & Woodhead, M. (2013). *Learning relationships in the classroom.* London, England: New York, NY: Routledge.

Fine, G.A. (1983). *Shared fantasy: Role playing games as social worlds.* Chicago: The University of Chicago Press.

Flanagan, M. (2010) Creating critical play, In R. Catlow, M. Garrett, and C. Morgana. (Eds.), *Artists Re: Thinking games* (pp. 49–53). Liverpool, England: Liverpool University Press.

Gardener, H. (1983). *Frames of mind: the theory of multiple intelligences.* New York, NY: Basic Books.

Henricks, T. (2015). *Play and the human condition.* University of Illinois Press: Urbana.

Huizinga, J. (1949). *Homo ludens.* London: Routledge.

Jackson, J. (2009). Game-based teaching: What educators can learn from video-games. *Teaching Education.* 20(30), 291–304.

Jensen, E. (2008). *Brain based learning: The new paradigm of teaching* (2nd ed.). Corwin Press: Thousand Oaks.

Laurie, L. (2016, January 20). In defense of cubes. *League of game makers*, Retrieved from http://www.leagueofgamemakers.com.

Loebenberg, A. (2019, June 17). Sneak Attack Anthropology: Experiences with Games in the College Classroom. Retrieved from http://analoggamestudies. org/2018/06/sneak-attack-anthropology-experiences-with-games-in-the-college-classroom/

Miller, E., & Cohen, J.D. (2001). An integrative theory of prefrontal cortex function. *Annual Review of Neuroscience.* 24, 167–202.

Singer, D., Goliknoff, R., and Hirsch-Pasek, K. (2006). Why Play = Learning: A Challenge for parents and Educators. In *Play = Learning: How play motivates and enhances children's cognitive and social-emotional growth* (pp. 2–14). New York: Oxford University Press.

Spinka, M., Newberry, R., & Bekoff, M. (2001). Mammalian play: Training for the unexpected. *Quarterly Review of Biology.* 76, 141–168.

Stotz, P.R. (2008). Describing quality from the child's perspective (Doctoral dissertation). Retrieved from Dissertations and Theses @ Proquest database. (AAT3333080)

Vygotsky, L.S. (1978). *Mind in Society.* Cole, M., John-Steiner, V., & Scribner, S.(eds). Cambridge: Harvard University Press.

Waskul, D. (2006). The role playing game and the game of role-playing' in *Gaming as culture.* Jefferson: McFarland and Company.

Wilson, D. (2015). The Eurogame as heterotopia. In E. Thorner, E. L. Waldren, & A. Trammell (Eds.) *Analog Game Studies, Vol. 2* (pp. 43–49). Pittsburgh, PA: Carnegie Mellon University ETC Press.

Woods, S. (2012). *Eurogames: The design, culture and play of modern European board games.* Jefferson, NC: McFarland & Co.

Index

Ableizhi, 14–15, 17

Ableizhi school, 15, 16–18

Ableizhi school curriculum: diverse instructional practices, 18; dramatizations and creative approaches, 19; letters learning lesson, 17–18

Ableizhi school curriculum, play integration: cultural learning, 20, 21, 23, 24; discussion about, 23–25; dramatizations of learning, 21; Kogi parents and, 21–23; math lessons, 19–21; natural world in, 19–20; overview, 18–21, 23–25; traditional teachings from home and, 23

Ableizhi teachers, 15–25

Adrien, E., 133

adult-guided play, 48

adult learners: adult play and, 131, 147; higher education and, 130, 131; play in higher education and, 131. *See also* play and curriculum for adult learners

adult play, 129; adult learners and, 131, 147; children's play and, 149; play studies literature on, 5

adult play in ECTE programs, 129; play pedagogy and, 6, 24–25, 132–34, 152

adult play in higher education, 129; adult learners and, 131; to create new pedagogies for students, 181–82; mental health and, 5–6. *See also* games and college students

Almon, J., 63

Arhuaco, 13–14

Ashbrook, P., 95

authentic assessment, in free play in elementary science study, 98, *99*, 104–6, *105*

Bassok, D., 163

Bergen, D., 182

block play, in math learning, 73–74, 86

Bowman, Sarah, 185

brain development: executive function, 7, 181, 182, 183, 185, 190, 191, 194; life cycle changes and, 182; LPFC and, 183

brain development and play, 183; college students and, 7, 181; in games at college studies, 181

brain in education studies, 182

brain research, 7; games and, 182–83; play and, 182–83

Braun, V., 55

Bruner, J., 7, 96

About the Contributors

Marleah Blom is currently assistant professor in the child studies program within the Department of Education and is the recipient of the 2019 President's Excellence in Teaching Award in the category of Innovative Excellence in Teaching at Concordia University in Montréal, Canada. She holds an undergraduate degree in Psychology and Theatre, a Master of Arts degree in Creative Arts Therapies (Drama Therapy), and a Ph.D. in Education. Marleah has worked with diverse groups of children and adults in a variety of settings including daycare, hospital, clinical, school, and university environments. Her research interests center on play, creativity and innovation, teaching and learning in higher education, early childhood education, teacher beliefs and practices, teacher education, and faculty development. She believes firmly in the value of play for learning, growth, and change for learners of any age.

Laurel Bongiorno is the Dean of the Division of Education and Human Studies at Champlain College in Burlington, Vermont. She is an early childhood specialist with research interests in play, art and creativity, and leadership.

Juana Gaviria-Loaiza received her Ph.D. in 2018 from the University of Delaware in Human Development and Family Sciences. Juana's research interests focus on caregiver-child interactions, how caregivers foster children's language and socioemotional development, and how different programs and policies support these relationships. She is particularly interested in cultural differences in parenting, teaching practices, and children's experiences and outcomes, as well as in low-income Hispanic children and families. She has participated in multiple research projects including an *Early Reading First* project and a parent-child interaction intervention into Early Head Start home visits. Juana is from Medellin, Colombia.

Myae Han is professor of early childhood Education in the Department of Human Development and Family Sciences at the University of Delaware. Her areas of research include literacy and play, early intervention and implementation. She is a past president of The Association for the Study of Play (TASP) and Literacy Development in Young Children (LDYC) SIG at the International Literacy Association. She is current Chair-elect of Early Education Child Development (EECD) SIG at the American Educational Research Association. She has directed various federal and state funded grant projects including three *Early Reading First* grants funded by US Department of Education, *Early Head Start University Partnership* grant, *Child Care Research Partnership* grant funded by US Department of Health and Human Services.

Alison Hooper is assistant professor of early childhood education in the College of Education at the University of Alabama. She received her Ph.D. in Human Development and Family Studies from the University of Delaware. Her research focuses on child care access and quality, specifically focused on quality improvement in home-based child care. Previously, she worked as a research project coordinator with the Delaware Institute for Excellence in Early Childhood and as a kindergarten teacher.

Cailin Kerch is clinical assistant professor of early childhood and elementary Education at the University of Alabama (PhD from the University of Alabama at Birmingham in Early Childhood Education). Her master's of education in educational leadership is from Lehigh University. Cailin was a pre-kindergarten, elementary school teacher, and school leader for over a decade. Her current research interests include social emotional learning in early childhood settings, play, and related professional development.

Miranda D'Amico is associate dean of student academic services and professor of education at Concordia University. She holds a PhD in Educational and Counseling Psychology and is trained as a school psychologist with a focus on the psycho-educational assessment and evaluation of individuals with developmental and intellectual disabilities. She is the co-founder of the Centre for the Arts in Human Development, where she is the co-director of research. She has been the Coordinator of Educational Psychology since 1986 and served as both undergraduate and graduate program director in Child Studies. With various publications, including a textbook entitled Educational Psychology: Reflection for Action, Miranda's research interests include: the cognitive and emotional development of individuals with special needs; school and community-based inclusion and advocacy of individuals with disabilities; and the assessment and evaluation of the efficacy of creative arts therapies and arts-based approaches on individuals with special needs.

Beth Ferholt is associate professor of early childhood education in the Department of Early Childhood and Art Education at Brooklyn College, City University of New York. She is an affiliated faculty member in the Program in Urban Education at the Graduate Center and in the School of Education and Communication at Jönköping University. Ferholt's current research takes place within an ongoing collaboration with a Brooklyn public elementary school and preschools in Sweden. In this work young children, teachers, teachers in training and researchers imagine and create culture and knowledge, and study their processes of doing so, in playworlds, which are adult-child joint play activities that combine play with art and science for the benefit of all participants. Ferholt co-authored, with Monica Nilsson, Anna-Karin Grankvist, Elin Johansson and Jeanette Thure, Lek, lärande och lycka: Lekande och utforskande i förskolan (Play, learning and joy: Playing and exploring in preschool).

James E. Johnson is professor of early childhood education in the Department of Curriculum and Instruction in the College of Education at The Pennsylvania State University. His research and scholarly interests center on play and curriculum and culture. He is co-facilitator of the Play, Policy, and Practices Interest Forum of the National Association for the Education of Young Children, and Series Editor of *Play & Culture Studies* for The Association for the Study of Play. He recently authored a chapter in *The SAGE Handbook of Play and Learning in Early Childhood* entitled "Play provisions and pedagogy in curricular approaches," and most recently (with Viana Wu) "Perspectives on play in early childhood care and education" in *The Wiley Handbook of Early Childhood Care and Education* (2019).

Abby Loebenberg is an anthropologist with an interest in urban childhoods, a play advocate, and researcher. Based at the Barrett Honors College at Arizona State University as an Honors Faculty Fellow and Senior Lecturer, Dr. Loebenberg works with students on service-based projects that look to make a difference in the community through play advocacy. Dr. Loebenberg teaches a variety of inter-disciplinary seminar classes on both introductory and special topics using flexible pedagogical strategies, including playful ones, to encourage students to break out of habitual reproductive thinking strategies into critical, productive ones. Prior research papers have covered role-playing games and open-endedness in the classroom, virtual spaces and the challenges of digital gaming and children's consumption and collection practices.

Lora Lorentsen attended Northern Arizona University and graduated in the spring of 2019 with a B.S.Ed. in elementary education and a minor in secondary mathematics education. During her collegiate career she participated in various undergraduate research including studies regarding using play as a tool to teach science, using virtual reality devices as a classroom tool, and creating tactile activities for mathematics educators, specifically in calculus. Lorentsen spent most of her childhood in Sierra Vista, Arizona and also lived in Germany for three years during her youth. Beginning in August 2019, Lorentsen will begin her teaching career as a 7th-grade mathematics teacher at Mount Elden Middle School in Flagstaff, Arizona.

Robert L. Mack is an Honors Faculty Fellow at Barrett, the Honors College at Arizona State University. He teaches the signature course of the college, The Human Event, as well as courses on rhetoric, media, and psychoanalysis. He is co-author (with Brian L. Ott) of *Critical Media Studies: An Introduction*, 3rd ed., and his work has also appeared in *The Journal of the Fantastic in the Arts*, *The Journal of Communication and Religion*, and *The Quarterly Review of Film and Video*.

Heather J. Pinedo-Burns, Ed.D. is director of Hollingworth Preschool at Teachers College, Columbia University, a lab school where she guides her children, teachers, and families in a child-responsive program, fostering opportunities for wonder through play, inquiry, and collaboration. She earned a Doctorate of Education from the Department of Curriculum at Teaching at Teachers College, Columbia University. Previously, Dr. Pinedo-Burns attained a Bachelor of Arts in English and secondary education certification from State University of New York, College at Geneseo, and taught middle school English for the Rochester City School District. She currently serves as an adjunct instructor within the Department of Curriculum and Teaching at Teachers College. Her research interests include early childhood, narrative inquiry, and aesthetics and wonder. Consulting with schools and companies, Dr. Pinedo-Burns offers her expertise on curriculum development, professional development of teachers, early childhood pedagogy and differentiated instruction for pre-k-12 educators.

Meghan Schmidt attended Northern Arizona University and graduated in the spring 2019 with a B.S.Ed in Elementary and Special Education. During Meghan's time at NAU she participated in an undergraduate research study regarding the use of play as a tool to teach science. She enjoys living an active and healthy life style. Meghan was born in Bethesda, Maryland but spent most her life in Gilbert, Arizona. She is the youngest of four and was the first in her family to attend and graduate from college. Beginning of August 2019, Meghan will begin her first year of teaching 2nd grade at Emerson Elementary in Mesa, Arizona.

S. Lynneth Solis is researcher at Harvard Graduate School of Education's Project Zero. Her research investigates the cognitive and social processes by which young children learn about the world around them. She is interested in the role of sociocultural and pedagogical factors that support young children's learning through play in both formal and informal settings. Her work asks: What are the play behaviors, spaces, and opportunities children engage in to develop their understandings of the world? and What is the role of adults, culture, and pedagogy in shaping children's playful learning experiences? In particular, she investigates 1) the unique play experiences of children growing up in cross-cultural settings and 2) young children's exploration of scientific phenomena through play. She holds an Ed.D. in Human Development and Education and an Ed.M. in Mind, Brain, and Education from Harvard University.

Brian A. Stone is senior lecturer at Northern Arizona University. He teaches undergraduate methods courses in elementary science and social studies. He also directs the Professional Development School program at NAU. He is the STEAM editor for the International Journal of the Whole Child. Dr. Stone's research interests include science education, inquiry-based learning, child-centered practice, authentic assessment, integrated curriculum, multiage education, and play. Dr. Stone leads study tours every summer, which emphasize multiage education, integrated curriculum, and place-based education, and has taken students to Australia, New Zealand, Ireland, U.K., Germany, Austria, and Switzerland.

Sudha Swaminathan is professor of early childhood education, specializing in math and educational technology at Eastern Connecticut State University. She conducts research at the Center for Early Childhood Education on effective ways to enhance children's mathematical development during play and has explored the impact of various technology-based applications, including coding, on supporting and challenging children's socio-cognitive growth. To date, she has over 15 publications in journals such as the Young Children and Childhood Education; and has presented her work at national and international conferences on early childhood education, educational technology and educational research. She is the recipient of several grants, including two Spencer Foundation grants to study the effects of teacher interactions during children's math play. Dr. Swaminathan earned her masters and doctoral degrees in Early Childhood Education with a concentration in Math Education from the State University of New York at Buffalo.

Jeffrey Trawick-Smith is professor emeritus in the Center for Early Childhood Education at Eastern Connecticut State University. He has authored or edited six books and over 60 articles and chapters—most related to young children's culture, play, early math learning, and teacher-child interactions in preschool classrooms. His book, *Early Childhood Development: A Multicultural Perspective*, is in its seventh edition, is published in several languages, and is read throughout the world. His latest book, *Young Children's Play: Development, Disabilities, and Diversity* reviews research on culture and play—the very topics that are the focus of this book series. He is an active play researcher and has published and presented findings in refereed journals and at national and international conferences in early childhood education. He is a former preschool and kindergarten teacher.

Ilfa Zhulamanova is assistant professor at University of Southern Indiana. Her concentration area is early childhood education. Ilfa's research focuses on play and learning, teacher education, family diversity, and curriculum development in early childhood. She studied the foundations of Waldorf/ Steiner pedagogy and was a founder of a Waldorf kindergarten in her home country, Kyrgyzstan.